QUOTATIONS
AND SOURCES

ON DESIGN
AND THE DECORATIVE ARTS

general editor
Paul Greenhalgh

Paul Greenhalgh is Head of Art and Design
History at Camberwell College of Arts, London
Institute. He was formerly a lecturer at the Royal
College of Art, and a curator at the Victoria and
Albert Museum. He has published widely in
journals and magazines, and written two books,
Ephemeral vistas (1988, Manchester) and
Modernism in design (1990, London).

QUOTATIONS AND SOURCES

ON DESIGN
AND THE DECORATIVE ARTS

compiled and introduced by

Paul Greenhalgh

Manchester University Press
Manchester and New York

distributed exclusively in the USA and Canada by St. Martin's Press

Published by Manchester University Press
Oxford Road, Manchester M13 9PL, UK
and Room 400, 175 Fifth Avenue, New York, NY 10010, USA

Distributed exclusively in the USA and Canada
by St. Martin's Press, Inc.,
175 Fifth Avenue, New York, NY 10010, USA

British Library Cataloguing-in-Publication Data
A catalogue record for this book is available from the British Library

Library of Congress Cataloging-in-Publication Data applied for

ISBN 0-7190-3964-9 *hardback*
      0-7190-3965-7 *paperback*

Typeset in Stone Serif and Sans
by Koinonia Ltd, Manchester
Printed in Great Britain
by Bell & Bain Limited, Glasgow

CONTENTS

GENERAL EDITOR'S FOREWORD

This series of books is principally about the history of objects. When put so bluntly, there seems to be a certain absurdity in the suggestion that there might be a need for such an enterprise. After all, is that not what various other disciplines are already providing us with? The answer to this question, I fear, is no. The history of design, or material culture, or decorative arts, as it is variously understood, usually begins where others end. Many disciplines have objects of one kind or another at their centre, but the history of design stands alone in its analysis of the wide range of genres which fill people's lives: the furnishings, utensils, adornments, decorations, clothing, graphic materials, vessels, electrical and mechanical products which give form and meaning to the cultures they reside in.

The range of texts in this series has not been limited either by the social status of the objects concerned or by their production methods. There are volumes on mass-produced commodities designed as low-value disposables, as well as exclusive products designed for a very rarefied usage. This range means that the series is not particularly united by its taxonomy, but rather by the aims of the contributing authors. They seek to expose the meanings of the objects within the cultural context they were produced in. In order to do this they will adopt approaches from other disciplines; from archaeology, art history, anthropology, literary studies, the history of science and sociology. By the very nature of its subject matter, design history is, and always must be, interdisciplinary.

This is a gathering of sources on design and material culture. It covers the last two centuries and aims to do several things. It means to put into circulation sources which have drifted out of view; it re-presents and contextualises famous utterings on design; and, by grouping the quotations thematically, it intends to stimulate debate. I hope the reader will enjoy also the colourful language and the extraordinary vision of the contributors.

Paul Greenhalgh, Camberwell, April 1993

ACKNOWLEDGEMENTS

There are many people to thank. First, most emphatically, and above all others, Belinda Greenhalgh. Belinda typed in many of the passages, edited them, sought out material and criticised the selection. The book simply would not exist without her involvement with it.

The libraries and archives which gave me access made the task so much easier; Brighton University, the British Library, Camberwell College of Arts, the National Art Library, the Public Record Office, the Royal Society of Arts, the Ceramics Section of the Victoria and Albert Museum and the Wolfsonian Foundation (Miami). Friends and colleagues in the various institutions I am, or have been, attached to, have given me tremendous support through what has been a surprisingly tricky venture. I thank especially colleagues and friends in the following: the two Schools at Camberwell College of Arts, and the London Institute generally; the staff in the Ceramics Section, the N.A.L., and all of my friends at the Victoria and Albert Museum As usual, there are many individuals who have lent their support, sometimes directly, and sometimes without fully realising it I hope those I have forgotten will forgive my omission: Oriana Baddeley, Gail Brown, Deirdre Campion, Aeli Clark, Pete Clarke, Craig Clunas, Ray Crozier, Philip Dann, Elizabeth Esteve-Coll, Annette Fernandez, Andre Garo, Pascal Garo, David Gould, Eve Graves, Bill Greenhalgh, Judith Harper, Flora Hayes, Richard Hughes, Bridget Jackson, Wendy Kaplan, Helen Long, Jonathan Lopez-Glynne, John MacKenzie, the late Reverend Geoffrey Mann, Professor Gillian Naylor, Jennifer Opie, Jane Pavitt, Alan Read, Katharine Reeve, Sue Rigby, Beryl Robinson, Katrina Royal, Charles Saumaurez-Smith, Chris Stevens, Paul Toogood, Noel Upfold, Oliver Watson, and Stephen Young. I also thank anyone with whom I have sat, taken a drink, and talked about art and design; the list would fill a volume of this size. Finally, I thank the students of the Colleges of Art and Design in Great Britain; I'm glad they are there.

INTRODUCTION

We have all used collections of writings as a staple of our activity, and most of us have wondered why the compiler of the volume chose those particular pieces. We might even have been sceptical and angry at eccentricities and omissions.

As compiler of the present volume I submit myself up as eccentric and omiter. But having done this, I offer a few reasons as to why I have chosen the pieces herein, in the hope that the reader will forgive my excesses and lapses.

This is not an attempt to characterise the history of design and the decorative arts over the past two centuries. Rather, it is a gathering of pieces of writing on topics which are of particular interest. There are many other topics of interest, and indeed, many other interesting pieces of writing on these topics. So much is self-evident. The present volume is intended, more than anything else, to do two things: to widen the range of available material and to put design into a wider cultural and historical context.

The thematic structure is designed to help teachers and students alike in their use of the book, and to aid the informal reader who wishes to peruse a selection of extracts on a particular topic. It will become apparent, as one moves through the passages, that a significant proportion of the quotations are designed to trigger debate. There are starkly opposing views on certain issues. Depending on the writers one believes, the Industrial Revolution is either a blessing or a nightmare, the home is a machine, a boudoir, a formal arrangement or a nest, popular culture is an alienating scourge or a vital element in the cultural structure, and decoration is indispensable and dispensable.

The themes are not definitive or closed, and it is clear that some of the passages could have been included in more than one chapter. Ruskin's 'Nature of the Gothic', for example, might have been placed in any one of five. The overlap between Chapter 3, *'Technology and Everyday Life'* and Chapter 4, *'Uses of the Hand'* , and of both of these with Chapter 2, *'Morality, Politics and the Spirit for Reform'*, is marked. I urge the reader, therefore, to look through the book laterally as well as vertically, and to help in this process, I have indicated, at the end of the individual introductions to the chapters, other chapters where relevant material can be found.

Mainly because of the thematic structure, the chronology within chapters is not even; Chapter 1, *'The Role of Ornament'*, for example, concentrates on the decoration debates during the seminal period in which historicism triumphed and then came under fire from modernism. This seemed to me to be a succinct unit. However, 'the decoration debate', if it can be called that, became vibrant once more under the auspices of post-modernism, and has been of great relevance to craft practices during the later twentieth century. The last part of the chapter, therefore, contains material about late twentieth-century decoration. The chronological leaps, I hope, are compensated for by the thematic evenness.

The titles of the quotations are often mine. If the quotation had a title, or was taken from a longer, titled, piece, I left it unchanged where possible. If I had no title to use, or if the title of the longer piece I was extracting the quotation from was not appropriate, then I added a title. In general I simply took a word or phrase from the piece quoted, so that it was identified and characterised with minimum intervention from me. Check the sources section to find out the original title.

I selected these particular quotations for one of four reasons. First, I used material which I knew had not been reprinted since its original publication. In some cases, the author and passage alike have fallen into obscurity. About half of the book is such a rehabilitation.

Second, I went to the opposite extreme. There are a goodly number of passages which are well known. I wished to put these into a wider context of argument and debate, and, in a number of cases, to quote more of the passage than is customary, to show that perhaps the writer did not mean exactly what we have always taken him/her to mean. It might be a surprise, for example, to discover that some modernists were racist, that Louis Sullivan was not against ornament, and that Marx was not against individuality.

Third, I chose passages which are not necessarily by designers or writers on design; in some instances passages are not overtly on the subject of design in the strictest sense. I chose these in order to put design into a wider context of ideas and things. *Everything* here, I would argue, therefore, is *ultimately* about design. Charles Darwin, Adolf Hitler, Karl Marx, Adam Smith, Queen Victoria and Oscar Wilde, for example, said and did things which had drastic implications for the whole of visual culture. I stress, therefore, that no passage in the book was chosen simply *because* it was said by a famous person. Choice was connected to the meaning of the words.

My fourth reason was less disinterested. I chose some passages in the belief that the reader might enjoy them. Some of them are amusing, some shocking, and some are charmingly of their period. Some are sensationalist, and possibly offensive. I fully accept, of course, that the actual selection process could neither be objective nor value-free. But then, nothing ever is. I hope that this frisson of controversy serves to make the book palatable, especially for those who do not normally indulge in design and decorative art history.

For Belinda, who makes it happen,
and for Jack and Alex,
who, in their own sweet way, stop it
from happening

1

THE ROLE OF ORNAMENT

For a considerable part of the last two centuries ornament has been the subject of debate amongst those involved in the production and consumption of design. Speaking in broad terms, there seem to have been three subjects within this debate. First is what might be called the 'sense of appropriateness', or the relationship of the decorative elements of an object to its intended function. In one form or another this topic runs through the two centuries, constituting the dominant aesthetic thread. Second, there is ongoing discussion of the meaning of decoration, and what its most appropriate sources should be. The role of nature, of history, of design from outside Europe, and the constituent elements of a style, feature strongly in all this. Third, commentators became increasingly self-conscious, as the period wore on, of the position of the ornamental arts in relation to the other, principally 'high', arts. There is more implied in the terms 'high', 'fine', 'low', 'popular' and 'useful' than simply types of practice; they also refer to economic and social class boundaries.

The development of machine-made decorative detail complicated all three elements of the debate, as ornamentation became a more widely available design element. Indeed, the availability of decoration in the wider demographic sense meant that discussion of it tended to have a moral, social and even political underpinning.

There are three main chronological groups within the quoted passages. The first covers the second half of the nineteenth century, and demonstrates that whilst ornament was a contentious issue, it was nevertheless considered a necessary thing by virtually everyone. The second group belongs to the first decades of the twentieth century, and illustrates the powerful questioning, and finally rejection, of decoration, which occurred amongst modernist thinkers and makers. The third group is far more recent, and is concerned with the return of the interest in ornamentation in the so-called postmodern period, after decades of modernist anti-decorative theory and practice.

See also
Chapter 2 for the morality of ornamental art
Chapter 4 for hand-making and ornamentation
Chapter 7 for the impact of the design of other nations upon Europe
Chapter 8 for modernist and postmodernist thought
Chapter 9 for aesthetic discussion of issues relating to ornament

---

1   A.W.N. Pugin (British): 'On Ornament' (1841)

The two great rules for design are these: first, that there should be no features about a building which are not necessary for convenience, construction, or propriety; second, that all ornament should consist of enrichment of the essential construction of the building. The neglect of these two rules is the cause of all the bad architecture of the present time. Architectural features are continually tacked on buildings with which they have no connection, merely for the sake of what is termed effect.

---

2   Henry Cole (British): 'The Two Roles of Design' (1849)

Design has a twofold relation, having in the first place, a strict reference to utility in the thing designed; and, secondarily, to the beautifying or ornamenting that utility. The word *design*, however, with the many has become identified rather with its secondary than with its whole signification – with ornament, as apart from, and often even as opposed to, utility. From thus confounding that which is in itself but an addition, with that which is essential, has arisen many of those great errors in *taste* which are observable in the works of modern designers.

---

3   Ralph Nicholson Wornum (British): 'The Styles and Role of Ornament' (1851)

Style in ornament is analogous to hand in writing, and this is its literal signification. As every individual has some peculiarity in his mode of writing, so every age or nation has been distinguished in its ornamental expression by a certain individuality of taste, either original or borrowed . . . There are, of course, many varieties of every great style; but so long as the chief characteristics remain unchanged, the style is the same. From this point of view, therefore, the styles become comparatively few. We shall find that nine will comprise the whole number of

2

the great characteristic developments which have had any influence on European civilisation: namely – three ancient, the Egyptian, the Greek, and the Roman; three middle-age, the Byzantine, the Saracenic, and the Gothic; and three modern, the Renaissance, the Cinquecento, and the Louis Quatorze.

All styles are only so many different ways of using the same language, that of ornament . . .

Ornament is not a luxury, but, in a certain stage of the mind, an absolute necessity. When manufactures have attained a high mechanical perfection, or have completely met the necessities of the body, the energy that brought them to that perfection must either stagnate or be continued in a higher province – that of Taste; for there is a stage of cultivation when the mind must revolt at a mere crude utility. So it is a natural propensity to decorate or embellish whatever is useful or agreeable to us. But, just as there are mechanical laws which regulate all our efforts in pure uses, so there are laws of the mind which must regulate those aesthetical efforts expressed in the attempt at decoration or ornamental design.

---

4 Owen Jones (British): 'General Principles in the Arrangement of Form and Colour' (1856)

Proposition 1
The Decorative Arts arise from, and should be properly attendant upon, Architecture.

Proposition 2
Architecture is the material expression of the wants, the faculties, and the sentiments, of the age in which it is created.
Style in architecture is the peculiar form that expression takes under the influence of climate and materials at command

Proposition 4
True beauty results from that repose which the mind feels when the eye, the intellect, and the affections, are satisfied from the absence of any want

Proposition 8
All ornament should be based on geometrical construction.

Proposition 13
Flowers or other natural objects should not be used as ornaments,

3

but conventional representations founded upon them sufficiently suggestive to convey the intended images to the mind,
without destroying the unity of the object they are employed to
decorate.

*Universally obeyed in the best periods of Art, equally violated
when Art declines.*

Proposition 17
The primary colours should be used on the upper portions of
objects, the secondary and tertiary on the lower.

Proposition 20
*Each colour has a variety of hues, obtained by admixture with other
colours, in addition to white, grey, or black: thus we have of yellow, –
orange-yellow on the one side, and lemon-yellow on the other; so of
red, – scarlet-red, and crimson-red ; and of each every variety of tone
and shade.*

When a primary tinged with another primary is contrasted
with a secondary, the secondary must have a hue of the third
primary.

Proposition 21
In using the primary colours on moulded surfaces, we should
place blue, which retires, on the concave surfaces; yellow,
which advances, on the convex; and red, the intermediate
colour, on the undersides; separating the colours by white on
the vertical planes.

Proposition 23
No composition can ever be perfect in which any one of the
three primary colours is wanting, either in its natural state or in
combination.

Proposition 26
Colours on white grounds appear darker; on black grounds
lighter.

Proposition 27
Black grounds suffer when opposed to colours which give a
luminous complementary.

Proposition 28
Colours should never be allowed to impinge upon each other.

4

Proposition 35
Imitations, such as the graining of woods, and of the various coloured marbles, are allowable only, when the employment of the thing imitated would not have been inconsistent.

Proposition 36
The principles discoverable in the works of the past belong to us; not so the results. It is taking the end for the means.

Proposition 37
No improvement can take place in the Art of the present generation until all classes, Artists, Manufacturers, and the Public, are better educated in Art, and the existence of general principles is more fully recognised.

---

5   John Ruskin (British): 'A Definition of Decorative Art' (1859)

Observe, then, first – the only essential distinction between Decorative and other art is the being fitted for a fixed place ; and in that place, related, either in subordination or in command, to the effect of other pieces of art. And all the greatest art which the world has produced is thus fitted for a place, and subordinated to a purpose. There is no existing highest-order art but is decorative. The best sculpture yet produced has been the decoration of a temple front – the best painting, the decoration of a room. Raphael's best doing is merely the wall-colouring of a suite of apartments in the Vatican, and his cartoons were made for tapestries. Correggio's best doing is the decoration of two small church cupolas at Parma; Michael Angelo's, of a ceiling in the Pope's private chapel; Tintoret's, of a ceiling and side wall belonging to a charitable society at Venice; while Titian and Veronese threw out their noblest thoughts, not even on the inside, but on the outside of the common brick and plaster walls of Venice.

Get rid, then, at once any idea of Decorative art being a degraded or a separate kind of art. Its nature or essence is simply its being fitted for a definite place; and, in that place, forming part of a great and harmonious whole, in companionship with other art; and so far from this being a degradation to it – so far from Decorative art being inferior to other art because it is fixed to a spot – on the whole it may be considered as rather a piece of degradation that it should be portable. Portable art – independent of all place – is for the most part ignoble art. Your little

Dutch landscape, which you put over your sideboard today, and between the windows tomorrow, is a far more contemptible piece of work than the extents of field and forest with which Benozzo has made green and beautiful the once melancholy arcade of the Campo Santo at Pisa; and the wild boar of silver which you use for a seal, or lock into a velvet case, is little likely to be so noble a beast as the bronze boar who foams forth the fountain from under his tusks in the market-place of Florence. It is, indeed, possible that the portable picture or image may be first rate of its kind, but it is not first-rate because it is portable; nor are Titian's frescoes less than first-rate because they are fixed; nay, very frequently the highest compliment you can pay to a cabinet picture is to say – 'It is as grand as a fresco.'

Keeping, then, this fact fixed in our minds, – that all art *may* be decorative, and that the greatest art yet produced has been decorative, – we may proceed to distinguish the orders and dignities of Decorative art.

---

6 C. L. Eastlake (British): 'The Degradation of Decorative Art' (1872)

We fall into the double error of adopting endless varieties of style at one time, and yet allowing buildings raised for totally opposite purposes to resemble each other in form. The same fallacy is repeated throughout the whole system of British manufacture. We copy the bronzes of France, the mosaics of Italy, the pottery of China, the carpets of Turkey, with indifferent success; and, not content with this jumble, we invest objects constructed of one material with the form and ornamental character which should be the attributes of another. By this means decorative art has been degraded in this country to a level from which it is only now beginning to rise.

---

7 Albert Racinet (French): 'The Role of Ornamental Art' (1873)

Most assuredly, however, we would not say that the productions of [ornamental] art can dispense with obedience to certain principles and superior laws, to which every artistic conception must conform.

Thus, an ornamental composition can only be perfectly beautiful when it produces in the spectator that sentiment of repose and satisfaction which results from the equilibrium and perfect harmony of the elements of which it is composed. The laws of proportion, the laws of balancing and symmetry, the subordination of details to the whole, variety in unity, all these rules, dictated by instinct and proclaimed by science, are binding on the art of ornamentation as on all others.

But yet, whilst painting and sculpture are more or less fettered by sense and logic, or by the necessity of the imitation and exact rendering of natural objects; whilst architecture must comply with various conditions – solidity, the purpose of the building, and the correlation of exterior aspect with interior use; ornament, and especially that kind which now occupies us – the decoration of coloured surfaces – has a sphere of action, doubtless more modest, but yet enjoying much greater liberty.

Many means exist by which this end may be attained, many ways of arriving at this combination of proportion and harmony which gives birth to the sentiment of the beautiful.

If ornament may borrow from other arts their various characteristics – from architecture its general forms and the interest attaching to repetitions and variations of the same motive; from sculpture its real or imitated reliefs; from painting the charms of episodic subjects and of natural colouring – it may, without diverging from its proper sphere, find inexhaustible resources.

From the simplest geometric figure – a square, a lozenge, or a triangle, the repetition and intermingling of which frequently suffice to form an interesting whole – to the most ingeniously complicated interlacings, the most capricious arabesques, and those chimerical compositions in which the line, the flower, the animal and the human figure are mixed and blended together, what a vast domain for the ornamentalist, who thus finds himself master of that fantastic and charming world, which depends not on nature but on the imagination! What captivating and even seductive liberty, if such freely-ranging caprice were not to be regulated by taste and judged by the effect produced, which must be, whatever the means employed, harmony in form as well as in colour!

Thus, the place which ornament occupies in the artistic scale is, though a secondary, yet an important one. If it is less ambitious than other forms of art, if it does not attempt like them to raise our souls and make them vibrate with the deepest feelings, it responds to one of the most instinctive needs of our nature, that of embellishing the objects around us.

Sometimes united to the creations of the higher arts in order to complete them, sometimes applied to the commonest objects, which it relieves and ennobles, it is the natural link between industry and art, of which it represents one of the most familiar, practical, and varied forms.

---

8 Richard Redgrave (British): 'On Utility which must be Considered before Ornamentation' (1876)

[A]s construction necessarily implies a purpose, utility must precede ornament. In all arts applied to articles for the use, convenience, and comfort of man, from the building which shelters him and the objects of his care, to the meanest utensil which he values enough to desire to render it ornamental, the utility and fitness for intended purpose is, or ought to be the first consideration. It has been said that design must commence with the choice of the first structural form and the best use of the materials to be employed, and afterwards proceed to the enhancing, enriching and ornamenting of that utility, or in other words, in accordance with the well-known rule, we must ornament construction, not construct ornament.

This seems an obvious and an almost unnecessary proposition, but it is often completely overlooked; if, however, it were kept prominently in view, it would correct so many grave errors, that it is worth being earnestly enforced and constantly repeated. Thus, with respect to the external structure of both public and private edifices, the errors that arise out of useless constructive ornamentation have already been noticed. Nor are the faults *within* the building, its furniture, its decoration, or its utensils, likely to be less grave, in consequence of the neglect of the principle of the prior claims of utility.

The way in which utility must control decoration is not always as patent as might be inferred, and oftentimes requires most attentive study and research. Thus, after the consideration of the general uses of any building, must come that of its individual apartments, regulating and characterising the decorative treatment of each ; and the hall, the library, the dining and withdrawing room, should each be considered having regard to their separate uses.

---

9 Ernest Chesneau (French): 'Decoration' (1886)

To satisfy taste while we satisfy the demands of utility: the problem stated in these apparently simple terms is, in reality, a very hard one; it is the whole mystery of decorative art.

---

10   Paul Gauguin (French): 'Notes on Decoration at the Paris Universal Exhibition' (1889)

Of course this exhibition is the triumph of iron, not only with regard to machines but also with regard to architecture. And yet architecture is at its beginnings, in that, as an art, it lacks a style of decoration consistent with the material which architecture uses. Why, alongside this severe, rugged iron, are there such flabby substances as underfired clay; why, alongside these geometric lines of a new type, is there all this old stock of old ornaments modernised by naturalism? To the architect-engineer belongs a new decorative art, such as ornamental bolts, iron corners extending beyond the main line, a sort of gothic lacework of iron. We find this to some extent in the Eiffel Tower.

Imitation bronze statues clash alongside iron. Always imitations! Better to have monsters of bolted iron.

Also, why repaint iron so it looks like butter, why this gilding as if in the Opera? No, that is not good taste. Iron, iron, and more iron! Colours as serious as the material used and you'll have an imposing construction, suggestive of molten metal . . .

Decoration involves so much poetry. Yes, gentlemen, it takes a tremendous imagination to decorate any surface tastefully, and it is far more abstract art than the servile imitation of nature. In the Dieulafoy Gallery at the Louvre, have a close look at the bas-reliefs of the lions. I maintain that enormous genius was required to imagine flowers that are the muscles of animals or muscles that are flowers. All of the dreamy, mystical Orient is to be found there.

Decoration, which is appropriate to the material and to the place where that material is to be used, is an art which seems to be disappearing and requires study over a long period of time, a special genius. It is true that here too the official manner has distorted taste. Sèvres, not to name names, has killed ceramics. No one wants them, and when some Kanaka ambassador comes along, bang, they stick a vase in his arms, the way a mother-in-law would fling her daughter at you, to get rid of her. Everybody knows this, but Sèvres is inviolable; it's the glory of France.

11 Louis Sullivan (American): 'We should Refrain Entirely from the Use of Ornament for a Period of Years' (1892)

I take it as self-evident that a building, quite devoid of ornament, may convey a noble and dignified sentiment by virtue of mass and proportion. It is not evident to me that ornament can intrinsically heighten these elemental qualities. Why then, should we use ornament? Is not a noble and simple dignity sufficient? Why should we ask more?

If I answer the question in entire candour, I should say that it would be greatly for our aesthetic good if we should refrain entirely from the use of ornament for a period of years, in order that our thought might concentrate acutely upon the production of buildings well-formed and comely in the nude. We should thus perforce eschew many undesirable things, and learn by contrast how effective it is to think in a natural, vigorous and wholesome way. This step taken, we might safely inquire to what extent a decorative application of ornament would enhance the beauty of our structures – what new charm it would give them.

If we have become well grounded in pure and simple forms we will revere them; we will refrain instinctively from vandalism; we will be loath to do aught that may make these forms seem less pure, less noble. We shall have learned, however, that ornament is mentally a luxury, not a necessary, for we shall have discerned the limitations as well as the great value of unadorned masses. We have in us romanticism, and feel a craving to express it. We feel intuitively that our strong, athletic and simple forms will carry with natural ease the raiment of which we dream, and that our buildings thus clad in a garment of poetic imagery, half hid as it were in choice products of loom and mine, will appeal with redoubled power, like a sonorous melody overlaid with harmonious voices.

I conceive that a true artist will reason substantially in this way; and that, at the culmination of his powers, he may realise this ideal. I believe that architectural ornament brought forth in this spirit is desirable, because beautiful and inspiring; that ornament brought forth in any other spirit is lacking in higher possibilities . . .

. . . It must be manifest that an ornamental design will be more beautiful if it seems a part of the surface or substance that receives it than if it looks 'stuck on', so to speak. A little observation will lead one to see that in the former case there exists a peculiar sympathy between the ornament and the structure, which is absent in the latter. Both structure and ornament obviously benefit by this sympathy; each enhancing the value of the other. And this, I take it, is the preparatory basis of what may be called an organic system of ornamentation.

---

12 Walter Crane (British): 'The Claims of Decorative Art' (1892)

An archbishop at an Academy dinner, doubtless with an amiable desire to administer consolation to those less favoured ones whose works did not adorn the walls around him, is reported to have said, in effect: 'Never mind. It is not given to every one to be a Raphael, a Phidias, or a Michael Angelo (the exhibition being, by implication, of course full of them); but let them not therefore despair, let them turn their attention to Decorative Art, for there was a large field in which they might yet distinguish themselves.'

Now, although I do not suppose that even an archbishop could be found now to say anything of this kind, so rapidly have we advanced, yet it struck me at the time as the expression of a very curious view of art. It was not the unfortunate selection of names, all of which stood for artists preeminently decorative; it was not the placid assumption that the Academy represented both the best judgment upon, and the best work in, art which the country produced; it was not this so much as the assumption that what is called decorative art belonged distinctly to a lower category, that its demands upon the mind, both of the artist and the spectator, were much less, and, in short, the whole thing was of lower aim, and required less skill and power to produce than what is called pictorial art. If, however, we are justified in drawing conclusions from the history and practice of art, they seem to invert this view altogether.

I have no wish to set the sisters one against the other, or make odious comparisons, and indeed there is no need to do so, as, in my belief, both kinds of art in their higher development join hands. Their true relative position, indeed, may be expressed by the two limbs of a pair of compasses, inseparable and mutually dependent and helpful. It is certain that painting and sculpture, as commonly understood, cannot be in a good state, cannot reach any perfection, where the multitudinous arts that surround and culminate in them – that frame them, in short – are not also in vigorous health and life. As well expect flowers to bloom without roots and stems, light, heat, and air, as to think that beautiful pictures or statues, or the sense that produces and admires them, can exist where there is no beauty in everyday things, no sources of harmonious thought about us, or delight of the eye in pleasant colour or form in things of daily use and surrounding. I would go further, and say that where decorative or applied art is in a wholesome condition good pictorial or dramatic art will follow on as natural effect in the chain of evolution from certain ascertainable causes.

13 Siegfried Bing (German, resident in France): 'The Difference between the Fine and Decorative Arts' (1895)

Painting is an abstract art, requiring only one creator. A painter may emerge spontaneously, in advance of the culture of his time, without being influenced by any external pressure. But conversely, the decorative arts develop only under pressure from pre-existing need, and in favourable surroundings. If the painter's task is limited to giving shape to the content of his imagination, the mission of decorative art is to adapt itself to the taste and habit of others.

14 James Ward (British): 'What Ornament Is' (1896)

Ornament is the proper enrichment of an object or surface with such forms, or forms and colours, as will give the thing decorated a new beauty, while strictly preserving its shape and character. It is the function of ornament to *emphasise* the forms of the objects it decorates, not to *hide* them. Decoration is not necessarily ornament; for instance, the lovely sprays of plants with birds and cognate subjects, painted on Japanese pottery, may be called beautiful decoration, but cannot, in our sense of the word be called ornament; for however realistic ornament may be, it must show that it has passed through the mind of man, and been acted on by it. This kind of decoration might be a literal transcript from nature, and neither emphasises the boundaries of the decorated surface nor harmonises with them. It possesses an exquisite beauty of its own, for the drawing and colour and the style of execution are good. With the exception of frets and diapers, true ornament is rare in Japanese art.

15	Hector Guimard (French): 'On Nature' (1899)

For construction, do not the branches of the trees, the stems, by turn rigid and undulating, furnish us with models?

16	Eugène Grasset (French): 'The Three Elements of Ornament' (1907)

Strictly speaking, ornament has three main principles.

Firstly, it is conceived completely in the abstract, secondly, the concrete, by which the object is created within the limits of the material which is being used, and lastly, the conceptual, or the desired ornamental interpretation. This last category of ornament is referred to as stylisation, the outcome of a voluntary act of reflection which transforms the natural object. These principles are no more than a point of departure for the artist, upon which he depends in order to conceive the ornament which he is looking for. Our imagination, left to its own devices, is still inadequate compared to the vast array of natural objects which become the themes for development, and upon which each talent can elaborate its inexhaustible fund of ideas. There is another condition which we must bear in mind when considering ornament; that is, that the most important natural characteristic of each object should be preserved because this ensures that the ornament enjoys an originality of construction. It should never be a creature created from many elements. All 'artist-decorators' must abide by these three principles of ornament and to apply them in the appropriate circumstances to the programmes and goals which they pursue.

17	Lewis F. Day (British): 'Mere Ornament' (1908)

The object of ornament is to ornament something; it has primarily nothing to do with story, poetry, or any other purpose than that . . .

The only reason, and the one excuse, for ornament is beauty – its very name will bear no other interpretation – and its beauty consists in its decorative, not in its symbolic, quality. It is perfect only when it fulfils a purpose perfectly, and its purpose is in the main modest. Ornament is essentially subsidiary; in many cases it is mere background, the merit of which is self-effacement. They lose sight of this who clamour for poetic significance, who think to disparage 'mere' ornament when they say, 'It doesn't excite me.' It is not its business to excite, but rather to soothe. The defect of meaningful ornament is that it asks too much attention, and ends in irritating us. Fancy living with carpets and curtains which excite you!

The merest ornament is not so meaningless as those who misinterpret it suppose. Is there no meaning in the solution of a decorative problem? Perhaps not for those who look at ornament without ever suspecting what the artist was about! Every adequate design stands for the solution of a problem – as for example: to occupy a given space; to divert attention from its awkward proportions, and to devise within it, therefore, lines or shapes which will draw the eye away from them; whilst keeping ornament in harmony with its architectural or other purpose and subservient to a general scheme of decoration, to adapt it to some particular means of execution; to produce a certain effect of gaiety, or restfulness, or dignity, as the case may be. And that is only the beginning of the problem. Yet, because the answer may not be in the words of nature, nor laden with symbols, nor labelled with a tag of rhyme, it is called unmeaning! It is the epithet which is unmeaning.

What is meant by 'meaningless'? And what right has anyone to say that *any* ornament is meaningless? For all he knows, the most arbitrary of meandering lines may signify the continuity of human life, the endlessness of life eternal.

---

18 Adolf Loos (Austrian): 'Ornament and Crime' (1908)

The human embryo goes through all the phases of animal life whilst it is inside the womb. When man is born, his instincts are those of a new-born dog. His childhood runs through all the changes corresponding to the history of mankind. At the age of two he looks like a Papuan, at four like one of an ancient Germanic tribe, at six like Socrates, at eight like Voltaire . . .

The child is amoral. So is the Papuan, to us. The Papuan kills his enemies and eats them. He is no criminal. But if a modern man kills someone and eats him, he is a criminal or a degenerate. The Papuan tattoos his skin, his boat, his rudder, his oars; in short, everything he can get his hands on. He is no criminal. The modern man who tattoos himself is a criminal or a degenerate ...

What is natural for a Papuan and a child, is degenerate for modern man. I have discovered the following truth and present

14

it to the world: cultural evolution is equivalent to the removal of ornament from articles in daily use.

19   G. Woolliscroft Rhead (British): 'The Classes of Ornament' (1913)

There are three great classes of ornamental design: symbolic, which is a figurative expression of a definite idea; mnemonic, which consists of written characters, signs, hieroglyphics, &c.; aesthetic, in which the purpose is solely decorative, without any distinct or definite meaning other than an appreciation of the beautiful.

The two first divisions, however, not only overlap each other but may be said to be intimately connected, as in Egyptian art (for example), which is in the nature of a symbolic language, both divisions or classes figure largely. Further, there are few examples of either symbolic or mnemonic art which are not also aesthetic in their purpose and intention.

20   Le Corbusier (C.E. Jeanneret) (Swiss, resident in France): 'The Decorative Art of Today' (1925)

Why do the objects that concern us here have to be called *decorative art*? This is the paradox: why should chairs, bottles, baskets, shoes, which are all objects of utility, all *tools*, be called *decorative art*? The paradox of making art out of tools. Lets be clear. I mean, the paradox of making *decorative* art out of tools. To make art out of tools is fair enough, if we hold with Larousse's definition, which is that ART is *the application of knowledge to the realisation of an idea*. Then yes. We are indeed committed to apply all our knowledge to the perfect creation of a tool: know-how, skill, efficiency, economy, precision, the sum of knowledge. A good tool, an excellent tool, the very best tool. This is the world of *manufacture*, of industry; we are looking for a standard and our concerns are far from the personal, the arbitrary, the fantastic, the eccentric; our interest is the norm, and we are creating type objects

So the paradox certainly lies in terminology.

But we are told that decoration is necessary to our existence. Let us correct that: art is necessary to us; that is to say, a dis-interested passion that exalts us. Decoration: baubles, charming entertainment for a savage. (And I do not deny that it is an excellent thing to keep an element of the savage alive in us – a small one.) But in the twentieth century our powers of judgment have developed greatly and we have raised our level of consciousness. Our spiritual needs are different, and higher worlds than those of decoration offer us commensurate experience. It seems justified to affirm: *the more cultivated a people becomes, the more decoration disappears.* (Surely it was Loos who put it so neatly.)

So, to see things clearly, it is sufficient to separate the satisfaction of disinterested emotion from that of utilitarian need. Utilitarian needs call for tools brought in *every respect* to that degree of perfection seen in industry. This then is the magnificent programme for *decorative art* (decidedly, an inappropriate term!) . . .

Previously, decorative objects were rare and costly. Today they are commonplace and cheap. Previously, plain objects were commonplace and cheap; today they are rare and expensive. Previously, decorative objects were items for special display: the plate which the peasant family hung on the wall and embroidered waistcoat for holidays; grist for the propaganda of princes. Today decorative objects flood the shelves of the Department Stores; they sell cheaply to shop-girls. If they sell cheaply, it is because they are badly made and because decoration hides faults in their manufacture and the poor quality of their materials: decoration and disguise. It pays the manufacturer to employ a decorator to disguise the faults in his products, to conceal the poor quality of their materials and to distract the eye from their blemishes by offering it the spiced morsels of glowing gold-plate and strident symphonies. Trash is always abundantly decorated; the luxury object is well made, neat and clean, pure and healthy, and its bareness reveals the quality of its manufacture. It is to industry that we owe this reversal in the state of affairs: a cast-iron stove overflowing with decoration costs less than a plain one; amidst the surging leaf patterns flaws in the casting cannot be seen . . .

Today there is a lively aesthetic awareness and a taste for a contemporary art responding to very much more subtle requirements and to a new spirit. As a result there is a distinct evolution towards ideas reflecting the new spirit; the experience of decoration as art from 1900 to the war has illustrated the impasse of decoration and the fragility of the attempt to make our tools expressive of sentiment and of individual states of mind. There has been a reaction to this obtrusive presence, and it is being rejected. Day after day, on the other hand, we notice among the products of industry articles of perfect convenience and utility, that soothe our spirits with the luxury afforded by the elegance of their conception, the purity of their execution, and the efficiency of their operation. They are so well thought out that we feel them to be harmonious, and this harmony is sufficient for our gratification . . .

Without a revolution, barricades, or gun-fire, but as a result of simple evolution accelerated by the rapid tempo of our time, we can see decorative art in its decline, and observe that the almost hysterical rush in recent years towards quasi-orgiastic decoration is no more than the final spasm of an already foreseeable death . . .

---

21   Theo van Doesburg (Dutch): 'Decoration' (1930)

The new architecture is anti-decorative. Instead of dramatizing a two-dimensional surface or serving as a superficial ornament, colour like light becomes an elementary means for pure architectural expression. This is literally what we must master in the new process of creating architecture.

Modern architects in almost all countries have already designed many buildings stimulated by these principles which demonstrate the fundamental spirit of architecture. They have not restricted themselves to the construction of country houses, hotels, streetplans and factories, but have expanded the problems related to the single house to include those related to *urbanism*.

---

22   Henry-Russell Hitchcock and Philip Johnson (American): 'The Avoidance of Applied Decoration' (1932)

Absence of ornament serves as much as regular horizontality to differentiate superficially the current style from the styles of the past and from the various manners of the last century and a half. Applied ornament may not have been significant or important in the architecture of the past, but it certainly existed. It is easier to defend the claim that the finest buildings built since 1800 were those least ornamented. The failure of revivalism probably lay quite as much in the inability to recreate the conditions of craftsmanship which once made applied ornament aesthetically valid, as in the impossibility of adapting the spirit of old styles to new methods of construction.

It would be ridiculous to state categorically that there will never be successful applied ornament in architecture again. It is nevertheless clear that conditions are today even less propitious for the production of ornament than they were during the last century. Since the middle of the eighteenth century the quality of the execution of ornament has steadily declined. Even the renaissance of craftsmanship sponsored by the Mediaevalists failed to turn the tide. On the whole each generation of traditionalists has been worse served in this respect than its predecessor . . .

Besides architectural detail, related subordinate works of sculpture and painting have on occasion been successfully used to decorate contemporary buildings without degenerating into mere applied ornament. Mural painting should not break the wall surface unnecessarily. Yet it should remain an independent entity without the addition of borders or panelling to fuse it with the architecture. Baumeister and Ozenfant, among others, have done work of this order. But there is no reason why painting less abstract should not find its place quite as satisfactorily on the walls of contemporary buildings. It is most important that mural painting should be intrinsically excellent; otherwise a plain wall is better. It need not be related, except in scale and shape, to the wall on which it is placed. Contemporary architecture cannot expect to dictate the evolution of contemporary painting, but it offers fields more considerable than the framed canvas panel.

Sculpture also ought not to be combined or merged with architecture.It should retain its own character quite separate from that of its background. This was true of the best Greek sculpture and often of that of other periods. It is particularly important today that sculpture should be isolated; for it is actually applied, its suggestion of solid mass is carried over to the wall surface it decorates. Thus far contemporary architecture has served rather as an admirable background for wholly separate units of painting and sculpture not designed for their specific location. But there is an opportunity here for collaboration which may well in the future lead to brilliant results . . .

The current style sets a high but not impossible standard for decoration: better none at all unless it be good. The principle is aristocratic rather than puritanical. It aims as much at making monstrosities impossible, at which the nineteenth century so signally failed, as at assuring masterpieces, at which the nineteenth century had no very extraordinary success.

23 Herbert Read (British): 'The Function of Decoration' (1934)

Before passing on to the possibilities of compensatory qualities in machine art I would like to refer to the function of decoration.

Again there is some confusion of terminology. A form in itself may be 'decorative', but that usually implies the relation of an object to its setting. We *decorate* a room when we paint the woodwork and paper the walls, but that sense merely implies that we give it colour. When we decorate a work of art, an *objet d'art*, as it is then usually called, we add to its form an extra thing which is known as *ornament*. Ornament can be added to almost any work of art – we add carved capitals and friezes to architecture, colour and pictures to pottery; even the cabinet picture is not complete without its ornamental frame. All such ornament is *applied* to the work of art, and this is where the word *applied* has its original and proper sense. But by one of those monstrous mis-applications of words that can confuse thought for centuries, the epithet was taken from ornament and given to art. Applied ornament became applied art, and all the commissions of enquiry, all the museums and schools of art in the country, have laboured under this confusion for a century or more. The necessity of ornament is psychological. There exists in man a certain feeling which has been called *horror vacui*, an incapacity to tolerate an empty space. The feeling is strongest in certain savage races, and in decadent periods of civilization. It may be an ineradicable feeling; it is probably the same instinct that causes certain people to scribble on lavatory walls, others to scribble on their blotting-pads. A plain empty surface seems an irresistible attraction to the most controlled of men; it is the delight of all uncontrolled children. Whilst I think that a little discipline would be a very good thing, I by no means wish to urge the total suppression of the instinct to fill blank spaces . . . At present, all I wish to insist on, is that the instinct is not necessarily aesthetic. All ornament should be treated as suspect. I feel that a really civilised person would as soon tattoo his body as cover the form of a good work of art with meaningless ornament. The only real justification for ornament is that it should in some way emphasise form. I avoid the customary word 'enhance', because if form is adequate, it cannot be enhanced. Legitimate ornament I conceive as something like mascara and lipstick – something applied with discretion to make more precise the outlines of an already existing beauty.

Since both our educationalists and manufacturers have for so long been blind to the formal elements in art, they have tended to regard ornament as the only essential element, and their failure has been largely due to this misguided attempt to contort and twist and otherwise deform the naturally austere and precise forms of manufactured articles into the types of ornament they mistake for art.

---

24 Sonia Delaunay (French): 'My Painting and my Decorative Work' (no date)

There was no gap between my painting and my decorative work and . . . the minor art had never been an artistic frustration but a free expansion, a conquest of new space. It was an application of the same research.

---

25 Charles Jencks (American): 'The Death of Modern Architecture' (1977)

A Post-Modern building is, if a short definition is needed, one which speaks on at least two levels at once: to other architects and a concerned minority who care about specifically architectural meanings, and to the public at large, or the local inhabitants, who care about other issues concerned with comfort, traditional building and a way of life. Thus Post-Modern architecture looks hybrid and, if a visual definition is needed, rather like the front of a Classical Greek temple. The latter is a geometric architecture of elegantly fluted columns below, and a riotous billboard of struggling giants above, a pediment painted in deep reds and blues. The architects can read the implicit metaphors and subtle meanings of the column drums, whereas the public can respond to the explicit metaphors and messages of the sculptors. Of course everyone responds somewhat to both codes of meaning, as they do in a Post-Modern building, but certainly with different intensity and understanding, and it is this discontinuity in taste cultures which creates both the theoretical base and 'dual coding' of Post-Modernism. The dual image of the Classical temple is a helpful visual formula to keep in mind as the unifying factor while different departures from Modernism are presented in this book. The buildings most characteristic of Post-Modernism show a marked duality, conscious schizophrenia . . .

Happily we can date the death of modern architecture to a precise moment in time. Unlike the legal death of a person, which is becoming a complex affair of brain waves versus heartbeats, modern architecture went out with a bang. That many people didn't notice, and no one was seen to mourn, does not make the sudden extinction any less of a fact, and that many designers are still trying to administer the kiss of life does not mean that it has been miraculously resurrected. No, it expired finally and completely in 1972, after having been flogged to death remorselessly for ten years by critics such as Jane Jacobs; and the fact that so many so-called modern architects still go around practising a trade as if it were alive can be taken as one of the great curiosities of our age (like the British Monarchy giving life-prolonging drugs to 'The Royal Company of Archers' or 'The Extra Women of the Bedchamber').

Modern Architecture died in St Louis, Missouri on July 15, 1972 at 3.32 p.m. (or thereabouts) when the infamous Pruitt-Igoe scheme, or rather several of its slab blocks, were given the final *coup de grace* by dynamite. Previously it had been vandalised, mutilated and defaced by its black inhabitants, and although millions of dollars were pumped back, trying to keep it alive (fixing the broken elevators, repairing smashed windows, repainting) it was finally put out of its misery. Boom, boom, boom.

Without doubt, the ruins should be kept, the remains should have a preservation order slapped on them, so that we keep a live memory of this failure in planning and architecture. Like the folly or artificial ruin – constructed on the estate of an eighteenth century English eccentric to provide him with instructive reminders of former vanities and glories – we should learn to value and protect our former disasters. As Oscar Wilde said, 'experience is the name we give our mistakes', and there is a certain health in leaving them judiciously scattered around the landscape as continual lessons.

Pruitt-Igoe was constructed according to the most progressive ideals of CIAM (the Congress of International Modern Architects) and it won an award from the American Institute of Architects when it was designed in 1951. It consisted of elegant slab blocks fourteen storeys high with rational 'streets in the air' (which were safe from cars, but as it turned out, not safe from crime); 'sun, space and greenery', which Le Corbusier called the 'three essential joys of urbanism' (instead of conventional streets, gardens and semi-private space, which he banished). It had a separation of pedestrian and vehicular traffic, the provision of play space, and local amenities such as laundries, creches and gossip centres – all rational substitutes for traditional patterns. Moreover, its Purist style, its clean, salubrious hospital metaphor, was meant to instil, by good example, corresponding virtues in the inhabitants. Good form was to lead to good content, or at least good conduct; the intelligent planning of abstract space was to promote healthy behaviour.

26 Robert Venturi (American): 'Ornament and Shelter' (1978)

Ornament was equated with crime by Adolf Loos as long ago as 1906, and symbolism was associated with discredited historical eclecticism; appliqué on shelter would have been considered superficial by theorists of the Modern Movement and contrary to the industrial techniques integral to Modern architecture.

But we like emphasising shelter in architecture, thereby including function in our definition; and we like admitting symbolic rhetoric in our definition which is not integral with shelter, thereby expanding the content of architecture beyond itself and freeing function to take care of itself.

27 Tom Wolfe (American): 'Glass Boxes' (1981)

Every new $900,000 summer house in the north woods of Michigan or on the shore of Long Island has so many pipe railings, ramps, hob-tread metal spiral stairways, sheets of industrial plate glass, banks of tungsten-halogen lamps, and white cylindrical shapes, it looks like an insecticide refinery. I once saw the owners of such a place driven to the edge of sensory deprivation by the whiteness & lightness & leanness & cleanness & bareness & spareness of it all. They became desperate for an antidote, such as coziness & color. They tried to bury the obligatory white sofas under Thai-silk throw pillows of every rebellious, iridescent shade of magenta, pink, and tropical green imaginable. But the architect returned, as he always does, like the conscience of a Calvinist, and he lectured them and hectored them and chucked the shimmering little sweet things out.

Every great law firm in New York moves without a splutter of protest into a glass-box office building with concrete slab floors and seven-foot-ten-inch-high concrete slab ceilings and plasterboard walls and pygmy corridors – and then hires a decorator and gives him a budget of hundreds of thousands of dollars to turn these mean cubes and grids into a horizontal fantasy of a Restoration townhouse. I have seen the carpenters and cabinetmakers and search-and-acquire girls hauling in more cornices, covings, pilasters, carved moldings, and recessed domes, more linenfold panelling, more (fireless) fireplaces with festoons of fruit carved in mahogany on the mantels, more chandeliers, sconces, girandoles, chestnut leather sofas, and chiming clocks than Wren, Inigo Jones, the brothers Adam, Lord Burlington, and the Dilettanti, working in concert, could have dreamed of.

Without a peep they move in! – even though the glass box appals them all.

These are not merely my impressions, I promise you. For detailed evidence one has only to go to the conferences, symposia, and jury panels where the architects gather today to discuss the state of the art. They profess to be appalled themselves. Without a blush they will tell you that modern architecture is exhausted, finished. They themselves joke about *the glass boxes*. They use the term with a snigger. Philip Johnson, who built himself a glassbox house in Connecticut in 1949, utters the phrase with an antiquarian's amusement, the way someone else might talk about an old brass bedstead discovered in the attic.

In any event, the problem is on the way to being solved, we are assured. There are now new approaches, new movements, new isms: Post-Modernism, Late Modernism, Rationalism, participatory architecture, Neo Corbu, and the Los Angeles Silvers. Which add up to what? To such things as building more glass boxes and covering them with mirrored plate glass so as to reflect the glass boxes next door and distort their boring straight lines into curves.

---

28 Eva Zeisel (American): 'The Straight Line and Curve' (1984)

For the first years of this century, from Vienna to Chicago, from Berlin to Paris, architects, designers, sociologists, and economists discussed the bad taste of 1900, pushing themselves away from this intensively personal world of sentimentalism, historicism, escapist romanticism, and ecstatic assertions of the present.

Searching for a new style, they engaged in passionate discussions of such gentle topics as the beauty of everyday objects (in Germany) and architecture (in Chicago). They 'fought' for a new style, they 'preached its evangelium', they declared 'the new truths' against 'the old truths', they 'battled' for them and sung 'hymns' to them. Style became a 'weapon' of German culture. The Futurists proclaimed a catastrophic break with the past. The word 'Naissance' was coined to herald the birth of something totally new.

As early as 1900 a 'document' by Peter Behrens declared the elimination of all historic and natural forms, predicting a new style. Soon after, a German professor exclaimed: 'Hurrah, hurrah for simplicity and the straight line'. Adolf Loos praised the exactitude of the compass' sweep 'against the uncertainty of the accident of dreams of humanity and the mystery of becoming'.

Years later, Le Corbusier still referred to the styles of his youth and wrote that, in those days, objects were supposed to be companions of our joys and sufferings – to have a soul and to spread radiant atmosphere. Now, he protested, things should be mute servants, not friends who have a soul. He called objects instruments, armatures, and *utillage*.

Faced with the overwhelming richness of emotional communicativeness which existed at the turn of the century, the virtue of the straight line lay in its restraint, its unwillingness to enter into an emotional dialogue with the viewer. Simple, straight lines were far from the emotionalism that had been communicated by the compound curve which Walter Crane called the 'expressive line'.

But emotionalism was not the only thing to be suppressed. The person himself, his whole identity was to be eliminated. Keeping in mind Gustav Eiffel's self-elevating 'I-built-that-thousand-foot-tower', we should not be surprised that the generation after him so vigorously departed from such overbearing pronouncements of individualism. When we understand what came before, we can see why the Bauhaus declared itself against the 'cult of I' and denounced all individual design solutions as 'arbitrary'. A decade before the declarations of the 1920's, the Austrian architect Otto Wagner had written that the city dweller preferred to disappear in the masses as 'numbers'. Later Gropius would declare that people, like machine parts, were interchangeable, that all men have the same needs at the same hour each day of their lives . . .

It was only around the 1920's in Germany that geometric forms were endowed with an ideology and that the Modern Movement systematically formulated its tenets. If the modernists wanted to stop the intensely emotional individual expressions they had inherited they made the right choice to reduce its formal language to rectilinear form . . . The aim of standardization and the ideal of the monolithic shape reduced the scope of aesthetic play. Arbiters of modern design still consider the acute angle and the compound curve 'gratuitous and sometimes extravagant.'

The exclusion of all but right angles, and of all but vertical and horizontal directions, resulted in a language devoid of communicative strength. Modern design was consciously deprived of the most effective means of making emotional contact between maker and the viewer. It was made purposely mute.

Some hundred and thirty years ago a popular American magazine recalled the observation of the painter, William Hogarth – that the S-curve was the line of beauty. Should any child practice forming this letter, it said, he would be able to see beauty in nature that was invisible to the mere definer of straight lines.

Let us then again admit this magical S-curve and instead of educating our public, simply try to please his eye and hand. Then, perhaps some fifty years from now, the museum walls will look down on our work bearing the legend: 'REJOICE! REJOICE! REJOICE!'

---

29   His Royal Highness, Charles, Prince of Wales (British): 'Decoration' (1989)

There seems to be a growing feeling that functional buildings with no hint of decoration give neither pleasure nor delight. The training of the modern architect rarely encompasses the rules of ornament or the study of past examples of applied decoration. There is no longer a universal language of symbolism, and the gropings of some critics towards the imposition of 'meaning' on what they call post-modern architecture has been fairly unfruitful.

This apparent vacuum can in fact easily be filled. There is a latent national interest in decoration. You only have to look at the thriving D.I.Y. industry! Long-lasting traditions of ornament go back to our Celtic forebears, and a glance into any ancient parish church can reveal amazing decorative secrets.

Many people think that a revival of classicism can help. It is certainly a universal language but it is not one that can be applied easily unless it is thoroughly learned. It is not the simple pastiche that some critics claim it to be: learning the classical language of architecture does not mean that you only produce endless neo-Georgian-style houses. Classicism provides an incredibly rich inventory of infinite variety.

In Britain there has always been a parallel stream of the Gothic and the Arts and Crafts Movements. These rich traditions rest in the hands of skilled craftsmen whose rare talents need constant nurturing to ensure their continuation. They are there, so why don't we use them more often?

We need to reinstate architecture as the mistress of the arts and the crafts. I would suggest that the consumers are ahead of the professionals here. They seem to feel, as I do, that living in a factory-made world is not enough. Beauty is made by the unique partnership of hand, brain and eye. The results should be part of all new architecture, helping it to enrich our spirits.

2
MORALITY, POLITICS AND THE
SPIRIT FOR REFORM

Much of this chapter is concerned with the psychological and physical effects of industrialisation upon the populations of both Europe and America. Britain was the first nation to go through this trauma, and so logically a lot of the earlier quotations concern Britain.

Design is never an innocent activity. There is always a motive force behind it, and usually there is more than one. The designer, under normal circumstances, is dedicated to the solving of the technical, aesthetic and commerical problems the object poses. These are immediate and clear goals, and they may or may not have direct socio-political ramifications. But design practice is virtu- ally always ideologically located in a wider sense; the appearance of the object, its technological and material make-up, its mode of production and the circumstances of its consumption, are all morally and politically mediated, in ways which are usually beyond the designer's control. Through the last two centuries, the horns of the dilemma at the centre of European and American culture, upon which design practice has been constantly speared, are the *drudg- ery of production* and the *promise of consumption*. The massive increase in the amount of goods in circulation has been paid for with a radical transformation of the work practices and life styles of the masses. In the first part of our period, places to consume in were far less evident than those constructed for production. Into the twentieth century, commentators were increasingly alarmed at the sea of consumables that surrounded the masses and apparently destroyed their sense of self.

This chapter contains some political, philosophical and literary tracts that were not written specifically *about* design but which clearly have major implications for it. The voracious advances of trade and industry occupied the attentions of the key thinkers of the age, and inspired some of the best novels. Indeed, philosophy, politics and literature frequently conjoined in their critique of the processes of industrial modernisation.

There are also passages which are centrally concerned with

design, quotations that are prescriptive with regard to the design process. Mass-production, however one chooses to understand that term, implied clear moral and political options for many designers and thinkers. If one was opposed to it, one had to under-mine it by transforming the work process; normally this was to be accomplished by dispensing with the division of labour and replac-ing it with a work system that put responsibility back with the worker. If one went along with mass-production, then the key issue was how one created a socially acceptable designed environment.

Also included in this chapter is material about State participation and intervention in the design process, including the organisation of design education and design promotion. The State, and State-related bodies, realised early in the period that design had politico-economic implications. Their most noticeable contributions came in the form of schools of design, and various types of trade display, including international exhibitions.

See also
Chapter 3 for the effects of technology and the division of labour
Chapter 4 for hand-making as an antidote to alienation
Chapter 5 for consumption theory
Chapter 7 for attitudes to race and nationalism
Chapter 8 for modernist solutions to moral and political issues

---

1 Prince Hoare (British): 'A Plea for Government Support for the Arts' (1806)

The importance of the arts, as well to the greatness as to the moral character of a nation, having been stated, in the obvious reflections offered in the foregoing pages, it will not be the presumptuous aim of the present chapter to enforce the con-sideration of the subject, by pointing out more strongly the public encouragement of the Arts of Design as a task incumbent on the high faculties of predominant states, as a debt for which they are responsible to a nation and to mankind. If, on contem-plating a duty of such magnitude, the extensive and capacious mind of an enlightened government find therein no adequate employment for thoughts of conscious greatness, no food for honourable ambition, no theme of virtuous praise, it is not within the hopes of the Writer of these sketches to suggest new excitements of attention . . .

. . . But should a wish for the accomplishment of unrivalled national fame, for the extension of peaceful human intercourse, for the establishment of more discriminate attachment to moral order, should such motives awaken a desire for the effectual progress of arts, so eminently subservient to those purposes, it is here desired to represent how inadequate to their protection and security must be all methods to which a powerful and permanent patronage does not lend its organising and supporting hand.

2 William Dyce (British): 'Design Education in Germany and France' (1840)

In Prussia the Schools of Art are classed under two heads, – 'Elementary Schools,' and 'Schools for Artisans.' As regards the former, besides two principal Elementary Schools at Berlin and Düsseldorf, under the superintendence of the Royal Academy, where each scholar pays about 12s. per annum, the Government has established about twenty elementary schools in the provinces. The pupils, who are generally of the poorer classes, are encouraged to proceed, and receive pecuniary assistance in their study, according as they show aptitude. Specimens of their work are forwarded to Berlin, and those who have distinguished themselves are rewarded with prizes, such as medals and useful publications; or, in remarkable cases, they receive pensions to enable them to pursue their studies in the metropolis. These pensions are as high as 300 thalers (about £45) per annum.

There are two schools for artisans, the 'Gewerbe Institut' and the 'Bau-Academie.' Of the former, it is difficult by a single expression to convey an accurate notion of the character of this establishment. Being intended for the general advancement of manufactures, its studies have reference to all the branches of science or art which any way conduce to that purpose.

The paramount object of the Institut is the creation of a race of intelligent and highly-cultivated artisans, to whose influence on the manufactures of the districts to which they belong the Government looks for the special benefits which are proposed by schools of more limited purpose. On this account, whatever may have been the occupation of the pupil previously to his entering school, no reference is made in the course of the instruction either to that or to his future purposes. If, however, during the progress of his studies, he displays remarkable scientific or artistical talent, he is transferred, as the case may be, to the University, to the Royal Academy, or to the Bau-Schule.

The young men who obtain admission to the Gewerbe

Institut, have generally been recommended on account of their having, in the elementary schools, shown some promise of ability; and the full development of this, whatever it may be, not by partial means, but by an admirable and extended system of education, is the great purpose of the Institut.

So far as taste is concerned, it was hoped that, by constituting the study of the principles of design and construction as part of the course, side by side with mechanics, chemistry, and other branches of physical science, the character of the pupils would be elevated in that respect in a degree suited to their other acquirements; and that whatever improvement took place in their scientific and practical knowledge, would also be seen in the refinement of their tastes; and accordingly, that the appreciation of art and its right application, wherever it was desirable, would be the inevitable result. Such has been the case. It is hardly necessary to say that these highly-instructed artisans seldom return to their native provinces as mere workmen; their knowledge and acquirements make them invaluable to manufacturers, as overseers and directors of their establishments; and thus, though the Gewerbe Institut does not profess specially to instruct designers for manufacture, it happens ultimately, in very many cases, that its pupils either personally conduct, or at least have the superintendence of, that branch of art. And apparently nothing can be more admirable than the preparation which is given in the school for an occupation of that sort. In the second class of the school (which is the elementary one), the pupils are taught geometrical, architectural, and free-hand drawing. They then have a course of mathematics and the elements of physics; after which they study machinery and the practical operations of manufacture. In this stage of their progress they learn, from working models and the demonstrations of the professor, every requisite of the design intended for a particular manufacture. They are taught, for instance, in the case of the figured silk, how to transfer a design to the ruled paper; how to read it off and pierce the cards; how to choose the silk which will produce the proposed effect; and, lastly, to set it up and work it in the loom. Or, in the case of calico-printing, they are shown the various operations of block and cylinder-printing, and the effects and combinations of colour which are possible in that process of industry.

It is obvious that preparatory study such as this might, if it were allowed to produce its full effect, leave comparatively little for the pupil to acquire in the practice of industrial design.

Exhibitions of specimens of manufacture are held from time

to time in Berlin. The object of these is to reward visible progress in manufacture by medals and other marks of approbation. It has been thought advisable to allow considerable intervals to elapse between these exhibitions, of which only two have already taken place – one in 1822, and the other in 1827.

Besides the schools expressly for the study of art, in all gymnasia, higher schools of citizens, normal schools, in most of the schools in towns, and in the better elementary schools in the country, the principles and practice of design are taught as an ordinary branch of public instruction, and that in the universities there are chairs of the History of Art.

Since the year 1815 great efforts have been made by the successive monarchs and administrations of Prussia to encourage the fine arts in that country. Museums, and other buildings of similar character, have been erected; sculptors, and more recently painters, have been employed in the execution of monumental works, and the cultivation of all those manufactures on which art can exercise any influence has been greatly promoted by the foundation of the 'Institution for Trades' (Gewerbe Institut). That these efforts have led to the happiest results has been proved by the (Great) Exhibition, which has furnished to Prussia a long-desired opportunity of showing what progress has there been made.

I have already mentioned, that the school at Munich is intended to bear chiefly on such branches of industry as are immediately connected with the fine arts; the school of Nuremberg on metal-casting, and that of Augsburg on calico-printing. Circumstances did not permit me to visit Augsburg, but the proofs I witnessed at Munich and Nuremberg of the efficiency of the schools, hold out the utmost encouragement, and give the best hopes of success to the establishment (School of Design), which in this country has lately been founded through . . . foresight and exertion.

The circumstances in which the school of Nuremberg is placed rendered it peculiarly interesting in relation to the objects of my inquiry. The town itself is a perfect mine of monuments of industrial art, the productions of a race of celebrated artifices, remarkable for having combined in their own persons the artist and the mechanic. In no place does there appear so widely spread the influence of taste. Not only in works, the costliness of which might have admitted of the employment of artists to furnish the designs, but in the most ordinary productions of handicraft, the love and knowledge of art manifest themselves . . .

31

France has long been celebrated for the attention which her rulers have given to the dissemination of artistic taste, and the cultivation of executive talent.

The Royal Free School of Paris was founded in 1767, under the title, 'L'Ecole Royale Gratuite de Dessin, de Mathématiques, de Construction et Sculpture d'Ornement, en faveur des Métiers relatifs aux Arts.' It was intended principally to benefit porcelain, tapestry, and carpet manufacture, the fabric of bronze, and other branches of industry practised in and about Paris; and with the exception of the addition of a greater number of professors, and the opening of an evening class at the beginning of this year (1838), the school remains as it was at its foundation.

The last of these is devoted to design for bronze manufacture. M. Lequien, the master, an able sculptor, who has occupied himself a good deal in designing for small bronze ornaments, and being annoyed to find the spirit and accuracy of his works so constantly destroyed by the chiselling and polishing subsequent to the casting, and necessary for the gilding or finishing operation in this fabric, determined, almost in self-defence, three years since, to open a school to instruct the workmen employed in this manufacture. These are of two kinds, the founders and chisellers. At present the school applies itself only to the latter; but M. Lequien hopes, by an increase of funds, to be enabled to provide an atelier for founders also, and thus to have the whole operation of producing a finished work in bronze performed in the school. The execution of bronze works for ornament he considers a kind of translation of art into a different language, and it is a thorough knowledge of the language only that he proposes to impart. With this view, his pupils are merely taught the art of copying accurately and with understanding what is placed before them, the ultimatum of their studies being the reproduction on any assigned scale of a given design adopted to their particular purpose.

The school, which is extremely well attended, is open in the morning to his private pupils; and in the evening to the public, at a charge of two francs per month.

On a review of the method of instruction adopted in the school of Lyons, so far as it is connected with manufacture, it appears to me to exhibit the true principle on which a school of design ought to be constituted, whether it confine itself to one branch of industry, or extend its operations over the whole field of ornamented manufacture. By the account I have given of it, the instruction will be observed to be twofold; one part relating to the general study of art, and the other to the process of manufacture to which art is to be applied; the latter naturally giving rise to what constitutes the ultimate purpose of the school; viz. the practice of the particular species of design which is adapted to the reproductive capabilities of the fabric.

Thus it will be seen that the elements of the education of an industrial artist, which in the German system are divided among two or three separate schools, are here to be found united in one; that is to say, the relation of ornamental design to taste, and the principles of fine art, and its practical relation to manufacture, equally form the business of the school of Lyons.

There is no circumstance, indeed, in France, connected with the application of design, not merely to the silk manufacture but to every branch of industry, that deserves more especial notice than the high estimation in which industrial artists are held, and the free and unrestrained exercise of their judgment and taste, which is consequently allowed to them, in all matters over which their peculiar abilities ought properly to give them control. So entire is the confidence which the Lyonnese manu-facturer reposes in his designer, that I have been assured by the head of one of the principal houses there, that in many cases he did not see the patterns till they were produced in silk, being quite satisfied that in every matter where taste was concerned the artist must know better than he. In short, a French pattern-designer is looked upon in his sphere precisely in the same light as a professor of fine art. You may employ him or not, as you think fit; but, having given a commission, it is he, not you, who is responsible for the merits of his performance; and this, as I have stated, does not terminate in the design merely – his taste and judgment must be equally allowed to control the manner and process of reproduction.

Those who are not much conversant with the very different state of matters in this respect at home, may think I attach too much importance to the authority which is accorded to French pattern-draftsmen by manufacturers; but a very little considera-tion will be sufficient to make this appear in another light. For myself I am quite persuaded, that if there is one cause more powerful than another which has contributed to retard, or which now presents an obstacle to, the progress of taste in British manufacture, it is the degraded position which pattern-designers occupy – a position in which their talents find no scope for development, and their taste and judgment as artists are set at nought.

33

In Lyons, the commercial value of taste is reckoned so high, that when a young man displays remarkable powers, a house will admit him to a partnership in order completely to monopolise his services. Even in general employment, a Lyonnese pattern-designer in good practice realises as much as 10,000 francs per annum; which, considering the comparative value of money in Lyons and any town in England, must be reckoned a sum much beyond the conceptions of remuneration on the part of English manufacturers. But why is this? For this obvious reason: the French manufacturer incurs little or no expense for the purchase of foreign designs; he does not employ agents to obtain, *per fas et nefas,* a pattern of every new article that appears in the London or Paris market; he never suffers the loss (so frequent in this country) arising from his having manufactured the same pirated design simultaneously with three or four other houses; and therefore it is that he can afford to pay his artist highly. Though the sum he thus expends may appear large, the outlay on patterns in France is not greater than it is in England, if indeed it be so great. But the difference is this: that the money which in France is paid directly to the artist, is in England frittered away on expedients for superseding the employment of original designers; expedients which, if law and honesty are to be taken into account, cannot be reckoned other than illegitimate, and which, if prudent, must, I fear, be thought very short-sighted, because the great bulk of patterns executed in England according to the present system must inevitably want the stamp of novelty and originality, which is not only the characteristic of the French, but is really the advantage which the French manufacturer gains by paying liberally for the assistance and judgment of highly-educated artists.

Everyone admits, that the great evidence, which we find in France, of the knowledge and love of art in the cheaper kinds of manufacture, is due to the ample opportunities of study provided for the common people. For myself I do not hesitate to state, as the conviction forced upon me by the inquiries I have made, that in those opportunities, embracing the innumerable elementary schools, public exhibitions, and other gratuitous means of fostering taste, the secret of the influence of the Schools of Design, properly so called, is to be found, and not in the completeness of their system of tuition; and that, if we wish the (British) Government school to prosper, the ground must thus be broken for it, otherwise it cannot, in the nature of things, take root, or bring forth any fruit . . .

In the matter of education, the foreign schools of design deal with artists or designers, i.e. inventors, as if they were to become workmen, and with the workmen as if they intended to be artists: the designer is brought down to the level of the workman by the practical study of industry, and the workman is elevated to the level of the artist by the study of art. When the process of reproduction is purely mechanical, the province of the designer extends to the very verge of the process; when artistical, the power and knowledge of the workman ought to come up to that of the author of the design.

---

3   Karl Marx (German): 'Alienation' (1844)

We have now to grasp the real connection between this whole system of alienation – private property, acquisitiveness, the separation of labour, capital and land, exchange and competition, value and devaluation of man, monopoly and competition – and the system of money . . .

. . . We shall begin with a contemporary economic fact. The worker becomes poorer the more wealth he produces and the more his production increases in power and extent. The worker becomes an ever cheaper commodity the more goods he creates. The devaluation of the world increases in direct relation to the increase in value of the world of things. Labour does not only create goods; it also produces itself and the worker as a commodity, and indeed in the same proportion as it produces the goods.

This fact simply implies that the object produced by labour, its product, now stands opposed to it as an alien being, as a power independent of the producer. The product of labour is labour which has been embodied in an object and turned into a physical thing; this product is an objectification of labour. The performance of work is at the same time its objectification. The performance of work appears in the sphere of political economy as a vitiation of the worker, objectification as a loss and as servitude to the object . . .

. . . All these consequences follow from the fact that the worker is related to the product of this labour as to an alien object. For it is clear on this presupposition that the more the worker expends himself in work the more powerful becomes the world of objects which he creates in face of himself, the poorer he becomes in his inner life, and the less he belongs to himself . . .

What constitutes the alienation of labour? First, that the

work is external to the worker, that it is not part of his nature; and that, consequently, he does not fulfil himself in his work but denies himself, has a feeling of misery rather than well-being, does not develop freely his mental and physical energies but is physically exhausted and mentally debased. The worker, therefore, feels himself to be at home only in his leisure time, whereas at home he feels homeless. His work is not voluntary but imposed, forced labour. It is not the satisfaction of a need, but only a means of satisfying other needs. Its alien character is clearly shown by the fact that as soon as there is no physical or other compulsion it is avoided like the plague. External labour, labour in which man alienates himself, is a labour of self-sacrifice, or mortification. Finally, the external character of work for the worker is shown by the fact that it is not his own work but work for someone else, that in work he does not belong to himself but to another person . . .

We arrive at the result that man (the worker) feels himself to be freely active only in his animal functions – eating, drinking, procreating, or at most also in his dwelling and in personal adornment – whilst in his human functions he is reduced to an animal. The animal becomes human and the human becomes animal.

Eating, drinking and procreating are of course also genuine human functions. But abstractly considered, apart from the environment of human activities, and turned into final and sole ends, they are animal functions . . .

Since alienated labour: (1) alienates labour from man; and (2) alienates man from himself, from his own active function, his life activity; so it alienates him from the species. It makes species-life into a means of individual life. In the first place it alienates species-life and individual life, and secondly, it turns the latter, as an abstraction, into the purpose of the former, also in its abstract and alienated form.

For labour, life activity, productive life, now appear to man only as means for the satisfaction of a need, the need to maintain his physical existence . . .

The animal is at one with its life activity. It does not distinguish the activity from itself. It is its activity. But man makes his life activity itself an object of his will and consciousness. He has a conscious life activity . . . Conscious life activity distinguishes man from the life activity of animals . . .

Private property is . . . the product, the necessary result, of alienated labour, of the external relation of the worker to nature and to himself.

Private property is . . . derived from the analysis of the concept of alienated labour; that is, alienated man, alienated labour, alienated life, and estranged man.

---

4 Queen Victoria (British): 'The Success of the Great Exhibition of 1851' (1851)

I wish you could have witnessed the 1st. May 1851, the *greatest* day of our history, the *most beautiful* and *imposing* and *touching* spectacle ever seen, and the triumph of my beloved Albert. It was truly astonishing, a fairy scene. Many cried, and all felt touched and impressed with devotional feelings. It was the *happiest, proudest* day of my life, and I can think of nothing else. Albert's dearest name is immortalised with this *great* conception, *his* own, and my *own* dear country *showed* me she was *worthy* of it. The triumph is *immense*, for up to the *last hour* the difficulties, the opposition, and the ill-natured attempts to annoy and frighten, of a certain set of fashionables and Protectionists, were immense; but Albert's temper, patience, firmness, and energy surmounted all, and the feeling is universal.

---

5 John Ruskin (British): 'The Nature of the Gothic' (1851)

You must either make a tool of the creature, or a man of him. You cannot make both. Men were not intended to work with the accuracy of tools, to be precise and perfect in all their actions. If you will have that precision out of them, and make their fingers measure degrees like cog-wheels and their arms strike curves like compasses, you must unhumanize them. All the energy of their spirits must be given to make cogs and compasses of themselves. All their attention and strength must go to the accomplishment of the mean act. The eye of the soul must be bent upon the finger-point and the soul's force must fill all the invisible nerves that guide it, ten hours a day, that it may not err from its steely precision, and so soul and sight be worn away, and the whole human being be lost at last – a heap of sawdust, so far as its intellectual work in this world is concurred: saved only by its Heart, which cannot go into the forms of cogs and compasses, but expands, after the ten years are over, into fireside humanity. On the other hand, if you will make a man of the working creature, you cannot make a tool. Let him but begin to imagine, to think, to try to do anything worth doing: and the engine-turned precision is lost at once. Out come all his roughness, all his dullness, all his incapability; shame upon shame, failure upon failure; pause after pause: but out comes the whole majesty of him also; and we know the height of it only when we see the clouds settling upon him. And, whether the clouds be bright or dark, there will be transfiguration behind and within them.

And now reader, look around this English room of yours, about which you have been proud so often, because the work of it was so good and strong, and the ornaments of it so finished. Examine again all those accurate mouldings, and perfect polishings, and unerring adjustments of the seasoned wood and tempered steel. Many a time you have exulted over them, and thought how great England was, because her slightest work was done so thoroughly. Alas ! if read rightly, these perfectnesses are signs of a slavery in our England a thousand times more bitter and more degrading than that of the scourged African, or helot Greek. Men may be beaten, chained, tormented, yoked like cattle, slaughtered like summer flies, and yet remain in one sense, and the best sense, free. But to smother their soul with them, to blight and hew into rotting pollards the suckling branches of their human intelligence, to make the flesh and skin which, after the worm's work on it, is to see God, into leathern thongs to yoke machinery with, – this is to be slave-masters indeed; and there might be more freedom in England, though her feudal lords' lightest words were worth men's lives, and though the blood of the vexed husbandman dropped in the furrows of her fields, than there is while the animation of her multitudes is sent like fuel to feed the factory smoke, and the strength of them is given daily to be wasted into the fineness of a web, or racked into the exactness of a line.

And, on the other hand, go forth again to gaze upon the old cathedral front, where you have smiled so often at the fantastic ignorance of the old sculptors: examine once more those ugly goblins, and formless monsters, and stern statues anatomiless and rigid; but do not mock at them, for they are signs of the life and liberty of every workman who struck the stone; a freedom of thought, and rank in scale of being, such as no laws, no charters, no charities can secure; but which it must be the first aim of all Europe at this day to regain for her children. Let me not be thought to speak wildly or extravagantly. It is verily this degrada-tion of the operative into a machine, which, more than any other evil of the times, is leading the mass of the nations everywhere into vain, incoherent, destructive struggling for a freedom of which they cannot explain the nature to themselves.

Their universal outcry against wealth, and against nobility, is not forced from them either by the pressure of famine, or the sting of mortified pride. These do much, and have done much in all ages; but the foundations of society were never yet shaken as they are at this day. It is not that men are ill-fed, but that they have no pleasure in the work by which they make their bread, and therefore look to wealth as the only means of pleasure. It is not that men are pained by the scorn of the upper classes, but they cannot endure their own; for they feel that the kind of layout to which they are condemned is verily a degrading one, and makes them less than men. Never had the upper classes so much sympathy with the lower, or charity for them, as they have at this day, and yet never were they so much hated by them: for, of old, the separation between the noble and the poor was merely a wall built by law; now it is a veritable difference in level of standing, a precipice between upper and lower grounds in the field of humanity . . .

We have studied and much perfected, of late, the great civilized invention of the division of labour; only we give it a false name. It is not, truly speaking, the labour that is divided; but the men: – Divided into mere segments of men – broken into small fragments and crumbs of life; so that all the little pieces of intelligence that are left in a man is not enough to make a pin, or a nail, but exhausts itself in making the point truly, to make many pins in a day; but if we could only see with what crystal sand their points were polished, sand of human soul, much to be magnified before it can be discerned for what it is – we should think there might be some loss in it also. And the great cry that rises from all our manufacturing cities, louder than their furnace blast, is all in very deed for this, – that we manufacture everything there except men; we blanch cotton, and strengthen steel, and refine sugar, and shape pottery; but to brighten, to strengthen, to refine, or to form a single living spirit, never enters into our estimate of advantages. And all the evil to which that cry is urging our myriads can be met only in one way: not by teaching or preaching, for to teach them is but to show them their misery, and to preach to them, if we do nothing more than preach, is to mock at it.

It can be met only by a right understanding, on the part of all classes, of what kinds of labour are good for men, raising them, and making them happy; by a determined sacrifice of such convenience, or beauty, or cheapness as is to be got only by the degradation of the workman; and by equally determined demand for the products and results of healthy and ennobling labour.

And how, it will be asked; are these products to be recognised, and this demand to be regulated? Easily: by the observance of three broad and simple rules:

1. Never encourage the manufacture of any article not absolutely necessary, in the production of which *invention* has no share.

2. Never demand an exact finish for its own sake, but only for some noble or practical end.

3. Never encourage imitation or copying of any kind, except for the sake of preserving records of great works . . .

---

6   G.W. Yapp (British): 'The Danger of Art Education' (1852)

Some people in this country believe that there is danger in teaching the people to draw, lest they should become unfitted for the duties of workmen, and aspire to become artists. A similar objection was made against Mechanics' Institutions when first introduced into this country. Experience has swept away the latter notion; and a little reasoning will be sufficient to meet the former. If a man have any talent for drawing – and scarcely any one is quite without it – that talent should be cultivated; a power undeveloped is frequently a powerful though hidden discontent. It may be true, that in some cases the teaching in Schools of Design has been calculated rather to make inferior artists than good draftsmen and designers: this is a mistake, against which it is necessary to be on the alert; and nothing is so likely to prevent such mistakes as making elementary instruction in drawing universal. General education, if it tend to increase the number of those who get their living, or attempt to do so, by literature, also furnish the public with the best of possible means of judging who among those would be authors are worthy to maintain their position. When the public is educated in art, there will be little danger of quack artists. Charlatanism is not the offspring of education, but of ignorance.

---

7   Elizabeth Gaskell (British): 'Morals and Manufacture' (1854)

'The whole machinery – I don't mean the wood and iron machinery now – of the cotton trade is so new that it is no wonder if it does not work well in every part all at once. Seventy years ago what was it? And now what is it not? Raw, crude materials came together; men of the same level, as regarded education and station, took suddenly the different positions of masters and men, owing to the mother-wit, as regarded opportunities and probabilities, which distinguished some, and made them far-seeing as to what great future lay concealed in that rude model of Sir Richard Arkwright's. The rapid development of what might be called a new trade, gave those early masters enormous power of wealth and command. I don't mean merely over the workmen; I mean over purchasers – over the whole world's market. Why, I may give you, as an instance, an advertisement, inserted into fifty years ago in a Milton paper, that so-and so (one of the half-dozen calico-printers of the time) would close his warehouse at noon each day; therefore, that all purchasers must come before that hour. Fancy a man dictating in this manner the time when he would sell and when he would not sell. Now, I believe, if a good customer chose to come at midnight, I should get up, and stand hat in hand to receive his orders.'

Margaret's lip curled, but somehow she was compelled to listen; she could no longer abstract herself in her own thoughts.

'I only name such things to show what almost unlimited power the manufacturers had about the beginning of this century. The men were rendered dizzy by it. Because a man was successful in his ventures, there was no reason that in all other things his mind should be well-balanced. On the contrary, his sense of justice, and his simplicity, were often utterly smothered under the glut of wealth that came down upon him; and they tell strange tales of the wild extravagance of living indulged in on gala-days by those early cotton-lords. There can be no doubt, too, of the tyranny they exercised over their work-people. You know the proverb, Mr. Hale, "Set a beggar on horseback, and he'll ride to the devil," – well, some of these early manufacturers did ride to the devil in a magnificent style – crushing human flesh under their horses' hoofs without remorse. But by-and-by came a reaction; there were more factories, more masters; more men were wanted. The power of masters and men became more evenly balanced; and now the battle is pretty fairly waged between us. We will hardly submit to the decision of an umpire, much less to the interference of a meddler with only a smattering knowledge of the real facts of the case, even though that meddler be called the High Court of Parliament.'

'Is there any necessity for calling it a battle between the two classes?' asked Mr. Hale. 'I know, from your using the term, it is one which gives a true idea of the real state of things to your mind.'

'It is true; and I believe it to be as much a necessity as that prudent wisdom and good conduct are always opposed to, and doing battle with ignorance and improvidence. It is one of the great beauties of our system, that a working-man may raise himself into the power and position of a master by his own exertions and behaviour; that, in fact, every one who rules himself to decency and sobriety of conduct, and attention to his duties, comes over to our ranks; it may not be always as a master, but as an overlooker, a cashier, a book-keeper, a clerk, one on the side of authority and order.'

'You consider all who are unsuccessful in raising themselves in the world, from whatever cause, as your enemies, then, if I understand you rightly,' said Margaret, in a clear, cold voice.

'As their own enemies, certainly,' said he quickly, not a little piqued by the haughty disapproval her form of expression and tone of speaking implied.

---

8   Charles Dickens (British): 'Coketown' (1854)

Let us strike the key-note, Coketown, before pursuing our tune.

It was a town of red brick, or of brick that would have been red if the smoke and ashes had allowed it; but as matters stood it was a town of unnatural red and black like the painted face of a savage. It was a town of machinery and tall chimneys, out of which interminable serpents of smoke trailed themselves for ever and ever, and never got uncoiled. It had a black canal in it, and a river that ran purple with ill-smelling dye, and vast piles of building full of windows where there was a rattling and a trembling all day long, and where the piston of the steam-engine worked monotonously up and down, like the head of an elephant in a state of melancholy madness.

---

9   Emperor Napoleon III (French): 'Art and Manufactures' (1855)

The improvement of manufactures is closely connected with that of the arts.

---

10   Karl Marx (German): 'The Potteries of Staffordshire' (1867)

The potteries of Staffordshire have, during the last twenty-two years, formed the subject-matter of three Parliamentary inquiries. The results are embodied in Mr. Scriven's Report of 1841 to

the 'Children's Employment Commissioners', in Dr. Greenhow's Report of 1860 published by order of the medical officer
of the Privy Council (Public Health, Third Report, 1, 102-13),
and lastly in Mr. Longe's Report of 1862, printed in the Children's Employment Commission, First Report dated 13 June
1863. For my purpose it is enough to take some of the deposi-
tions of the exploited children themselves from the reports of
1860 and 1863. From the children we may deduce the situation
of the adults, especially the girls and women, and in a branch of
industry, indeed, alongside which cotton spinning appears as a
very agreeable and healthy occupation.

William Wood, 9 years old, 'was 7 years 10 months when he
began to work' He 'ran moulds' (carried ready-moulded articles
into the drying-room, afterwards bringing back the empty
mould) from the very beginning. He came to work every day in
the week at 6 a.m., and left off at about 9 p.m. 'I work till 9
o'clock at night six days in the week. I have done so for the last
seven or eight weeks.' Fifteen hours of labour for a child of 7! J.
Murray, 12 years of age, says: 'I turn jigger and run moulds. I
come at 6. Sometimes I come at 4. I worked all night last night,
till 6 o'clock this morning. I have not been in bed since the
night before last. There were eight or nine other boys working
last night. All but one have come this morning. I get 3 shillings
and sixpence. I do not get any more for working at night. I
worked two nights last week'. Fernyhough, a boy of 10: 'I have
not always an hour (for dinner). I have only half an hour
sometimes: on Thursday, Friday, and Saturday.'

Dr. Greenhow states that the average life-expectancy in the
pottery districts of Stoke-on-Trent and Wolfstanton is extra-
ordinarily low. Although only 26.6 per cent of the male population over the age of 20 are employed in the potteries in the
district of Stoke, and 30.4 per cent in Wolfstanton, more than
half the deaths among men of that age in the first district, and
nearly two fifths in the second district, are the result of pul-
monary diseases among the potters. Dr. Boothroyd, a medical
practitioner at Hanley, says: 'Each successive generation of
potters is more dwarfed and less robust than the preceding one'.
Similarly another doctor, Mr. McBean, states: 'Since I began to
practise among the potters 25 years ago, I have observed a
marked degeneration, especially shown in diminution of stat-
ure and breadth'. These statements are taken from Dr.
Greenhow's Report of 1860.

From the report of the Commissioners in 1863 the following:
Dr. J.T. Arledge, senior physician of the North Staffordshire

C

Infirmary, says: 'The potters as a class, both men and women, represent a degenerated population, both physically and morally. They are as a rule, stunted in growth, ill-shaped, and frequently ill-formed in the chest; they become prematurely old, and are certainly short-lived; they are phlegmatic and bloodless, and exhibit their debility of constitution by obstinate attacks of dyspepsia, and disorders of the liver and kidneys, and by rheumatism. But of all diseases they are especially prone to chest-disease, to pneumonia, phthisis, bronchitis, and asthma. One form would appear peculiar to them, and is known as potter's asthma, or potter's consumption. Scrofula attacking the glands, or bones, or other parts of the body, is a disease of two-thirds or more of the potters . . . That the "degenerescence" of the population of this district is not even greater than it is, is due to the constant recruiting from the adjacent country, and intermarriages with more healthy races'.

Mr. Charles Parsons, until recently the House Surgeon of the same hospital, writes in a letter to Commissioner Longe, amongst other things: 'I can only speak from personal observation and not from statistical data, but I do not hesitate to assert that my indignation has been aroused again and again at the sight of poor children whose health has been sacrificed to gratify the avarice of either parents or employers'. He enumerates the causes of the diseases of the potters, and sums them up in the phrase 'long hours'. In their report, the Commissioners express the hope that 'a manufacture which has assumed so prominent a place in the whole world, will not long be subject to the remark that its great success is accompanied with the physical deterioration, wide-spread bodily suffering, and early death of the workpeople . . . by whose labour and skill such great results have been achieved'. And all that hold of the potteries in England is true of those in Scotland.

---

11   F. Edward Hulme (British): 'The Foundation of the Schools of Design' (1882)

In the year 1837 the attention of the Government was aroused to the fact that a greater diffusion of the knowledge of the art of design was necessary to the safety of our manufactures in their competition with the productions of other countries, and it was resolved to establish Government Schools of Design. In the first establishment of these schools the object was not the stimulation of a general love of art amongst the people, nor the furnishing of various classes of the community with that special kind of drawing which bore upon their particular trades, but was avowedly and exclusively the education of designers for manufacturers, and to this end alone, at first, were all the efforts of the authorities and the studies of the schools directed.

This attempt to establish schools of design was the first great proof of the necessity of establishing schools of drawing, and that the new power should not be limited, as at first proposed, but spread as widely as possible. It soon became evident that the manufacturer, after all, only kept abreast of public demand, and that it was at least as necessary to diffuse a general appreciation of art as to secure good designing power in a few isolated instances, and since the International Exhibition of 1851 this view became rapidly strengthened. From 1837 to 1852 may be regarded as a period of experiment. In 1852 the central school of Somerset House was under the immediate control and management of the Board of Trade, and there were 17 provincial schools partly supported by local effort and partly by Government aid. The whole cost of the schools in London and the provinces, including management, figure in the estimates at £15,000 . . .

. . . The head school, as we have already seen, was established in London in 1837. Other schools were established in Bloomsbury, Birmingham, York, Manchester, and Spitalfields in 1842; Nottingham and Sheffield in 1843; Coventry and New-castle-upon-Tyne in 1844; Glasgow in 1845; Leeds and Norwich in 1846; Hanley and Stoke-upon-Trent in 1847; Paisley in 1848; Dublin in 1849; Belfast and Cork in 1850; and Macclesfield, Stonebridge, and Worcester in 1851. All these, it will be noticed, are in well-known seats of various manufactures. In 1853 the head school was transferred to Marlborough House, and in 1857 it was once more moved, taking up at South Kensington what we may now conclude to be its final home.

---

12   William Morris (British): 'Art and the People' (1883)

I do not want art for a few, any more than education for a few, or freedom for a few.

No, rather than art should live this poor thin life among a few exceptional men, despising those beneath them for an ignorance for which they themselves are responsible, for a brutality that they will not struggle with, – rather than this, I would that the world should indeed sweep away all art for a while, as I said before I thought it possible she might do; rather than the wheat should rot in the miser's granary, I would that the earth had it, that it might yet have a chance to quicken in the dark.

---

13 Oscar Wilde (Irish): 'Art Should Never Try to be Popular' (1891)

The public has always, and in every age, been badly brought up. They are continually asking art to be popular, to please their want of taste, to flatter their absurd vanity, to tell them what they have been told before, to show them what they ought to be tired of seeing, to amuse them when they feel heavy having eaten too much, and to distract their thoughts when they are wearied of their own stupidity. Now art should never try to be popular. The public should try to make itself artistic. There is a very wide difference.

---

14 Bertha (Potter) Palmer (American): 'Women were the Originators of Most of the Industrial Arts' (1893)

It will be shown that women, among all the primitive peoples, were the originators of most of the industrial arts, and that it was not until these became lucrative that they were appropriated by men, and women pushed aside. While man, the protector, was engaged in fighting or the chase, woman constructed the rude semblance of a home. She dressed and cooked the game, and later ground the grain between the stones, and prepared it for bread. She cured and dressed the skins of animals, and fashioned them awkwardly into garments. Impelled by the necessity for its use, she invented the needle, and twisted the fibres of plants into thread. She invented the shuttle, and used it in weaving textile fabrics, in which were often mingled feathers, wool, and down, which contributed to the beauty and warmth of the fabric. She was the first potter, and molded clay into jars and other utensils for domestic purposes, drying them in the sun. She originated basket-making, and invented such an infinite variety of beautiful forms and decorations as put to shame modern products. She learned to ornament these articles of primitive construction by weaving in feathers of birds, by a very skilful embroidery of porcupine quills and vegetable fibres, and by use of vegetable dyes.

15 Arnold Bennett (British): 'The Potteries' (1902)

Beneath them, in front, stretched a maze of roofs, dominated by the gold angel of the Town Hall spire. Bursley, the ancient home of the potter, has an antiquity of a thousand years. It lies towards the north end of an extensive valley, which must have been one of the fairest spots in Alfred's England, but which is now defaced by the activities of a quarter of a million people. Five contiguous towns – Turnhill, Bursley, Hanbridge, Knype, and Longshaw – united by a single winding thoroughfare some eight miles in length, have inundated the valley like a succession of great lakes. Of these five Bursley is the mother, but Hanbridge is the largest. They are mean and forbidding of aspect – sombre, hard-featured, uncouth; and the vaporous poison of their ovens and chimneys has soiled and shrivelled the surrounding country till there is no village lane within a league but what offers a gaunt and ludicrous travesty of rural charms. Nothing could be more prosaic than the huddled, red-brown streets; nothing more seemingly remote from romance. Yet be it said that romance is even here – the romance which, for those who have an eye to perceive it, ever dwells amid the seats of industrial manufacture, softening the coarseness, trans-figuring the squalor, of these mighty alchemic operations. Look down into the valley from this terrace-height where love is kindling, embrace the whole smoke-girt amphitheatre in a glance, and it may be that you will suddenly comprehend the secret and superb significance of the vast Doing which goes forward below. Because they seldom think, the townsmen take shame when indicted for having disfigured half a county in order to live. They have not understood that this disfigurement is merely an episode in the unending warfare of man and nature, and calls for no contrition. Here, indeed, is nature repaid for some of her notorious cruelties. She imperiously bids man sustain and reproduce himself, and this is one of the places where in the very act of obedience he wounds and maltreats her. Out beyond the municipal confines, where the subsidiary industries of coal and iron prosper amid a wreck of verdure, the struggle is grim, appalling, heroic – so ruthless is his havoc of her, so indomitable her ceaseless recuperation. On the one side is a wrestling from nature's own bowels of the means to waste her; on the other, an undismayed, enduring fortitude. The grass grows; though it is not green, it grows. In the very heart of the valley, hedged about with furnaces, a farm still stands, and at harvest-time the sooty sheaves are gathered in.

16 Francis Jourdain (French): 'The People, Design and the State' (1904)

The incoherence in which we live from the point of view of the rapport between Art and the State makes aesthetic evolution, from which we hoped for decisive results some years ago, very miserable, very difficult and very hesitant . . . If the crowds made their own judgment without inquiring for the opinion of the State, the meddling of a Minister in the aesthetic question would hardly matter. Unfortunately, by a kind of atavism born of sad servility, the public shows an irresistible and childlike need to hang on to a tutor, a teacher, a prophet, a master who can show them what to like and hate. In this way, an artist noticed or chosen by the State becomes a genius, and the misunderstood genius, or someone simply kept in the background by the Offices of the Rue de Valois, can become so grotesque or dangerous that it becomes necessary to hunt him down.

17 Robert Tressell (British): 'The Plight of Edwardian House Decorators' (1910)

Frank Owen was the son of a journeyman carpenter who had died of consumption when the boy was only five years old. After that his mother earned a scanty living as a needle-woman. When Frank was thirteen he went to work for a master decorator who was a man of a type that has now almost disappeared, being not merely an employer but a craftsman of a high order.

He was an old man when Frank Owen went to work for him. At one time he had had a good business in the town, and used to boast that he had always done good work, had found pleasure in doing it and had been well paid for it. But of late years the number of his customers had dwindled considerably, for there had risen a new generation which cared nothing about craftsmanship or art, and everything for cheapness and profit. From this man and by laborious study and practice in his spare time, aided by a certain measure of natural ability, the boy acquired a knowledge of decorative painting and design, and graining and signwriting.

Frank's mother died when he was twenty-four, and a year afterwards he married the daughter of a fellow workman. In those days trade was fairly good and although there was not much demand for the more artistic kinds of work, still the fact that he was capable of doing them, if required, made it comparatively easy for him to obtain employment. Owen and his wife were very happy. They had one child – a boy – and for some years all went well. But gradually this state of things altered: broadly speaking, the change came slowly and imperceptibly, although there were occasional sudden fluctuations.

Even in summer he could not always find work: and in winter it was almost impossible to get a job of any sort. At last, about twelve months before the date that this story opens, he determined to leave his wife and child at home and go to try his fortune in London. When he got employment he would send for them.

It was a vain hope. He found London, if anything, worse than his native town. Wherever he went he was confronted with the legend: 'No hands wanted'. He walked the streets day after day; pawned or sold all his clothes save those he stood in, and stayed in London for six months, sometimes starving and only occasionally obtaining a few days or weeks work.

At the end of that time he was forced to give in. The privations he had endured, the strain on his mind and the foul atmosphere of the city combined to defeat him. Symptoms of the disease that had killed his father began to manifest themselves, and yielding to the repeated entreaties of his wife he returned to his native town, the shadow of his former self.

That was six months ago, and since then he had worked for Rushton & Co. Occasionally when they had no work in hand, he was 'stood off' until something came in.

Ever since his return from London, Owen had been gradually abandoning himself to hopelessness. Every day he felt that the disease he suffered from was obtaining a stronger grip on him. The doctor told him to 'take plenty of nourishing food', and prescribed costly medicines which Owen had not the money to buy.

Then there was his wife. Naturally delicate, she needed many things that he was unable to procure for her. And the boy – what hope was there for him? Often as Owen moodily thought of their circumstances and prospects he told himself that he would be far better if they could all three die now, together.

He was tired of suffering himself, tired of impotently watching the sufferings of his wife, and appalled at the thought of what was in store for the child.

Of this nature were his reflections as he walked homewards on the evening of the day when old Linden was dismissed. There was no reason to believe or hope that the existing state of things would be altered for a long time to come.

Thousands of people like himself dragged out a wretched existence on the very verge of starvation, and for the greater number of people life was one long struggle against poverty. Yet practically none of these people knew or even troubled themselves to inquire why they were in that condition; and for anyone else to try to explain to them was a ridiculous waste of time, for they did not want to know.

---

18   Eric Gill (British): 'The Factory System and Christianity' (1918)

The Factory System is unchristian because:

It puts the service and glory of man before the service and glory of God.

It promotes the comfort of man and destroys the worship and praise of God.

It puts the making of money before the making of goods.

It puts quantity before quality – for quantity can be determined by measurement, whereas quality demands imagination and cannot be measured.

It deprives the workman of responsibility for his work.

It is subject only to 'efficient causes' and not to 'final causes'.

It depends upon the notion that 'it is more blessed to receive than to give'.

It destroys the personal relationship of maker to buyer.

It promotes the war of classes (masters *versus* men).

It prevents Trades Unions from becoming Trades Guilds.

It promotes the notion that leisure time is more to be desired than work time, for it deprives the workman of any power to express his own ideas in his work or to get any amusement out of it, thus causing him always to look forward to the time when he will stop work.

It flatters the consumer to capture his custom, and covers the land with damnable advertisements.

It subdivides labour so that the workman becomes merely a tool.

It puts a premium upon mechanical dexterity and a discount upon intellectual and spiritual ability in the workman.

It undermines the family, for it drags both men and women into its net and destroys home work and home life.

It depends upon militarism, for without the support of the military the system would have been destroyed in its beginnings and the strike is only rendered abortive because in the last resort the soldiers can be brought out to shoot down the strikers.

It promotes wars, for it destroys local markets and makes trade dependent upon 'world markets' and financial magnates. Over-production is inevitable and when there is over-production there must be a struggle for fresh markets.

19 Government Official (French): 'The Internationally Agreed Definition of an "Expo."' (1928)

The provisions of the present convention apply only to international exhibitions which are official or officially recognised.

The expression 'official' or 'officially recognised international exhibition' shall be deemed to include every display, whatever its designation, to which foreign countries are invited through the diplomatic channel, which is not generally held periodically, of which the principal object is to demonstrate the progress of different countries in one or several branches of production, and in which, as regards admission, no distinction in principle is made between buyers and visitors.

The provisions of the said convention do not apply to the following:-

1. Exhibitions having a duration of less than three weeks;

2. Scientific exhibitions organised on the occasion of international congresses, provided that their duration does not exceed the period mentioned in 1;

3. Exhibitions of the fine arts;

4. Exhibitions organised by one country in another country on the invitation of the latter . . .

. . . The duration of any international exhibition should not exceed six months; provided always that the International Bureau may authorise, in the case of a general exhibition, a longer period which shall not in any circumstances exceed twelve months.

20 Theodor Adorno and Max Horkheimer (German): 'The Culture Industry' (1944)

Under monopoly capitalism all mass culture is identical, and the lines of its artificial framework begin to show through. The people at the top are no longer so interested in concealing monopoly: as its violence becomes more open, so its power grows. Movies and radio need no longer pretend to be art. The truth that they are just business is made into an ideology in order to justify the rubbish that they deliberately produce. They call themselves industries; and when their directors' incomes are published, any doubt about the social utility of the finished products is removed.

Interested parties explain the culture industry in technological terms. It is alleged that because millions participate in it, certain reproduction processes are necessary that inevitably require identical needs in innumerable places to be satisfied with identical goods. The technical contrast between the few production centres and the large number of widely dispersed consumption points is said to demand organization and planning by management. Furthermore, it is claimed that standards were based in the first place on consumers' needs, and for that reason were accepted with so little resistance. The result is the circle of manipulation and retroactive need in which the unity of the system grows even stronger. No mention is made of the fact that the basis on which technology acquires power over society is greatest. A technological rationale is the rationale of domination itself. It is the coercive nature of society alienated from itself. Automobiles, bombs, and movies keep the whole thing together until their levelling element shows its strength in the very wrong which is furthered. It has made the technology of the culture industry no more than the achievement of standardization and mass production, sacrificing whatever involved a distinction between the logic of the work and that of the social system. This is the result not of a law of movement in technology as such but of its function in today's economy. The need which might resist central control has already been suppressed by the control of the individual consciousness.

---

21   Hannah Arendt (American): 'The Permanence of the Work of Art' (1958)

Among the things that give the human artifice the stability without which it could never be a reliable home for men are a number of objects which are strictly without any utility whatsoever and which, moreover, because they are unique, are not exchangeable and therefore defy equalization through a common denominator such as money; if they enter the exchange market, they can only be arbitrarily priced. Moreover, the proper intercourse with a work of art is certainly not 'using' it; on the contrary, it must be removed from the whole context of ordinary use objects to attain its proper place in the world. By the same token, it must be removed from the exigencies and wants of daily life, with which it has less contact than any other thing. Whether this uselessness of art objects has always pertained or whether art formerly served the so-called religious needs of men as ordinary use objects serve more ordinary needs does not enter the argument. Even if the historical origin of art were of an exclusively religious or mythological character, the fact is that art has survived gloriously its severance from religion, magic, and myth.

22 Andy Warhol (American): 'I Accept Things' (1967)

The world fascinates me. It's so nice, whatever it is. I approve of what everybody does; it must be right because somebody said it was right. I wouldn't judge anybody. I thought Kennedy was great but I wasn't shocked at his death: it was just something that happened . . . it isn't for me to judge it . . . I'm very passive. I accept things. I'm just watching, observing the world.

23 Linda Nochlin (American): "Why have there been no Great Women Artists?" (1971)

Why have there been no great women artists? The question is crucial, not merely to women, and not only for social or ethical reasons, but for purely intellectual ones as well. If, as John Stuart Mill so rightly suggested, we tend to accept whatever *is* as 'natural', this is just as true in the realm of academic investigation as it is in our social arrangements: the white Western male viewpoint, unconsciously accepted as *the* viewpoint of the art historian, is proving to be inadequate. At a moment when all disciplines are becoming more self-conscious – more aware of the nature of their presuppositions as exhibited in their own languages and structures – the current uncritical acceptance of 'what is' as 'natural' may be intellectually fatal. Just as Mill saw male domination as one of many social injustices that had to be overcome if a truly just social order were to be created, so we may see the unconscious domination of a white male subjectivity as one among many intellectual distortions which must be corrected in order to achieve a more adequate and accurate view of history.

A feminist critique of the discipline of art history is needed which can pierce cultural-ideological limitations, to reveal biases and inadequacies *not merely in regard to the question of women artists, but in the formulation of the crucial questions of the discipline as a whole.* Thus the so-called woman question, far from being a peripheral subissue, can become a catalyst, a potent intellectual instrument, probing the most basic and 'natural' assumptions, providing a paradigm for other kinds of internal questioning, and providing links with paradigms established by radical approaches in other fields. A simple question like 'Why have there been no great women artists?' can, if answered adequately, create a chain reaction, expanding to encompass every accepted assumption of the field, and then outward to embrace history and the social sciences or even psychology and literature, and thereby, from the very outset, to challenge traditional divisions of intellectual inquiry.

---

24 Adolfo Sanchez Vasquez (Mexican): 'Truly Popular Art' (1973)

Under the conditions of capitalism, which is interested in encouraging a privileged, elite art and in impeding the distribution of true art, it is possible to create an art which addresses itself to the majority, not to the masses, that is, a truly popular art, both in a quantitative and a qualitative sense. There are quite a number of examples of this. But the hostility of capitalism to art can create a situation in which truly popular art is not 'popular', not accepted by the majority, while an art which is actually antipopular, mass art, is 'popular' by virtue of the conditions under which production and consumption are carried out in capitalist society.

Once we have discarded the false concepts which equate popular art and mass art or popular art and artistic 'populism', we must select a qualitative criterion in order to define what we mean by truly popular art. This can be none other than the depth and richness with which art expresses the desires or aspirations of a people or a nation in a particular historical stage of its existence. We therefore agree with the concept of popular literature expressed by the great Italian Marxist Antonio Gramsci: 'Question of how or why literature is popular. Beauty is not enough. What is required is an intellectual and moral content which is the elaborate and complete expression of the most profound aspirations of a determinate public, of the nation-people in a certain phase of historical development'.

Gramsci assets that 'beauty' is not enough when it is not sparked by a profound ideological and moral content . . .

Popular art is a profound expression of the aspirations and interests of the people in a given historical stage, and as such it maintains a certain relationship with politics.

25   Judy Chicago (American): 'The Problem of the Female Role' (1977)

I am beginning to see that in taking on the Project [the Dinner Party] I took on the real nexus of the problem that has prevented women from overcoming their oppression: (1) the enormity of the task of changing attitudes on a large scale; (2) the problems of the female role conditioning and how it prevents women from working at all, much less facing the challenge of changing their condition; and (3) the absence of support in society. These three things all loomed up in front of me. Had I been able to get more support from society, the task would have been easier.

26   Pierre Bourdieu (French): 'Culture' (1979)

One cannot fully understand cultural practices unless 'culture', in the restricted, normative sense of ordinary usage, is brought back into 'culture' in the anthropological sense, and the elaborated taste for the most refined objects is reconnected with the elementary taste for the flavours of food.

27   Germaine Greer (Australian): 'The Nature of Women's Struggle' (1979)

If we look fearlessly at the works of dead women and do not attempt to erect for them a double standard in the mistaken notion that such distortion of the truth will benefit women living and working today, we will understand by analogy a good deal about our own oppression and its pathology. We will see all the signs of self-censorship, hypocritical modesty, insecurity, girlishness, self-deception, hostility towards one's fellow-strivers, emotional and sexual dependency upon men, timidity, poverty and ignorance. All these traits of the oppressed personality are only to be expected; the astonishing and gratifying thing is that so many women conquered all of these enemies within some of the time, most often when they were young, before marriage and childbirth or poverty and disillusionment took their toll. Their defeats can teach us about the nature of the struggle; their successes assure us that we too can do it.

---

28 **Leon Krier (British): 'Architecture is not Political' (1985)**

Architecture is not political. It is an instrument of politics, for better or for worse.

---

29 **Jean Baudrillard (French): 'Opinion Polls, Advertisements, and the End of Alienation' (1985)**

I will take the example of the opinion polls, which are themselves a mass medium. It is said that opinion polls constitute a manipulation of democracy. This is certainly no more the case than that publicity is a manipulation of need and of consumption. It too produces demand (or so it claims) and invokes needs just as opinion polls produce answers and induce future behaviour. All this would be serious if there were an objective truth of needs, an objective truth of public opinion. It is obvious that here we need to exercise extreme care. The influence of publicity, of opinion polls, of all the media, and of information in general would be dramatic if we were certain that there exists in opposition to it an authentic human nature, an authentic essence of the social, with its needs, its own will, its own values, its finalities. For this would set up the problem of its radical alienation. And indeed it is in this form that traditional critiques are expressed.

Now the matter is at once less serious and more serious than this. The uncertainty which surrounds the social and political effect of opinion polls (do they or do they not manipulate opinion?), like that which surrounds the real economic efficacy of publicity, will never be completely relieved – and it is just as well! This results from the fact that there is a compound, a mixture of two heterogeneous systems whose data cannot be transferred from one to the other. An operational system which is statistical, information-based, and simulational is projected onto a traditional values system, onto a system of representation, will, and opinion. This collage, this collusion between the two, gies rise to an indefinite and useless polemic. We should agree neither with those who praise the beneficial use of the media, nor with those who scream about manipulation, for the simple reason that there is no relationship between a system of meaning and a system of simulation. Publicity and opinion polls would be incapable, even if they wished and claimed to do so, of alienating the will or the opinion of anybody at all, for the reason that they do not act in the time-space of will and of representation where judgment is formed. For the same reason, though reversed, it is quite impossible for them to throw any light at all on the public opinion or individual will, since they do not act in a public space, on the stage of a public space. They are strangers to it, and indeed they wish to dismantle it. Publicity and opinion polls and the media in general can only be imagined; they only exist on the basis of a disappearance, the disappearance from the public space, from the scene of politics, of public opinion in a form at once theatrical and representative as it was enacted in earlier epochs. Thus we can be reassured: they cannot destroy it. But we should not have any illusions: they cannot restore it either.

It is this lack of relationship between the two systems which today plunges us into a state of stupor. That is what I said: stupor. To be more objective one would have to say: a radical uncertainty as to our own desire, our own choice, our own opinion, our own will. This is the clearest result of the whole media environment, of the information which makes demands on us from all sides and which is as good as blackmail.

We will never know if an advertisement or opinion poll has had a real influence on individual or collective wills, but we will never know either what would have happened if there had been no opinion poll or advertisement.

The situation no longer permits us to isolate reality or human nature as a fundamental variable. The result is therefore not to provide any additional information or to shed any light on reality, but on the contrary, because we will never in the future be able to separate reality from its statistical, simulative projection in the media, a state of suspense and of definite uncertainty about reality. And I repeat: it is a question here of a completely new species of uncertainty, which results not from the *lack* of information but from information itself and even from an *excess* of information. It is information itself which produces uncertainty, and so this uncertainty, unlike the traditional uncertainty which could always be resolved, is irreparable.

This is our destiny: subject to opinion polls, information, publicity, statistics; constantly confronted with the anticipated statistical verification of our behaviour, and absorbed by this permanent refraction of our least movements, we are no longer confronted with our own will. We are no longer even alienated, because for that it is necessary for the subject to be divided in itself, confronted with the other, to be contradictory. Now, where there is no other, the scene of the other, like that of politics and of society, has disappeared. Each individual is forced despite himself or herself into the undivided coherency of statistics. There is in this a positive absorption onto the transparency of computers, which is something worse than alienation.

---

30 Cheryl Buckley (British): 'Women as Designers' (1990)

Patriarchal ideology identified women with certain types of art – the lesser or applied arts – and specific artistic abilities – subtlety in the use of colour, a fascination for complex patterns and a love of subject matter drawn from nature or domestic life such as flowers, children and the home. Within this framework, women could work with some success as designers.

3
TECHNOLOGY AND EVERYDAY LIFE

There is no doubt that technological advance has been one of the key differentiating factors between ourselves and, say, the world of 1800. There is no doubt either that crucial scientific breakthroughs, which made technological development possible, occurred during the period we now generally label the Industrial Revolution.

We should not, however, fall into the trap of suggesting either that technology was, as it were, 'invented' during the Industrial Revolution, or that technology causes cultural development in a direct or determined way. The relationship of technology to culture, and hence to design, is complex; we should never allow ourselves the luxurious assumption that when a new technology becomes available it immediately has an effect on the appearance of things, or even that designers bother to use it in the short term. For example, the technologies which built the American skyscrapers of the 1930s, were largely available to the architects who built America's tall buildings in the 1890s. The dramatic visual difference between the two groups of buildings is thus *not* explained by technology alone.

'Technics' are a staple necessity in the survival of all societies, and are not peculiar to the period covered here. But it would be wrong to suggest that the nineteenth and twentieth centuries are not profoundly different from previous ages; one of the central causes of this difference was the extraordinary way in which technological innovation occurred in tandem with dramatic growths in population and trade. These three provoked an effective transformation in the structure of European and American society. Technology was not the cause of change or even the leading agent; it was a catalyst, an enabler and a partner in change. Societies have to decide to use technology in an organised way before it can have any effect. And the reasons why societies do determine to use technology rarely spring from the nature of the technologies themselves, but from ulterior motives.

There are various types of quotation here. A significant proportion are polemics either for or against mechanisation. Others are classic descriptions, justifications and explanations of new materials and methods of production. There are also descriptions of the growth of technology in urban and domestic life; electricity, for example, is used as a key technology and treated in several passages which show its steady evolution into a staple energy. The intention is that the cumulative effect of the passages will be to convince the reader that technology transforms society not so much by dictating to it as by unevenly infiltrating it. Arguably, the end result is the same.

See also
Chapter 2 for the moral effects of technology on society
Chapter 4 for the response to mechanisation by those committed to hand-craft work
Chapter 5 for the relationship of commerce to technology
Chapter 6 for aspects of the use of technology in the home
Chapter 8 for modernist enthusiasm for mechanisation

---

1 Josiah Wedgwood (British): 'The Capabilities of Electricity' (1766)

I am much pleas'd with your disquisition upon the Capabilitys of Electricity, & should be glad to contribute in any way you can point out to me, towards rendering Doctor Priestleys very ingenious experiments more extensively usefull, & whatever is the result of your farther thoughts, & the Doctors experiments on this subject I am ready, so far as I can be concern'd, to ratify & confirm your resolutions. But what dareing mortals you are! to rob the Thunderer of his Bolts, – & for what? – no doubt to blast the oppressors of the poor & needy or else to execute some public piece of justice in the most tremendous & conspicuous manner, that shall make the great ones of the Earth tremble! – But peace to ye Mortals, no harm is intended, – Heavens once dreaded bolt is now called down to amuse your wives & daughters, – to decorate their tea boards & baubles! – well – if you think this business may be pursued without presumption, & with safety to ourselves, I sho^d. very gladly meet you at Warrington, if you let me know when you can spare a day for that purpose. I beg my respectfull compliments to the Doctor & wish him all possible success in his delightfull & ingenious researches into the secrets of nature.

2   Adam Smith (British): 'The Division of Labour' (1776)

To take an example, therefore, from a very trifling manufacture: but one in which the division of labour has been very often taken notice of, the trade of the pin-maker; a workman not educated to this business (which the division of labour has rendered a distinct trade), nor acquainted with the use of the machinery employed in it (to the invention of which the same division of labour has probably given occasion), could scarce, perhaps, with his utmost industry, make one pin a day, and certainly could not make twenty. But in the way in which this business is now carried on, not only the whole work is a peculiar trade, but it is divided into a number of branches, of which the greater part are likewise peculiar trades.

One man draws out the wire, another straights it, a third cuts it, a fourth points it, a fifth grinds it at the top for receiving the head; to make the head requires two or three distinct operations; to put it on is a peculiar business, to whiten the pins is another; it is even a trade by itself to put them into the paper; and the important business of making a pin is, in this manner, divided into about eighteen distinct operations, which in some manufacturies, are all performed by distinct hands, though in others the same man will sometimes perform two or three of them. I have seen a small manufactory of this kind where ten men were employed, and where some of them consequently performed two or three distinct operations. But though they were very poor, and therefore but indifferently accommodated with the necessary machinery, they could, when they exerted themselves, make among them about twelve pounds of pins a day. There are in a pound upwards of four thousand pins of middling size. Those ten persons, therefore, could make among them upwards of forty-eight thousand pins in a day. Each person, therefore, making a tenth part of forty-eight thousand pins, might be considered as making four thousand eight hundred pins in a day. But if they had all been wrought separately and independently, and without any of them having been educated in this peculiar business, they certainly could not each of them have made twenty, perhaps not one pin in a day; that is certainly, not the two hundred and fortieth, perhaps not the four thousand eight hundred part of what they are at present capable of performing, in consequence of a proper division and combination of their different operations.

The improvement of the dexterity of the workman necessarily increases the quality of the work he can perform; and the division of labour, by reducing every man's business to some one simple operation, and by making this operation the sole employment of his life, necessarily increases very much the dexterity of the workman . . . the advantage which is gained by saving the time commonly lost in passing from one sort of work to another is much greater than we should at first view be apt to imagine it. It is impossible to pass very quickly from one kind of work to another that is carried on in a different place and with quite different tools. A country weaver, who cultivates a small farm, must lose a good deal of time passing from his loom to the field, and from the field to his loom. When the two trades can be carried on in the same workhouse, the loss of time is no doubt much less. It is even in this case, however, very considerable. A man commonly saunters a little in turning his hand from one sort of employment to another. When he first begins the new work he is seldom very keen and hearty; his mind, as they say, does not go to it, and for some time he rather trifles than applies to good purpose. The habit of sauntering and of indolent careless application, which is naturally, or rather necessarily acquired by every country workman who is to change his work and his tools every half hour, and to apply his hand in twenty different ways almost every day of his life, renders him almost slothful and lazy, and incapable of any vigorous application even on the most pressing occasions. Independent, therefore, of his deficiency in point of dexterity, this cause alone must always reduce considerably the quantity of work which he is capable of performing.

It is the great multiplication of the productions of all the different arts, in consequence of the division of labour, which occasions, in a well-governed society, that universal opulence which extends itself to the lowest ranks of the people. Every workman has a great quantity of his own work to dispose of beyond what he himself has occasion for; and every other workman being exactly in the same situation, he is enabled to exchange a great quantity of his own goods for a great quantity, or, what comes to the same thing, for the price of a great quantity of theirs. He supplies them abundantly for what they have occasion for, and they accommodate him as amply with what he has occasion for, and a general plenty diffuses itself through all the different ranks of the society . . .

3 Richard Trevithick (British): 'The Maiden Voyage of the First Steam Car' (1804)

Yesterday we proceeded on our journey with the engine; we carry'd ten tons of Iron, five waggons, and 70 Men riding on them the whole of the journey. It's above 9 miles which we perform'd in 4 hours & 5 Mints, but we had to cut down some trees and remove some Large rocks out of the road. The engine, while working, went nearly 5 miles per hour; there was no water put into the boiler from the time we started until we arriv'd at our journey's end. The coal consumed was 2 Hundred. On our return home, about 4 miles from the shipping place of the Iron, one of the small bolts that fastened the axel to the boiler broak, and let all the water out of the boiler, which prevented the engine returning until this evening. The Gentleman that bet five Hundred Guineas against it, rid the whole of the journey with us and is satisfyde that he have lost the bet. We shall continue to work on the road, and shall take forty tons the next journey. The publick until now call'd mee a schemeing fellow but now their tone is much alter'd.

4 *The Times* (British): 'The Engine is the Favourite' (1808)

We are credibly informed that there is a Steam Engine now pre-paring to run against any mare, horse, or gelding that may be produced at the next October Meeting at Newmarket; the wagers at present are stated to be 10,000 to 1; the engine is the favourite. The extraordinary effects of mechanical power are already known to the world; but the novelty, singularity and powerful applica-tion against time and speed has created admiration in the minds of every scientific man. – TREVITHIC, the proprietor and patentee of this engine, has been applied to by several distin-guished personages to exhibit this engine to the public, prior to its being sent to Newmarket; we have not heard this gentle-man's determination yet; its greatest speed will be 20 miles in one hour, and its slowest rate will never be less than 15 miles.

5 Thomas Carlyle (British): 'The Mechanical Age' (1829)

Were we required to characterise this age of ours by any single epithet, we should be tempted to call it, not an Heroical, Devo-tional, Philosophical or Moral Age, but, above all others, The

Mechanical Age. It is the Age of Machinery, in every outward and inward sense to that word; the age which, with its whole undivided might, forwards, teaches and practises the great art of adapting means to ends. Nothing is now done directly, or by hand; all is by rule and calculated contrivance. For the simplest operation, some helps and accompanists, some cunning abbreviating process in readiness. Our old modes of exertion are all discredited, and thrown aside. On every hand, the living artisan is driven from his workshop, to make room for a speedier, inanimate one.

There is no end to machinery. Even the horse is slipped of his harness, and finds a fleet fire-horse yoked in his stead. Nay, we have one artist that hatches chickens by steam; the very brood-hen is to be superseded! For all earthly, and for some unearthly purposes, we have machines and mechanic furtherances; for mincing our cabbages; for casting us into magnetic sleep. We remove mountains and make seas our smooth highway; nothing can resist us. We war with rude Nature; and, by our resistless engines, come off always victorious, and loaded with spoils.

But leaving these matters for the present, let us observe how the mechanical genius of our time has diffused itself into quite other provinces. Not the external and physical alone is now managed by machinery, but the internal and spiritual also. Here too nothing follows its spontaneous course, nothing is left to be accomplished by old natural methods. Everything has its cunningly devised implements, its pre-established apparatus; it is not done by hand, but by machinery. Thus we have machines for Education: Lancastrian machines; Hamiltonian machines; monitors, maps and emblems. Instruction, that mysterious communing of Wisdom with Ignorance, is no longer an indefinable tentative process, requiring a study of individual aptitudes, and a perpetual variation of means and methods, to attain the same end; but a secure, universal, straightforward business, to be conducted in the gross, by proper mechanism, with such intellect as comes to hand ...

Has any man, or any society of men, a truth to speak, a piece of spiritual work to do; they can nowise proceed at once and with the mere natural organs, but must first call a public meeting, appoint committees, issue prospectuses, eat a public dinner; in a word, construct or borrow machinery, wherewith to speak it and do it. Without machinery they were hopeless, helpless; a colony of Hindoo weavers squatting in the heart of Lancashire.

With individuals, in like manner, natural strength avails little. No individual now hopes to accomplish the poorest enterprise singlehanded and without mechanical aids; he must make interest with some existing corporation, and till his field with their oxen. In these days more emphatically than ever, 'to live, signified to unite with a party, to make one'. Philosophy, Science, Art, Literature, all depends on machinery.

---

6 Arnold Toynbee (British): 'The Industrial Revolution in England' (1886)

Every page of [Adam Smith's] the *Wealth of Nations* is illuminated with an illimitable passion for freedom of industry and trade. In the spirit of that book still more than in the facts contained in it, the dawn of a new epoch is visible. The *Wealth of Nations* is the great proclamation of the rights of industry and trade.

Let us pause and inquire what the proclamation really meant. We shall find, if we consider it closely, that it contained two assertions; first, an assertion of the right of the workman to legal equality and independence; secondly an assertion that industrial freedom is essential to the material prosperity of the people. The first assertion – rather implied than insisted on – reflected the political ideas of the age. It is significant that the same year which witnessed the enunciation of the industrial rights of man in the publication of the *Wealth of Nations* witnessed the enunciation of the political rights of man in the Declaration of American Independence. All around, indeed, men pointed out signs of the dissolution of the old social and political system. 'Subordination' said Dr. Johnson, who could compress keen observation into pregnant sentences – 'subordination is sadly broken down in this age. No man, now, has the same authority which his father had – except a gaoler'. The second assertion contained in this proclamation expressed the inarticulate desire for the removal of ancient restrictions once approved by both masters and men, a desire created by the rapid growth of material prosperity. Just now I said that in the middle of the last century there was comparatively little movement of workmen from place to place; but Adam Smith's fierce attack on the law of settlement shows that migration was on the increase. The world was, in fact, on the eve of an industrial revolution, and it is interesting to remember that the two men who did most to bring it about, Adam Smith and James Watt, met, as I have mentioned, in Glasgow, when one was dreaming of the book, and the other of the invention, which were to introduce a new industrial age.

For *The Wealth of Nations* and the steam engine (with the great inventions, like the spinning jenny and the power loom, which accompanied or followed it) destroyed the old world and built a new one. The spinning wheel and the hand loom were silenced, and manufactures were transferred from scattered villages and quiet home steads to factories and cities filled with noise. I cannot stop to describe to you this vast revolution in detail; I must try to carry you quickly over a period of seventy years, making as strongly as I can the principal features of the change. Rapid as the revolution was it did not come at once. In the cotton trade, for instance, first the hand-wheel was thrown away, and mills with water frames and spinning jennies were built on the sides of streams; then the mule was invented, which supplied the weaver with unlimited quantities of yarn, and raised his wages and increased the demand for loom-shops, causing even old barns and cart-houses hastily pierced with windows to be adapted to that purpose; finally there came the introduction of the power-loom, the general application of steam to drive machinery, and the erection of gigantic factories that we see around us at the present time. By these last changes the final blow was struck at the little master, half-manufacturer half-farmer, and in his place sprang up the great capitalist employer, the owner of hundreds of looms, the employer of hundreds of men, buying and selling in every market on the globe.

The revolution, however, was not entirely due to the substitution of steam for hand power in production; it was partly the result of an enormous expansion of internal and external trade. The expansion of internal trade was the effect of unparalleled improvements in the means of communication, the establishment of the canal system, the construction of new roads by Telford, and the introduction of railways. The expansion of external trade was caused by the great war of 1793, which, closing the workshops of the Continent, opened every port in Europe to English iron and cotton. We should naturally expect such radical changes to give rise to new industrial and commercial problems, and this was the case. In the literature of this period we find, for the first time, discussions of those intricate questions of over-production and depression of trade with which we are now only too familiar – questions, remember, which never embarrassed an earlier age. On these points, however, I do not intend to speak tonight. I must proceed instead to a brief examination of a subject which is perhaps the most vital of those I have considered; I mean the effects of the revolution in the external forms of industry upon its inner life.

These effects were terrible. In the new cities – denounced as dens where men came together not for the purposes of social life, but to make calicoes and hardware, or broadcloths – in the new cities, the old warm attachments, born of ancient, local contiguity and personal intercourse, vanished in the fierce contest for wealth amongst thousands who had never seen each other's faces before. Between the individual workman and the capitalist who employed hundreds of 'hands' a wide gulf opened: the workman ceased to be the cherished dependant, he became the living tool of whom the employer knew less than he did of his steam-engine.

---

7 Carl Hering (American): 'The Advance of Electricity and its Associated Industries' (1890)

The following general figures may be of interest here. The proceedings of the Electrical Light Association gives the following figures for the United States for the beginning of 1890: 2,700,000 incandescent lamps, 230,000 arc lamps, 500,000 horse power used for lighting; over 600 hundred miles of electrical railroads completed and in construction; 750,000 miles of telegraph lines; over 120,000 miles of telephone lines. The following, from the beginning of 1890, is taken from the *Electric World*:

> *The number of electric lighting companies in the United States and Canada operating central stations at the beginning of 1886 was 450. This number had increased at the beginning of 1877 to 750, at the beginning of 1889 to nearly 1,200, and, at the beginning of 1890 to 1,277, including 25 in Mexico and Central America. Meantime 266 gas companies engaged in electric lighting at present (1890) is 1,543. The number of isolated or private incandescent and arc light plants at the beginning of 1887 was about 1,000 each. Now there are 3,925 private plants in the United States, 175 in Canada, and 200 in Mexico and Central America, making 4,300 in all. The number of arc lamps in use in 1882 was 6,000. This number doubled each year for four years, and has since grown rapidly until there are now 235,000 arc lamps in use. The number of incandescent lights has increased from 525,000 in November, 1886, to 3,000,000 at present. The number of electric motors now in operation in the country is estimated at 15,000, many of them from 15 to 50 horse power. There are nearly 200 electric railways in over 125 towns and*

cities, and these have in operation or under contract 1,884 cars on 1,260 miles of track . . .'

The introduction of the incandescent lamp as a commercial lamp may be said to have begun between ten and twelve years ago, although it was known and had been used a number of years prior to that, yet it had not been developed sufficiently to come into general use.

One of the most important steps in its development, made at that time, was to make the incandescent carbon long and slender instead of short and thick; this was without doubt that which made it a practical success as a commercial lamp. This step is claimed to have been made by Edison . . .

As a convertor of electrical energy into light, it is still very inefficient; an arc lamp will give as much as five to ten times as much light per Watt as the incandescent. It is claimed to have been found that only a very small fraction of he electrical energy of an incandescent lamp is converted into light, almost all of it being converted to heat. If this is the case, and it seems likely, it is great waste of energy to produce light with incandescent lamps, in the same way as it is a great waste to use gas for illuminating purposes, or even using coal for driving steam engines. There is, therefore, very much room for improvement of incandescent lamps, which will probably be in its being replaced by a radically different lamp, rather than in improvements of its present form.

---

8   Oscar Wilde (Irish): 'On the Uses of Machines' (1891)

Up to the present, man has been, to a certain extent, the slave of machinery, and there is something tragic in the fact that as soon as man had invented a machine to do his work he began to starve. This, however, is, of course, the result of our property system and our system of competition. One man owns a machine which does the work of five hundred men. Five hundred men are, in consequence, thrown out of employment, and, having no work to do, become hungry and take to thieving. The one man secures the produce of the machine and keeps it, and has five hundred times as much as he should have, and probably, which is of much more importance, a great deal more than he really wants. Were that machine the property of all, everybody would benefit by it. It would be an immense advantage to the community. All unintellectual labour, all monotonous, dull labour, all labour that deals with dreadful things, and involves unpleasant conditions, must be done by machinery. Machinery must work for us in coal mines, and do all sanitary services, and be the stoker of steamers, and clean the streets, and run messages on wet days, and do anything that is tedious or distressing. At present machinery competes against man. Under proper conditions machinery will serve man. There is no doubt at all that this is the future of machinery; and just as trees grow while the country gentleman is asleep, so while Humanity will be amusing itself, or enjoying cultivated leisure – which, and not labour, is the aim of man – or making beautiful things, or reading beautiful things, or simply contemplating the world with admiration and delight, machinery will be doing all the necessary and unpleasant work. The fact is, that civilization requires slaves. The Greeks were quite right there. Unless there are slaves to do the ugly, horrible, uninteresting work, culture and contemplation become almost impossible. Human slavery is wrong, insecure, and demoralizing. On mechanical slavery, on the slavery of the machine, the future of the world depends. And when scientific men are no longer called upon to go down to a depressing East End and distribute bad cocoa and worse blankets to starving people, they will have delightful leisure in which to devise wonderful and marvellous things for their own joy and the joy of everyone else. There will be great storages of force for every city, and for every house if required, and this force man will convert into heat, light, or motion, according to his needs. Is this Utopian? A map of the world that does not include Utopia is not worth even glancing at, for it leaves out the one country at which Humanity is always landing. And when Humanity lands there, it looks out, and, seeing a better country, sets sail. Progress is the realization of Utopias.

9   *The Household* (British): 'The Everyday Use of Electric Light' (c.1905)

Light is produced wherever electricity is forced along a conductor which resists its passage, or is not sufficient to convey the quantity of electricity without great resistance, causing friction, heat, and light. The arc light is caused by the passage of the electric current across the space between two pieces of carbon; the points of which are raised by the current to a white heat. The ordinary incandescent light is caused by forcing a current along a carbon filament, which is not sufficient to carry the quantity of the current without great resistance. This resistance causes the filament first to become red-hot, and then to glow with a bright white light. The morsel of carbon would be instantaneously burnt up, but that the air has been exhausted from the small glass globe in which it is placed; by which means a vacuum is formed, and combustion prevented, so that the filament will glow brightly for a thousand hours or more, and still be unconsumed.

It is evident that the wires conveying the electric current can far more easily be conveyed into houses than gas-pipes, because they can be conveyed along walls, or even between floors and ceilings, by means of very small apertures; and they can also be fixed at any convenient place on the walls, and conveyed, in the same manner as telegraph-wires, to any point where they are wanted. In some of the systems lately introduced this is done on the principle of induction apparatus or secondary generators. Thus, a primary electric current, a high pressure, is conveyed along a wire main laid along the street, and carrying a current of prodigious tension; and in as many places as the light is required along the course of this primary conductor, a secondary generator or coil is arranged, capable of carrying off a current of larger comparative quantity and lower pressure, in order to supply a certain number of lamps of any of the various kinds that have been invented for the electric light. In other cases the current is used direct, or from what are called secondary or storage batteries.

The arc light is not universally becoming to colours or complexions; but much can be done by the use of tinted glasses; and ladies will have to choose the colours of their evening dresses with a special view to the electric light when it becomes general. It is said that at present nothing looks so well under its influence as pink, and the various shades of red. Incandescent lamps are usually pleasant enough . . .

The proportion of heat given off by electric lights is about one-twentieth of the heat given off by gas, for the same amount of illumination; so it is much cooler. The danger of fire is much diminished by the use of electricity. The incandescent lamp may be ever so near to curtains or hangings, but they will not catch fire; matches and tapers are never required, as a small switch turns the light on or off; and there is no danger of explosion. Then the electric light does not destroy the most elaborate gilding; it does not promote or produce dirt in any way; and thus a certain amount of economy follows its reign. So much bearing have these peculiarities upon the real cost of lighting, that many people consider the electric light is even now scarcely dearer than gas, where it can be laid on. But though no more startling discoveries are now to be expected in this branch of practical science, every year makes the electric light a shade cheaper, by the avoidance of little wastes and leakages, which secure a slightly higher percentage of duty for the power expended. Many of the dynamo-electric machines, for instance, looked at casually, appear nearly the same as those made under the same name ten years before. In broad outlines they are the same; but every machine, nevertheless, shows many little constructional differences, which in one way or another produce a better return; and all this is tantamount to some reduction in the cost of lighting . . .

The chief question which at present is regarded as open, or awaiting practical decision, concerns the choice between the two methods of supplying the current for domestic use, which have already been alluded to. The greater part of London has been allotted to a company which proposes to use the system of induction, or secondary generators. This may perhaps be thought to decide the matter; but such is by no means the case, and many skilled electricians regard the upshot of such an extensive experiment with very grave anxiety. This system depends upon the fact that if a current is sent alternately along a wire, which we will call the main wire – that is, if the current be *reversed* in direction at short intervals, perhaps many times in a second – and another wire be arranged parallel with this main wire, but not touching or having any other direct connection with it, at every reversal of the current in the main wire, a current is 'induced' along the secondary wire. On this system the consumers are supplied by secondary wires as required, and matters are easily so arranged that currents either at higher or lower pressure are taken off. So far all is very convenient. But, in the first place, for a main wire thus to supply a large circuit, its current must be of enormous tension, such as would be fatal to a human being; and in the second place, the *alternating currents*, which are a necessity of the system, are many times more painful and dangerous, if accidentally taken through the body, than a steady or continuous current of the same tension. For instance, if a current of the quantity and tension sufficient to supply a single arc light, such as a scientific lecturer uses in an electric lantern to demonstrate before an audience, were by any inadvertence taken through his hands, if it be a continuous current he would simply take a small shock and think no more of it; but were it an alternating current of the same measurement, the effects of even such a current would be painful, and

71

might give perceptible shock to the system . . .

It cannot be very long before dwellers in most large towns will be enabled at a very moderate cost to enjoy a system of lighting which in health, cleanliness, and steadiness of illumination offers so many advantages.

10 Gregor Paulsson (Swedish): 'Design and Machinery' (1919)

Now that we have the machines let us, instead of imitating former products and techniques, try to design goods that are characteristic of machine production . . . Do not let us imitate former designs. Let us, with the help of these technical aids, produce the new.

11 Peter Behrens (German): 'Technology and Cultural Life' (1922)

No one is likely to underestimate the influence which the Great War and its consequences will exert on future generations. Our interim impression is that we have witnessed the collapse of a high economic civilization, a collapse which not only affects ourselves, but all the countries of the Old World. The sophistication of this civilization found its most typical expression in the unprecedented progress of its technology. It seemed then as though all endeavours were subsumed within the general perspective of mathematically-based thinking. And this view was reflected in the world about us. We admired the massive curves of those great iron halls and the bold sweep of those bridges: we succumbed to the aggressive impact of those machines whose construction seemed so audacious and so cogent, though we kept telling ourselves that such an impact on our senses was fortuitous and pseudo-aesthetic, given that no artistic conception underlay their construction.

And indeed technology has thus far contrived to reach a peak only in terms of material existence, for the unity of the material and the spiritual – that is, the values of culture – has never achieved formal expression. Indeed, nobody has given a moment's thought to it. The engineer in his ascent from success to success, has turned increasingly away from anything which has no immediate bearing on his own field.

Thus our times present on all sides the symptoms of disunity. Wherever we look, we see a welter of contradictory trends. We acknowledge the considerable accomplishments of the construction engineer, but we are equally aware of the decadence and mediocrity of our modern city architecture. The bold forms of our transport vehicles are a constant source of pleasurable surprise, yet at the same time the quality of the general utensils and industrial products on display in our shops indicates a nadir of taste which can scarce be imagined any lower.

This may prompt present day intellectuals in particular to see technology as the medium and expression of a calculating, analytical and imperialistic era. And they may be inclined to turn back and seek out far-off times and places by way of an art of introversion and soulful simplicity. For them the machine has utterly destroyed the heart of the creative urge and the created work. They have a presentiment that our technological and materialistic civilization is reaching its peak, and that a return to spiritual and cultural values awaits us in the near future.

Here we see the opposite tendency. Both cases are the same: both the engineer and the man of sensibility are opting out of a commitment to the totality of lived experience.

No one would seriously wish to give up the achievements of modern technology. More than at any other time in history, we are dependent on its greatest and cheapest facilities. Indeed, precisely because we are economically weak at the present time, we have no choice but to make our lives more simple, more practical, more organised and wide ranging. Only through industry have we any hope of fulfilling our aims. It alone can save us from our economic misery. But those people who object to seeing a split between mechanisation and the life of the spirit are equally in the right. It is thus a question of historic importance whether it is possible for technology to free itself from its role as an end unto itself and become a medium for the expression of our cultural life.

---

12   *Daily Mail* (British): 'Manufactured Wood' (1922)

The discovery of 'Manufactured Wood' marks the commencement of a new era in the art of Bungalow equipment. This wonderful new process of manufacturing wood has not only made possible the faithful reproduction of the most beautiful woodwork of any period or style, it has also brought the cost of artistic interior fittings and decorations within the reach of all.

'Manufactured Wood' Productions can be obtained at one-third the cost of hand-carved woodwork, yet it is practically impossible to distinguish them from the most expensive, genuine hand-work. They look like wood, feel like wood, and last like wood – the only difference is in the cost.

We give you a cordial invitation to visit our showrooms and inspect the numerous examples of 'Manufactured Wood' Productions, or we will gladly send you a copy of our illustrated booklet giving full details of this modern discovery. Why not write to-day?

---

13   Theo van Doesburg (Dutch): 'The Idea of the Machine in Art' (1923)

Personal taste and also admiration for the machine (machine-art) are of no importance whatsoever in establishing unity between art and life. The ideal of the machine in art is as illusory as the ideals which inspired Naturalism, Futurism, Cubism and Purism among other movements, and it remains more dangerous than metaphysical speculation.

---

14   Dorothy Belasco (British): 'Electricity and the Home' (1924)

More and more is labour-saving becoming an absolute necessity in the modern home. It was the prodigious amount of work in the past that was inseparable from running even the smallest of households that forced the householder to voice the demand for labour-saving devices, and consequently the easier running of the domestic machinery. Indeed, the idea of the labour-saver was almost a revolution on the part of those whose lives were spent in the domestic sphere. How important these developments are on the national life cannot but be recognised. Our stability as a people, and our greatness as a nation depend almost entirely on our home life, which is indeed the backbone of our existence. With the hurry and scurry and strenuous endeavour of modern life, the home has to take its rightful place, namely, where it is possible to rest and recuperate. Consequently its running should involve the minimum amount of trouble and worry.

We are not naturally a race of restaurant habitués, and our achievements are largely born of the home. Thus it can be readily understood the great value that electricity has here. Domestic difficulties cease, and we are not now dependent as we were on domestic help in order to run our homes, and the home expenditure is materially lessened.

Of late years electricity in the home has been developed into almost undreamed of possibilities, and the resultant luxurious living conserves our energies for the real battles of life . . .

Indeed a fixed charge of a single low rate per unit can, with arrangement, be recorded on one meter for all purposes, lighting, heating and cooking. Electrical heating of the home has, of course, been employed for some years, but there is a great revolution in the stoves and radiators of the past; these formerly looking rather cold and unsightly unless the power was being used. Nowadays this is all changed, and the very latest heating stoves give the appearance of coal fires. The actual heating apparatus, which is at the back and fitted with a special constructed deflector which ensures directed radiant heat, can be turned on and off at will. It makes not the slightest difference to the coal fire effect, the light of which can be turned on and off quite independently. The consumption of power for this firelight, coming as it does from the power circuit and not from the lighting, is almost nil.

It is remarkable how a warm appearance will give the feeling of warmth, and so these latest stoves give all the social comfort of a coal fire combined if necessary with as much heat as is desired.

Of course, for ordinary heating purposes, there is no end to the number of stoves that can be employed. All of them can be moved about as desired, according to the length of the flex, and they can be obtained in all different sizes. Apart from the fireplace stoves, the portable radiant heaters are much to be desired. Fitted with a reflector and wire guard, they can be placed in any position on ledge, table, etc., and are excellent to take the chill off a bathroom or similar small space.

The heating of water for baths or ordinary hot water supply is expensive, unless one can arrange for cheap power, which is a personal matter to be arranged with the electrical supply company.

There are two systems in use in this connection, the first of which is really impracticable in this country as the expense is far too great to make it a good working proposition. It is a system used largely in Holland and America where there is a large power system, the water being put through an electrical geyser which consumes anything from 8-12 kilowatts an hour, quite apart from the fact that the system requires a special main right up to the geyser.

D

The method generally in use here is the tank system, which will use anything from 300-600 watts an hour. A tank holding 40 gallons of water, generally running on a fixed consumption of 300 watts, is the most useful. This system does not incur the expense of having a special cable, the power coming off the ordinary power supply. As this is a regular consumption, it is possible to have definite charge arrangements with the companies, irrespective of any of their power being used.

Cooking by electricity is a great boon to the housewife. It is, of course, absolutely necessary to have a power circuit in the house, which means a separate meter. The possession of an electric cooking stove is a great saving in labour; there is no preparation for use, there is no cleaning up, and after the switch has been turned off there is always enough heat for any slow cooking.

Such a stove is clean, simple, healthy and economical to use, being always easily regulated. An ordinary cooking stove, large enough for six to eight persons, will consume about three and a half – four and a half units. The householder is often introduced to electric cooking by the means of table cookery appliances. A great variety of apparatus is now sold for heating foods and liquids, toasting and grilling. These find favour by their attractive appearance and general handiness.

These cookers are generally operated from a convenient lamp socket or wall plug, and the table can be fitted with connections at each end for the users of these appliances.

All these cooking gadgets can come off the light circuit, but if power is in the home, it is much cheaper to take off this. And now we come to the lighting of the home – a very important factor in domestic comfort. Here electric lighting more than comes into its own.

The very simplicity of control, and the efficiency and cheapness in use, make it very much to be desired. The modern electric lamp has a white and beautifully concentrated light, the correct illuminating effect being obtained by the use of reflectors and shades designed with regard to optical requirements. All this makes electrical lighting of indispensable value to the house.

There are a few points to bear in mind in connection with this lighting. Voltages vary from 100-150. Where there is an alternating current it is possible to use a transformer, so that a 50-volt half-watt lamp will be more efficient and use less current than a higher voltage. This transformer, though, can only be used for lighting and not for power.

About eight years ago the half-watt lamp was introduced which would go on any circuit, providing it was the right voltage for the supply. An ordinary 1-watt lamp gives a soft light and can be used without a shade. A half-watt lamp is really more efficient, the light being very concentrated, and using only half the current. Half-watt lamps generally require to be diffused by a shade of some kind.

The position of the lamps must also be considered. For general purposes in the centre of the room hanging from the ceiling is excellent, but not in the dining-room, where a head light is somewhat confusing. A far better idea is to use a table standard, or, what are very popular, electric candle lights. Wall lights also can be used here to great advantage. There are very many different kinds of lamps, from the very small candle to the large floor standard, and of course many and various are the shades and fittings. The modern reproductions of the old coaching lamps are having an enormous vogue. If they are not being used as hall lanterns they form delightful shades for Empress Standards on finial posts. They are of course out of keeping in the drawing-room.

15 Walter Gropius (German): 'What Technology can Give Us' (1925)

Smooth and sensible functioning of daily life is not an end in itself, it merely constitutes the condition for achieving a maximum of personal freedom and independence. Hence, the standardisation of the practical processes of life does not mean new enslavement and mechanisation of the individual but rather frees life from unnecessary ballast in order to let it develop all the more richly and unencumbered.

16 Lewis Mumford (American): 'Machine Worship' (1934)

What we call, in its final results, 'the machine' was not, we have seen, the passive by-product of technics itself, developing through small ingenuities and improvements and finally spreading over the entire field of social effort. On the contrary, the mechanical discipline and many of the primary inventions themselves were the result of deliberate effort to achieve a mechanical way of life: the motive in back of this was not technical efficiency but holiness, or power over other men. In the course of development machines have extended these aims and provided a physical vehicle for their fulfilment.

Now, the mechanical ideology, which directed men's minds toward the production of machines, was itself the result of special circumstances, special choices and interests and desires. So long as other values were uppermost, European technology had remained relatively stable and balanced over a period of three or four thousand years. Men produced machines partly because they were seeking an issue from a baffling complexity and confusion, which characterized both action and thought: partly, too, because their desire for power, frustrated by the loud violence of other men, turned finally toward the neutral world of brute matter. Order had been sought before, again and again in other civilizations, in drill, regimentation, inflexible social regulations, the discipline of caste and custom: after the seventeenth century it was sought in a series of external instruments and engines. The Western European conceived of the machine because he wanted regularity, order, certainty, because he wished to reduce the movement of his fellows as well as the behavior of the environment to a more definite, calculable basis. But, more than an instrument of practical adjustment, the machine was, from 1750 on, a goal of desire. Though nominally designed to further the means of existence, the machine served the industrialist and the inventor and all the cooperating classes as an end. In a world of flux and disorder and precarious adjustment, the machine at least was seized upon as a finality.

If anything was unconditionally believed in and worshipped during the last two centuries, at least by the leaders and masters of society, it was the machine; for the machine and the universe were identified, linked together as they were by the formulae of the mathematical and physical sciences; and the service of the machine was the principal manifestation of faith and religion: the main motive of human action, and the source of most human goods. Only as a religion can one explain the compulsive nature of the urge toward mechanical development without regard for the actual outcome of the development in human relations themselves: even in departments where the results of mechanization were plainly disastrous, the most reasonable apologists nevertheless held that 'the machine was here to stay' – by which they meant, not that history was irreversible, but that the machine itself was unmodifiable.

17 Serge Chermayeff (Russian, resident in Britain and USA): 'Mass-produced Housing' (1935)

Technical invention has far outstripped social invention in its advance, and it is now necessary to invent some new economic methods which will prevent our suffering from the too rapid technical advance and enable us to obtain the full benefits of the work of our scientists and inventors. A great many processes, which can be used by the architect for the benefit of the many, are finding an outlet only in the work of a luxurious character for the economically privileged and are hailed as a sign of returning prosperity . . . We have the machine worked materials and the machine made goods. In fact, mass production, the inevitable purpose for which the first power driven machine, the modern tool, was invented, today can be utilised for the production of essential elements for the millions who at the moment lack them. Bricks alone are not enough. Mass production and prefabrication of all the essential structural parts of the simplest dwellings could contribute some form of standardised architecture such as has been attempted already in the USSR and the USA.

18 Royal Barry Wills (American): 'On Functionalism' (1941)

The exterior appearance of man may be the result of his way of life and he is undoubtedly the most marvellous machine on this planet – but he does look more seductive when clothed – especially as the years pile up. And there are practical reasons for it, over and above the risk of sitting on a thistle. Sheer 'functionalism' as expressed in the alleged 'house of the future' smacks strongly of downright nakedness to the usual sense of artistic morality and, it may be observed, the ravages of time deal as roughly with its bare externals as with our own.

19 John Steinbeck (American): 'Ford's Gadgets' (1945)

Two generations knew more about Ford's gadgets than about the clitoris, more about shifting gears than about the solar system.

20   John Gloag (British): 'Plastics are not Substitutes' (1945)

Apart from our normal, human resistance to unusual things, the inclination to regard plastics chiefly as substitutes is often supported by the hope that the rich confusion of the prospect they disclose may thus be simplified. The most august technical authorities sometimes display a tendency to emphasise the traditional materials that plastics could displace, even when they are elucidating the scope and novelty of their inherent properties. For example, Professor J.D. Bernal, in discussing the gifts that the technical industry may bestow on the world, writes: 'Already we have, in artificial silk and plastics such as bakelite, materials which are successfully displacing natural products; and this tendency may become more general.'

The accent here is on *displacement* . . .

. . . It is undesirable that one class of materials should ever dominate our environment: however versatile the components of that class might be, their universality would destroy variety, and, in the words of Mr. Winston Churchill '. . . the most fertile means from which happiness may be derived in life is from variety.'

It is clear that in some directions plastics will replace natural products. For instance, nylon bristles have already replaced hog's bristle in tooth brushes and hair brushes . . . We are not always aware of the extent of the service plastics are already performing in everyday life nor how far they influence or control the technique of industrial production. An excellent summary of the subject was furnished by Mr. C.F. Merriam . . . who . . . asked his listeners to imagine what would happen if there was a sudden and miraculous withdrawal of those materials from the world. He said: 'If you were using a modern telephone at the moment, the whole instrument, with the exception of a few small metal parts, would disappear. You wouldn't be able to go on knitting that sock you're holding, because the plastic needles would have vanished. If you were playing a game of table tennis, you'd find yourself hitting the air instead of the ball. If we were eating dinner, many of us who happen to wear false teeth would find it most uncomfortable because the dentures would have gone, leaving the teeth loose in the mouth. If you were riding a cycle or driving a car, the handle grips or steering wheel would suddenly feel cold and harsh because the plastic covering had been removed. The wireless set you're listening to might fade out because the case and some vital part had gone. The comb you might be passing through your hair would also vanish. And what about those buttons on your dress and those coloured zip-fasteners that hold you together? They would go as well . . . Perhaps the most astonishing result of this miracle would be that air warfare would cease for a time because pilots and crews of very fast aeroplanes couldn't withstand the rush of air, from which they are now protected by plastic windows and cockpit covers. And so you see plastics enter into our daily lives in quite a number of unexpected ways. I could give you many more instances, but I think I've said enough to show you that without plastics life would be rather different.'

21 T. S. Ashton (British): 'The Industrial Revolution' (1948)

In the short span of years between the accession of George III and that of his son, William IV, the face of England changed. Areas that for centuries had been cultivated as open fields, or had lain untended as common pasture, were hedged or fenced; hamlets grew into populous towns; and chimney stacks rose to dwarf ancient spires. Highroads were made – straighter, stronger, and wider than those evil communications that had corrupted the good manners of travellers in the days of Defoe. The North and Irish Seas, and the navigable reaches of the Mersey, Ouse, Trent, Severn, Thames, Forth and Clyde were joined together by threads of still water. In the North the first iron rails were laid down for the new locomotives, and steam packets began to ply on the estuaries and the narrow seas . . .

The industrial revolution is to be thought of as a movement, not as a period of time. Whether it presents itself in England, after 1760, in the United States and Germany after 1870, or in Canada, Japan and Russia in our own day, its character and effects are fundamentally the same. Everywhere it is associated with a growth of population, with the application of science to industry, and with a more intensive and extensive use of capital. Everywhere there is a conversion of rural into urban communities and a rise of new social classes. But in each case the course of the movement has been affected by circumstances of time and place. Many of the social discomforts that have been attributed to the industrial revolution in Britain were, in fact, the result of forces which (for all we know) would still have operated if manufacture had remained undeveloped and there had been no change of economic form.

22   Alvar Aalto (Finnish): 'Art and Technology' (1955)

The boundaries of art and technology are obviously not well defined. In the past these concepts were often considered the same thing or similar; different constellations of cultural significance appeared, according to whether it was a question of art, technology, handicraft, or whatever. Strictly speaking it is so even today within architecture, where the connection between art and technology is most obvious.

23   Peter Reyner Banham (British): 'The Machine Age' (1960)

Even a man who does not possess an electric razor is likely – in the Westernised world at least – to dispense some inconceivable product, such as an aerosol shaving cream, from an equally unprecedented pressurised container, and accept with equanimity the fact that he can afford to throw it away, regularly, cutting-edges that previous generations would have nursed for years. Even a housewife who does not possess a washing machine dispenses synthetic detergent from synthetic plastic packs on to synthetic fabrics whose quality and performance makes the jealously-guarded secrets of silk seem trivial. A teenager, curled up with a transistorised, printed-circuit radio, or boudoir gramophone, may hear a music that literally did not exist before it was committed to tape, reproduced at a level of quality that riches could not have bought a decade or so ago. The average automobile of today, running on such roads as have been specially contrived for it, provides transport more sumptuous in vehicles more gorgeous than palanquin-born emperors knew how to desire.

   Many technologies have contributed to this domestic revolution, but most of them make their point of impact on us in the form of small machines – shavers, clippers and hair-dryers; radio, telephone, gramophone, tape recorder and television; mixers, grinders, automatic cookers, washing machines, refrigerators, vacuum cleaners, polishers . . . A housewife alone often disposes of more horsepower today than an industrial worker did at the beginning of the century. This is the sense in which we live in a machine age.

24 Huw Beynon (British): 'Fordism' (1973)

The twentieth century has been the century of mass-production. The century in which the moving assembly line goes on producing millions upon millions of automobiles. The introduction of the assembly line at the beginning of this century was greeted with acclaim that approached adulation. The man responsible was seen as a miracle maker. And that man was Henry Ford. He became the hero of the mass-production saga. Wilde's dictum that 'under the right conditions technology will serve men' was taken for granted, for the right conditions were at hand. The age of plenty was around the corner. The technological euphoria of those early years mellowed in the face of mass unemployment and the 'speed-up' practised on the line. The hero became the villain in Chaplin's *Modern Times*. The little man crushed by the assembly line. Huxley's pessimistic *Brave New World* depicted a future where men were stunted by coercion and confused by a new religion – Fordism. A technocratic disenchanted world. Ford became plagued by a similar vision. So much so that he started to buy up parts of 'old America', opening folk museums, closing roads to the motor car.

Henry Ford was born the son of a farmer in Dearborn, Michigan, in 1863. He made his first automobile in 1893 and formed the Ford Motor Company in 1903 when he was forty. He dominated the affairs of the Company for the next forty years. Throughout his life he retained the prejudices and ideas of a small farmer. He was an anachronism. The multi-billion dollar small-town farmer who produced motor cars.

On 18 June 1903 Henry Ford and eleven other men met to form the Ford Motor Company. In its first year 1708 Ford passenger cars were produced. Ten years later, annual production figures reached the 200,000 mark. In 1915 half a million cars were produced and in 1919 the figures reached a million cars a year – only to soar again to over two million in 1923. Ford had made it. He had broken into the mass market for automobiles. And he was rich. In 1903 very little capital was needed to start a motor company and Ford and his eleven associates had started with $28,000. In its first ten years the company earned fifty-five million dollars. The following three years brought in over a hundred million dollars. By August 1916 the Company's assets stood at $300,000,000. Ford was a rich man. A rich man who wanted to control his own.

25   Sylvia Katz (British): 'Plastic, the Democratic Material' (1978)

The asset of plastics is that, unlike precious metals and stones, it is a universal material, available to everyone. Synthetic resin is transformed into articles that can be exclusive and expensive, or cheap rubbish. Plastics can also be superfluously decorative, but at the same time, according to Charles Spencer, can fill a social need: 'Perhaps there is something in plastics, as a kind of democratic material, capable of the most mundane and the most serious uses, identified with the "space" age, which pro- motes a down-to-earth, social conscience' . . . But as Alan Glanvill pointed out at the Society of Industrial Artists confer- ence in May 1975, plastics have suffered from the success of fulfilling this social need, for they have thus descended the social scale in the mind of the user.

26   Alan Altshuler and Daniel Roos (Americans): 'Can Automobility Endure?' (1984)

Do conditions loom in the foreseeable future that can be dealt with only by reducing the mass use of automobiles for personal travel? Many analysts have judged that they do, grouping po- tential threats to the future of automobility under two head- ings. The most pressing, in many assessments of the situation, are physical shortages of energy and limits on the capacity of the atmosphere to absorb auto emissions. If these problems can be surmounted, it can still be argued that the unpleasant side effects of automobility, such as traffic congestion and noise in urban areas, will become so great that societies will decide that the gain in personal mobility is not worth the cost to the community. Restrictions on auto use or decisions not to build the roads needed for growing traffic might follow. Further in the future, other challenges to automobility may come from improved urban transit systems, cheaper or faster air and rail links for intercity travel, or electronic communications systems that may reduce the desire for personal travel. Collectively these might halt or reverse the growth in auto use. But are these truly threats to widespread auto use in the long term, or are they only problems for certain vehicle technologies and operating prac- tices?

27 Adrian Forty (British): 'The Extent of Mechanisation in the Nineteenth Century' (1986)

It is important to remember that the extent of mechanisation in mid-nineteenth century industries was far less than was, and still is, supposed. As Raphael Samuel has shown, the manufacture of a great many products relied for a long time on the manual skill and strength of workmen. Even where machines were introduced, they were rarely applied to all the stages of production, and many processes continued to be carried out by hand: for instance in tailoring and dress-making, until late in the century, machines were employed only for a few types of sewing. Of all British manufacturing industries in the middle of the nineteenth century, only textile production had been extensively mechanised. In the many industries that continued to be based on manual labour, products were not necessarily made from start to finish by the same craftsmen: for example, the division of labour in the unmechanised pottery industry goes back as far as the early eighteenth century and it appeared in many other industries at the same time.

28 Andrea Branzi (Italian): 'The Megasystem of Furnishings and Fittings' (1988)

At the beginning of the last century, the home of a reasonably well-off family of four contained a set of objects comprising no more than 150-200 items, including crockery and clothing. The home of a comparable family today might contain 2500 to 3000 objects, including electric appliances and items used in the pursuance of hobbies but not such items as books, records, and tapes.

What occurred, through a slow but relentless process, was a true revolution, one in which the environmental presence once represented by architecture was replaced by industrial and nonindustrial objects. The number of these objects has continued to increase, and their uses and modes of function have actually created an almost unabridged gap in the metropolitan experience of man. He lives and works within a universe of objects that renews itself, grows more specialized and in fact constitutes his true interface with the world outside.

Today we can use old works of architecture and parts of ancient cities, or even primitive ones, as long as the available set of objects and services is functionally and culturally adapted to the activities that we wish to carry out there. We can live in houses built five hundred or a thousand years ago, if they contain the furnishings, facilities and sources of information that we need. All that we use of these works of architecture is a number of symbolic codes.

This change has not just shifted the center of gravity from architecture to design but has, in fact, created a new metropolitan theorem. This theorem recognizes that changes in the metropolis take place not only through the construction of architectural structures, road systems or urban services, but also through the renewal of the system of objects and of individual commodities that improve and transform the cultural and technical fitness of places for habitation, creating the city of the present inside that of the past and that of the future inside the present one.

This explains the great difficulty, indeed impossibility, of planning the present-day metropolis and its growth. It is made up of a swarm of microstructures, objects, and services that eludes any logic of planning and control. A swarm that invades the scene, fills the environment and provides a support for the use of the city, rendering it flexible and capable of coping with a wide variety of different requirements. We live in a megasystem of furnishings and fittings, within a gigantic 'light-scape,' in a wired-up territory in which an infinity of terminals are linked together, like an all-embracing interface, artificially ventilated and riddled with tunnels of information and signs that have nothing in common with architecture. Design is the only discipline that gets its hands dirty in this hybrid, compromised, but terribly real universe. It works with objects and commodities, and therefore at the heart of the true problems of this age.

4

USES OF THE HAND

Without doubt, the hand is the ultimate tool. Hand skills have been the basis of creation in all the visual arts since the earliest times, and undoubtedly, in one way or another, they still are.

There have always been makers of art-objects in all media. And objects of high artistic merit, made for contemplation rather than utility, are made today in all media just as they have been made through the millennia. At this point in time the makers of these objects, albeit in clay, metal, wood, stone or cloth, tend to be labelled as being part of the crafts. The chapter includes quotations from some of these makers towards the latter end, but on the whole it is concentrated elsewhere.

Before the real onset of mass-industrialisation, and certainly before manufacturing moved towards centralisation and systematisation, articles of everyday utility were normally produced with relatively little recourse to machinery, and often by a single artisan, or a small team of artisans. As the various industries grew and transformed, the work of these artisans was gradually replaced by, or appropriated into, larger production systems. In the textile industry in particular, skills which had hitherto been omnipotent began to wane in usefulness, and, hence, in economic power. Thus there grew a tension between the hand and the machine, the most famous instance of which was Luddism.

But many industries did not immediately replace the hand with the machine; indeed, technological redundancy was not new at the beginning of the nineteenth century, and so it would be wrong to associate such replacement only with this period. It was more normal for hand and machine to combine in various ways. Nevertheless, many commentators on these issues depicted the replacement of hand skills by machinery as being both sudden and universal. This was usually because they had ideological and political agendas which were not concerned with historical fidelity. They sensed a shift in the shape of society, and they associated it with the shifts in industrial practice. In the last quarter of the nineteenth century especially, hand-making was promoted as being the antidote to the social and psychological alienation, caused, the theory goes, by the mechanisation and centralisation of the manufacturing process.

The makers of art-objects referred to above were never 'in tension' with the machine; if anything, they benefited from it, by virtue of the fact that it made their hand-craft all the more exclusive.The quotations are less about these makers, but are concentrated more on what might be called the politics of hand-making in the first and second machine ages.

See also
Chapter 1 for ornamental art
Chapter 2 for the morality of hand-making
Chapter 3 for the development of technology in relation to hand-making
Chapter 7 for the influence of non-European hand-making

---

1   C. R. Cockerell (British): 'Mind, Hand and Mechanical Process' (1834)

I believe that the attempt to supersede the work of the mind and hand by mechanical process for the sake of economy will always have the effect of degrading and ultimately ruining art.

---

2   William Morris (British): 'Useful work versus Useless Toil' (1884-5)

There are two kinds of work – one good, the other bad; one not far removed from a blessing, a lightening of life; the other a mere curse, a burden to life.

What is the difference between them, then? This: one has hope in it, the other has not. It is manly to do one kind of work, and manly to refuse to do the other.

What is the nature of the hope which, when it is present in work, makes it worth doing?

It is threefold, I think – hope of rest, hope of product, hope of pleasure in the work itself; and hope of these also in some abundance and of good quality; rest enough and good enough to be worth having; product worth having by one who is neither a fool or an ascetic; pleasure enough for all for us to be conscious of it while we are at work; not a mere habit, the loss of which we shall feel as a fidgety man feels the loss of the bit of string he fidgets with.

3 Josef Hoffmann and Koloman Moser (Austrians): 'The Work Programme of the Wiener Werkstatte' (1905)

The boundless evil caused by shoddy mass-produced goods and by the uncritical imitation of earlier styles, is like a tidal wave sweeping across the world. We have been cut adrift from the culture of our forefathers and are cast hither and thither by a thousand desires and considerations. The machine has largely replaced the hand and the business-man has supplanted the craftsman. To attempt to stem this torrent would seem like madness.

Yet for all that we have founded our workshop. Our aim is to create an island of tranquillity in our own country, which, amid the joyful hum of arts and crafts, would be welcome to anyone who professes faith in Ruskin and Morris. We are calling for all those who regard culture in this sense as valuable and we hope that the errors we are bound to commit will not dissuade our friends from lending their support.

4 William Burton (British): 'Hand and Machine' (1911)

Before I entirely leave the question of hand-work, or craftsman-ship as we may call it in the broad sense as opposed to machine-work production on the large scale, let me enter a respectful but emphatic protest against the widely prevalent idea that hand-work is so sacrosanct that all hand-work, whether ancient or modern, must be essentially artistic and superior to the best that can be done by the use of modern machines. There is no commoner delusion than this, unless it be the idea, often loudly preached, that the workman in any craft should himself be the designer also. The entire history of human craftsmanship dem-onstrates on every hand the falsity of both these positions; there are, and always have been, good and bad craftsmen and good and bad designers.

5 Maurice Guillemot (French): 'An Exhibition of the Arts of Women' (1911)

Art is found in everything; and those objects which are made by women's hands claim an aesthetic character. If I can talk of the past, certain women nowadays in their desire to equal men in everything, would like to become lawyers, justices of the peace, doctors, voters, academics, much more than they want to be lacemakers or embroiderers; to them, those occupations are a ridiculous waste of their time. Working in the arts is nowhere as important to them as the vainglorious pursuits of the intellect – either publishing a successful book, or successfully defending someone in court – transitory glory.

One of Molière's characters, Chrysale, remarked that a woman's chief function was to make and mend clothes. It was alright for him to say that because he had never been forbidden more intellectual pursuits; he'd never been forced to do needlework or crochet – skills which have been relegated to a minor status, despite the fact that they enrich our homes, ourselves and our lives. The same can be said of lacework and embroidery.

6   Walter Gropius (German): 'The Bauhaus and Hand-made Products' (1935)

The *Bauhaus* workshops were really laboratories for working out practical new designs for present-day articles and improving models for mass-production. To create type-forms that would meet all technical, aesthetic and commercial demands required a picked staff. It needed a body of men of wide general culture, as thoroughly versed in the practical and mechanical sides of design as in its theoretical and formal laws. Although most parts of these prototype models had naturally to be made by hand, their constructors were bound to be intimately acquainted with factory methods of production and assembly, which differ radically from the practices of handicraft. It is to its intrinsic particularity that each different type of machine owes the 'genuine stamp' and 'individual beauty' of its products. Senseless imitation of hand-made goods by machinery infallibly bears the mark of a makeshift substitute. The *Bauhaus* represented a school of thought which believes that the difference between industry and handicraft is due, far less to the different nature of the tools employed in each, than to subdivision of labour in the one and undivided control by a single workman in the other. Handicrafts and industry may be regarded as opposite poles that are gradually approaching each other. The former have already begun to change their traditional nature. In the future the field of handicrafts will be found to lie mainly in the preparatory stages of evolving experimental new type-forms for mass-production.

There will, of course, always be talented craftsmen who can

turn out individual designs and find a market for them. The *Bauhaus*, however, deliberately concentrated primarily on what has now become a work of paramount urgency: to avert mankind's enslavement by the machine by giving its products a content of reality and significance, and so saving the home from mechanistic anarchy.

---

7 Walter Dorwin Teague (American): 'The Last Revolt Against Destiny' (1940)

The Victorian era had reason to blush at utility, for most of the utilities offered it by an adolescent Machine Age were indecently hideous. It was easy for Morris and his converts to set these crude mechanical products in humiliating contrast against the suave works of the old handicrafts, not stopping to think that the craft forms stood at the end of a long process of evolution while the machine forms stood at the beginning of another. The perfect adaptation of the older products to the uses for which they were intended, their simple, honest effectiveness and the deep-rooted, organic source of their beauty were serenely evident, and Morris's campaign had a brief prosperity. It could not succeed because it was a mere eddy in an irresistible current, a last revolt against destiny.

The object of work is not only its own joy. While there should and must be joy in work, its object also is the increase in material aids to the comfort and richness of life. Machines are capable of making more things and better things, making them faster and cheaper and available to more of us, than is possible through handwork alone. The end that Morris held most dear, the communal happiness of mankind, required that machine production should prevail, as a later generation of social revolutionists in Russia clearly realises. But Morris did a great constructive service: he was one of the first to revive appreciation of sound and honest work and re-establish rightness as the aim of all our mechanical endeavours.

---

8 Bernard Leach (British): 'The Artist Craftsman and Machine Production' (1945)

The war has brought British craftsmen face to face with the necessity of determining afresh their relationship to the society in which they live. The reaction started by John Ruskin and

William Morris against the trend of industry, economics and social morality has run its course and the accent which they laid upon handwork has been replaced during the last decade by the idea of better design for mass-production. Industry was in a state of experiment and expansion then. Now, however, the whole saturated world is being forced to realize to what abuses the misuse of power has led us. Changes are taking place in the basic order of our society and therefore, in the period of reconstruction which will follow the war, we have a possibility which never really presented itself to Morris and his friends of achieving for craftsmanship its true place in a modern community.

A first step towards clarity of thought on this still confused issue is to define the function of handwork and to bring to light the underlying nature of craftsmanship.

To differentiate between traditional handcrafts of the countryside, machine-crafts of the factory, and individual or artist-crafts of the studio, it is clarifying to bear in mind the gradual evolution of work through these three stages. Thence it becomes apparent that the artist as a worker (or, as Eric Gill put it, every creative worker an artist) is too recent a development for an understanding of his function in the social structure to have spread widely, and more particularly into the preceding field of industry.

The rather limited idea of functionalism prevalent amongst many modern artists, leading as it does to contentment with better design for the machine, makes it all the more necessary to state the case for the human being as a worker, as a craftsman and as a creative artist.

The artist-craftsman has only existed for a comparatively short time. Whilst, on one hand, his contribution to society is not clearly understood, the character of his reaction from a money and machine-ridden world, on the other, has tended hitherto to isolate him from life and has caused some of the work done during the last sixty years to be justly labelled as 'mediaevalist'. For this, he is partly to blame, and Morris himself, great man though he was, cannot altogether escape contemporary criticism on this ground. At that period a reaction such as his could not stem the outgoing tide, so his followers were left stranded on the Cotswolds and in other isolated corners of England consciously preserving traditions of handwork, hugging their special truth to themselves and guarding it with fanaticism.

Moreover, the difficulty of producing and distributing handmade goods in competition with industry is greater than people in general imagine. The individual craftsman working alone or with one or two assistants can only make a living by selling his work, as painting and sculpture are sold, to a public composed of collectors and enthusiasts. Trade sales depend to a great extent upon illustrated catalogues of standardized productions. But two unavoidable characteristics of individual production are variety and a small output. Thus catalogues are at a discount amongst craftsmen unless a group succeed in truly co-ordinating their activities and turning out a basic output at a low enough price for fairly normal purchase and use.

Moreover the full interplay of the capacities and require-ments of a team of more or less educated people is quite a different problem from the traditional co-operation of a group of peasants or of the 'hands' in a factory. Convictions, satisfac-tion in work as well conceived and executed as possible, sharing of responsibilities and profits, must all be based on common assent. Such an effort demands more than the solitary artist's giving of himself to his vocation, or on the other hand, the fellowship of a well-run factory. A way of life – a new social order in embryo – lies behind good work turned out in this way.

The employment of simpler types of local labour may modify but does not squarely face the issue because we can no longer return to the productive unconsciousness of country traditions which guided nine-tenths of the co-operative labour of former ages.

Factories have driven folk-art out of England and the artist-craftsman has been the chief means of defence against the materialism of industry and its insensibility to beauty; but the moment has come for a renewed attempt to bring art and work into closer relationship. It is in the consciousness and unity of such groups or teams that in this and a few other workshops a belief in the development of craftsmanship is gaining ground. The obsession with the individual 'artist' point of view appears to be lessening. Independence once achieved is very precious, but an exaggerated pride in its possession stands bluntly in the way of concurrence in either aim or action and the pride is only too often merely that of an artist on a dunghill. This is very evident in the effort to establish a tradition of work amongst a group of apprentices today. Those who are attracted to handcrafts are no longer simple-minded peasants but mainly conscious art-students anxious to establish their own work-shops at the earliest opportunity. Local lads with a half-educa-tion grow up with a normal expectation of pleasure after work which tends to prevent them from really entering a craftsman's life. Without a new inducement to work together no continuity of steady production can be expected, for crafts such as pottery depend, as it were, upon a slow passage of time: the gradual transfer of the bodily knowledge of the right usage of material in the intimate co-operation of small groups of workers.

. . . The machine has split the human personality: industrialism has brought humanity within sight of safety and leisure for the first time in history, but it has also landed us in the most appalling catastrophe the world has known.

In a machine age artist-craftsmen, working primarily with their hands, represent a natural reaction valid as individual expression, and they should be the source of creative design for mass-production whether they work in conjunction with industry or not. More and more people want to make or enjoy things which are projections of themselves and of their culture – expressions of life – and not mere means to ends. The majority of craftsmen feel that they can contribute best of all by sticking to their lasts. Some of us spend a part of our time teaching, but that is usually undertaken to eke out a meagre living. Few of us work in close contact with machine production and most of those who do so get the worst of the bargain. I have no brief for a puritanical refusal to do so, but it may be a good thing to give some of the reasons for what may otherwise be too readily interpreted as a kind of art-snobbery.

The inducements to make a link with industry are lacking: lacking in reward, in conditions, in probability of good, sound results. Before we can make any approach industry must want us. So far it does not know what we have to offer. It is a position with both sides to blame, or rather, if the matter is approached sympathetically, with neither; for the vicious circle which is just beginning to break down is the almost inevitable outcome of given conditions.

The gap between art and industry has to be bridged. It has grown imperceptibly until the cleavage is wide and misunderstandings on both sides considerable. An example can be found in the unsuccessful effort a few years ago by Stoke-on-Trent to obtain fresh ideas in design by inviting some well-known painters such as Sir Frank Brangwyn, R.A., and Dame Laura Knight, R.A., to decorate table wares. There was no guarantee that the artists selected knew the technique of the potter or that they could employ their sensibilities in process of manufacture. The result might have been foreseen, for the approach was external and the painted wares thus produced were marketed through the usual middleman channels where the comment both just and unjust was generally adverse.

Why were English craftsmen-potters not approached? Not necessarily, or perhaps most advisedly, to work in the factories themselves (though that experience might not have hurt them for a time), but for consultation for the beginning of a better mutual understanding, and in planning the training of a better type of designer for the industry. Why on earth have designers got to be brought from Paris? Pottery in France is not on a level with French painting or even French dress-making, whereas English studio pottery has gained a world-wide repute during the last twenty-five years . . .

With responsible control there would appear to be no deeper cleavage between tool and machine than between hand and tool, but the fact is that as soon as the creative intention ceases to control the processes of manufacture directly (as when re-duplicative work is delegated to the machine), a cleavage does take place. A deadening process begins which increases progressively with further mechanisation.

The words 'hand', 'tool' and 'machine' imply degrees of intimacy between conception and execution, and as soon as the function of the prime tool – the human hand – is recognized, the antagonism, as such, between hand and machine tends to lessen. At one end of the scale is creative thought expressing itself as directly as is humanly possible: at the other the automatic repetitions of mass-production are comparatively devoid of the irregular rhythm of life. Craftsmanship operates throughout, but with diminishing responsibility with the sub-division of labour and the increased employment of power-driven machines.

What all craftsmen are concerned with is the effort to make as excellent things as are possible within the necessarily strict limits of usefulness. These limits also apply to machine-made goods, but the distant control inherent in mass-production combined with the ca'canny of safe dividends to shareholders result in things which give neither maker or user full satisfaction.

Craftsmen, as the residual type of fully responsible workmen look upon industry in its present form as largely anti-social and upon craftsmanship in the widest sense as its antidote. By our way of life we imply another set of values, one in which neither money nor coercive power are ultimate standards. As craftsmen we believe in the best (and therefore the most responsible) work, and regard the lack of this incentive as one of the principal evils of our age.

We do not turn from science and the inventions of the

Western man as evils in themselves, but as powers which have not yet been fully used in the human interest. The birth of industrialism and its long development on English soil places upon us the burden of discovering the solution to the social problems which we have created.

We live in a machine age: as craftsmen we have the choice of using it or of being regarded as mere survivals. Every craftsman should be free to decide the degree to which he can extend his power over material without loss of control. Arbitrary rules forbidding him to use power-wheels or power-driven looms, for example, are ridiculous. The co-operative spirit of his workshop and the creative character of its output are the criteria of his sincerity.

In the work of the hand-craftsman there is a co-operation of hand and undivided personality which has no counterpart in the work of the designer for mass-production. Good hand-craftsmanship is directly subject to the prime source of human activity, whereas machine crafts, even at their best, are activated at one remove. For this reason above all others, artist craftsmanship justifies its existence near the heart of any culture worthy of the name even when it stands alone as an exemplar and reminder.

In this time of flux and reorganization we, as responsible craftsmen, have an essential contribution to make in clarifying and fighting for the basic principles of work – that work which is at one and the same time recreation and labour and in which use and beauty are inseparable.

Most of our slowly-built-up workshops have closed, many of them for good. Threads of tradition running back through centuries were preserved in some, and others were experimental laboratories in which artist craftsmen attempted the fusion of cross-currents of culture.

The regimentation of labour and the ordering of private lives according to the needs of the State – a condition likely to prevail for a long time whatever the outcome of the war – is forcing those of us still left at work to reconsider our fundamental relationship to society, and to take such steps as we can towards establishing a definite position within it. Within the framework of post-war England there is a place for the craftsman's contribution to national life, but it has yet to be secured by convictions held in common, made known to a wider public and protected by the Government. Without such protection the continued existence of free craftsmanship, with all its implications, is at stake.

9 Judy Chicago (American): 'Art and Craft' (1980)

I decided to learn china-painting in 1972 after seeing an antique porcelain plate and realizing that the quality of its color and surface was perfect for the images I had in mind. I never consciously thought about using a woman's history; in fact, I often used techniques that were outside mainstream art sensibility. Over the years I had worked with automotive paint, plastics, or fireworks, as these always seemed to offer unexplored visual possibilities.

Studying china-painting exposed me, for the first time, to the world of women's traditional arts. I learned a great deal from the women with whom I trained – not only about china-painting, but also about a very different way of being an artist. Most china-painters see teaching as part of their work. Their teaching takes a number of forms; they give classes and seminars, but most importantly, at least for me, they teach by example. During exhibitions, they sit in their booths and paint while crowds of people watch them. This act and the public response to it intrigued me; the china-painters' activity was in stark contrast with the isolated and private act of creation associated with twentieth-century 'high art'. Watching these women work out in the open helped me to do the same thing when the *Dinner Party* Project required a studio full of workers. Moreover, the enormous interest of the viewers at these demonstrations suggested that many people craved the opportunity to participate in art.

My learning experience with the china-painters was not totally positive, however. Many of them viewed me suspiciously, were outright hostile, or thought of me as someone who wanted to exploit them – despite all my efforts, both public and private, to honor them. This kind of reaction forced me to confront the conservatism and fear which, along with generosity and warmth, typify the 'subculture' of women's crafts.

During my apprenticeship with the china-painters, I often listened to their discussions about why china-painting wasn't considered art. Interestingly, these conversations focused on the technique of china-painting – which is exceedingly difficult – rather than its content. But it is the absence of personal content that distinguishes art from craft. It was as if the conflict I had experienced between my drive to be an artist and my conditioning as a woman mirrored a much deeper conflict in most of these women. Although many of them possessed the visual skills to express personal subject matter, they did not take themselves seriously nor did they believe that their experiences were important enough to express. This lack of self-esteem resulted not only in a continual dependence upon preformed patterns and designs, but also in a resistance to new ideas and unfamiliar thoughts. All this only reinforced my belief in the importance of addressing women's lack of self-worth as a crucial step in creating change and my determination to achieve this through art.

---

10   Alison Britton (British): 'The Vessel' (1981)

Clay is a material that has been prone to metaphor for centuries. It is such a malleable, versatile, simulatory substance, that practical objects have been formed in some disguise or other for probably almost as long as clay has been used. The first vessels to use clay are thought to have been woven reed containers plastered with a layer of sticky clay to make them waterproof. Even in this there is an ambiguity between 'pot' and 'basket'. Being a vessel is not very demanding. Once the functional requirements of holding are fulfilled, there is still room for plenty of interpretation and variety of outer form . . .

Vessels are basic, archetypal, timeless. A container is a fundamental prop (and symbol) of civilization. A container is an object made with a specific relation to people in mind . . .

---

11   Enid Marx (British): 'Traditional Art' (1981)

Traditional art – folk art – is, I think, very important. It has not been nearly as fully recognised in this country as it has been abroad, yet it is our roots, and without roots nothing can grow. As Gorden Russell said, hand work has a special quality which cannot be imitated by the machine; the machine has its own qualities. Nevertheless, the craft-based industries will always be dependent for good design on those designers who have been trained in handcraft skills: that is the only way to learn to understand the nature of materials, whether natural or synthetic. Designing for synthetic textiles, for example, is far more difficult than designing for natural ones; with synthetics it is necessary to discover, or introduce, qualities to validate them in their own right; they have for too long been used purely imitatively.

12 Patricia Mainardi (American): 'Quilts: The Great American Art' (1982)

Women have always made art. But for most women, the arts valued highest by male society have been closed to them for just that reason. They have put their creativity instead into the needlework arts, which exist in fantastic variety wherever there are women, and which in fact are a universal female art, transcending race, class and national borders. Needlework is the one art in which women controlled the education of their daughters, the production of the art, and were also the audience and critics. Needlework is therefore so important to women's culture that a study of the various textile and needlework arts should occupy the same position in Women's Studies that African art occupies in Black Studies – it is our cultural heritage. Because quilt making is so indisputably women's art, many of the issues women artists are attempting to clarify now – questions of feminine sensibility, of originality and tradition, of individuality versus collectivity, of content and values in art – can be illuminated by a study of this art form, its relation to the lives of the artists, and how it has been dealt with in art history. The contrast between the utilitarian necessity of patching and quilting and the beautiful works of art which women made of it, and the contrasts between the traditions of patchwork and quilting as brought to America and the quilts made here from colonial times to the present, give ample evidence that quilts are The Great American Art.

Although quilts had a functional purpose as bed coverings, they had another purpose equally important to their makers, and that is display. Early bedrooms frequently possessed only one piece of furniture, namely, the bed; and the quilt displayed on the bed was the central motif. Women exhibited their quilts, and still do, at state and country fairs, churches and grange halls, much as our contemporary 'fine' art is exhibited in museums and with much the same results. Good quilt makers were known and envied throughout their area, the exhibition of exceptionally fine craftswomanship and design influenced other women who returned home stimulated to do even finer work, and ideas of color and design were disseminated from one area to another causing recognizable historic and geographic trends.

13   Charles Poulsen (British): 'The Reign of King Ludd' (1984)

. . . The Nottingham riots of 1799. The stocking-knitters sent in a petition to Parliament for a minimum rate, which, as usual, was rejected. Crowds gathered in the streets, smashed windows and attacked the houses of the principal masters. Mills were broken into and knitting-frames destroyed; three hundred were smashed in one factory alone. The disorders continued for several days, during which time three hundred special constables were sworn in and soldiers patrolled the streets. A stocking frame was carried into the marketplace and ceremoniously destroyed. The manufacturers unofficially contacted the workmen and the town council, and offered improved rates and conditions. The riots ended at once.

In 1811 the proprietors of factories in the stocking trade around Nottingham began to receive threatening letters, declarations and manifestos, bearing the the signature 'King Ludd' or 'Ned Ludd' and an address given as 'Sherwood Forest' or 'Sherwood Castle'. Who this 'King Ludd' was, or if he ever existed, was never ascertained, but obviously a large secret organisation existed with a powerful individual or group controlling it. It may have been a name adopted from the legendary King Ludd who was said to have conquered London and built Ludgate long before the Romans came; it may have been taken from Ned Ludd, who, according to vague stories, was a half-witted boy in a stocking mill who in a fire of fury at persecution smashed the stocking frames. His address may have been a reference to Robin Hood. Many simple people believed that he actually existed and held court in the depths of the forest, sworn to redress the wrongs of the poor. Whoever they were, the 'Luddites' quickly became a force in Nottinghamshire, Lancashire and Yorkshire, able to summon on its missions large bodies of armed, disciplined and determined men, safeguarded and protected by the sympathies of most of the common people and even many within the professional classes.

The Luddites first appeared among the 'stockingers' of Nottinghamshire; their trade, relying largely on the European market, had been ruined by the long war and the blockades. They were skilled men who had served apprenticeships and knitted their wares on 'narrow' frames. Some mill owners had developed a 'wide' frame on which unskilled workers could knit large pieces which were cut and sown into form, instead of being made in one piece. These were cheap and soon fell apart, but sold well. These shoddy goods were ruining the market for domestic producers. Following a reduction in the price paid to out-workers, parties of Luddites raided the mills and destroyed the wide frames and the goods they produced. A thousand frames and large stocks of stockings were destroyed in a few weeks.

Luddites met secretly by night in armed groups, some of which carried firearms. They advanced on the machines, smashed or burnt them, and dispersed quickly; a primitive and limited form of guerrilla war. The cut-up work dropped off sharply, and earnings rose by as much as two shilling a dozen pieces.

King Ludd claimed to be acting within the law. Under their charter the Framework Knitters Company had been empowered by Charles II to examine goods and destroy those below accepted standards. Their actions were selective – they sought only to destroy the shoddy stockings along with the machines upon which they were made. The J.P.s rejected this viewpoint and sent 2,000 troops into the area.

The punishment for machine-breaking was transportation to the convict settlements of Australia for up to fourteen years . . . Parliament decided to raise the penalty to death.

---

14   Kerstin Wickman (Swedish): 'Women Saved the Swedish Textile Heritage' (1985)

While in England it was a man – William Morris – who studied old craft traditions, and revived vegetable dye recipes and old manufacturing methods, in Sweden it was a woman – *Lilli Zickerman* – who was in the 1890s embarked on a comprehensive inventory of Swedish domestic crafts and textile art in farmhouses all over the country. She investigated the patterns, techniques and materials of different areas. She photographed her finds and noted down facts, and this work led her, supported by Prince Eugen, himself an artist and patron of the arts, to form the association Swedish Handicraft *(Svensk Hemslojd)* in 1899. The end result was a large textile archive collection of 24,000 pictures, now in the Nordiska Museet (Scandinavian antiquities) and the National College of Art and Design, both in Stockholm: a permanent source of inspiration and instruction for young textile artists.

Lilli Zickerman was interested not so much in developing and renewing textile patterns and techniques as in preserving knowledge and a sense of quality and bringing the popular heritage to the urban masses. She wanted to preserve the skills that still lived and teach people to appreciate them. Some of her young assistants, inspired from what they learned from these inventories, renewed and developed old techniques and patterns into unique handicraft – tapestries, carpets, upholstery fabrics, etc. Lilli Zickerman can be seen as the spiritual ancestor of the generations of textile artists who followed in her footsteps. From the very outset, textile art acquired a powerful position in Sweden. Women became the first applied artists in something like our own sense of the term.

Textile pioneers were the women behind the Friends of Handicrafts Association (*Hand arbetets Vanner*), who had been engaged ever since 1874 in choosing elements of rural textile traditions for the drawing rooms of the urban middle class. The Association's overriding mission was the development and dissemination of textile art. To begin with, the patterns were prepared by female artists, but before long men were also submitting sketches and paintings to be woven or embroidered.

The female artists who did the rounds of Europe in the 1880s, together with their male colleagues, painting landscapes and café life, were told in the 1890s that great art could only be created by men. In Europe during the 1890s it was inopportune for women to assert their personal right to creativity and artistic expression. Applied arts – and textile art above all – provided them with a sanctuary. Carl Larsson's wife *Karin Larsson* both wove and embroidered patterns of high quality. Her furniture designs, put into effect by a local carpenter in the family's home community of Sundborn, were equally innovative. She practised in obscurity what Carl Larsson preached in public. But with the world-wide distribution of Carl Larsson's watercolours, it was Karin Larsson's achievement, the family home at Sundborn, which set the fashion for Swedish interior design during a very large part of the present century!

---

15   Peter Dormer (British): 'Micro-circuitry and the Applied Artist' (1986)

One of the interesting phenomena of the latter part of this century is the way that design, rather than fine art, is now generating new images and metaphors. In the past five years, design, especially in Europe and Japan, has been liberated from the black box/white box syndrome by the development of micro-circuitry. Objects can still be useful but are metamorphosed into the most surprising shapes. Micro-circuitry has forced the designer to think of the imagery his packaging presents, because there is no longer an excuse for making things according to the old 'function dictates form' principle.

For the applied artist, including the potter, this trend is exciting – on the one hand, it ought to suggest to the potter that he or she can offer skills in decoration and ornament to the design world (this has happened a little in England with Janice Tchlenko and Carol McNicholl). On the other hand, the new upsurge of ornamentalist design provides all decorative artists with a wider source of images, together with a greater chance of public acceptability as more and more people become used to the variety of ways in which a thing – anything – can look.

16   Agnes Walter (British): 'Making a Rag Rug' (1987)

First you get your hessian – we used washed potato sacks which, if we were lucky, we got free from the local shop, or sometimes your dad got them from his work lorry-driving. Then you take your rag strips – we mainly used cast-off outer clothes. There weren't jumble sales in our day, where we lived; occasionally we would sell a few things to the rag-and-bone man for some coppers, but mostly we used everything up ourselves; everybody did, so there wasn't anything to go in a jumble sale. The outer garments went into the rugs, the underwear was used as cleaning rags, and the woollens were unpicked and knitted up again. Some people who made rugs used to swap stuff, for the sake of the colours to make up a pattern; your grandmother used to do that with great glee.

You use a rag hook to poke the strips into the hessian backing; you can imagine it as darning the hessian, but leaving loops which form the pile of the rug. There were two or three working methods: you could cut short strips, which I always did because it was quicker. You just prod one strip at a time, leaving the two ends to form a pile; it made a loose, floppy rug. But your grandmother always used a long strip; she prodded it in about an inch and a half on each side of the hessian, making a completely reversible rug that was very heavy. They were very difficult to lift and shake; we used to clean them by banging them against the wall, but it took more than one person to bang grandma's rugs.

Your grandmother always had a rug on the go during the

winter, and she'd put a new one down on the hearth every spring, and move the older ones upstairs. When they got too worn, she'd cut off the good bits to use as mats. She made quite complicated patterns by drawing round plates and saucers and things. Your Auntie Ivy took some of the rugs after she died, but she didn't keep them long; everyone was saying at the funeral, 'Fancy taking those old things!' In the end she burnt them because people thought that, being home-made, they were common. But in your grandmother's day, there wasn't anything you could buy; you were poor, you made your own pillow-slips and everything. They put them out from the age of twelve; she was in service from then, till she married. Imagine, from that to your own home, your own things. She was very house-proud, though she got everything second-hand.

My rugs were never masterpieces like your grandma's. I used mainly navy blue, with bits of red here and there. You used to save the bright bits for the corners, and you used to look at other people's rugs, and your own old ones, for ideas. But I never had much time for rug-making, just the evenings sometimes, when I wasn't knitting or decorating, or just washing. Washing was hellish! There was no hot water in the house; you had to heat it all up in the copper, what we called the set-pot. First you had to light a fire under it, then when the water was hot, you had to ladle it out by hand, into the peggy tub. There was no soap powder in those days, only this green soap that you shredded. So when I was working, I didn't have much time for the rugs, but I always knitted a lot.

5
THE MARKETPLACE

Design, at its most basic level, is about rendering objects more desirable. The desire might be born of a need to have things function efficiently, but over the last two centuries, it has been more directly associated with appearances. Design refers to the beauty of the object, as much as to its functionability, and these two things are, regardless of the rhetoric of design reformers, often mutually exclusive.

One of the key motivations of manufacturers in making the object 'look good', is to be found in the marketplace. Sales and aesthetics go together, as indeed do aesthetics and fashion. It is arguable that, outside a vibrantly market-led economy, industrial design as we know it would barely exist at all. The world's Communist nations have, on the whole, demonstrated the truth of this.

If this volume were covering the entire European tradition, then the argument that design was inextricably linked to economy would be far less widely true. Over the last two centuries, consumerism has grown. There would have been no need for an expansion in industry, had there not been an expansion in the desire of society itself for the objects of industry. More than this, there has been a dramatic increase in the numbers of objects made *specifically to be traded*, as opposed to objects which fulfil a purpose that *makes them tradeable*. Production and consumption are therefore inextricably linked, and design, for better or or worse, is the enabler which acts between the two.

Many design reformers over the last two centuries, including the modern movement, have been embarrassed by the directness of the link between design and consumption. This is largely because much design reform has been inspired by the political left, and because the left has had a powerful say in the construction of the history of design as it has existed for much of the twentieth century. Design has been characterised, often deterministically, as having a myriad of healing powers, which, if unleashed, would cure many social ills. Whether it does or does not, first and foremost, design is locked in a relationship with commerce. This is not to say, of course, that design reform and commerce must always be incompatible. Indeed, improved trade was, for many Victorian reformers, the key aim.

The passages here mostly deal with consumerism. The extremes of enthusiasm and opposition are illustrated, but it has to be said that, especially after Marx, the majority of the most convincing and powerful writings on consumerism have been against it. The broad pattern to the chapter shows that positive attitudes to selling, up to the late modern period, tend to be clear, direct and untheorised. Recent thinkers have tended to accept consumerism as a normative human activity. Negative attitudes to consumerism focus upon three questions: first, who should do the consuming; second, what psychological harm does consumption cause or reflect, and third, what other forms of damage does a consumer-led society cause?

See also
Chapter 2 for moral implications
Chapter 3 for the effects of new technologies

---

1   **Josiah Wedgwood (British): 'The Worrying Threat of the American Market' (1765)**

I am afraid of encroaching too much upon your time & patience with my trifling concerns & shall therefore conclude them here. But permit me Sir just to mention a Circumstance of a more Public nature which greatly alarms us in this neighbourhood. The bulk of our particular manufacture you know is exported to foreign markets, for our home consumption is very trifleing in comparison to what is sent abroad, & the principal of these markets are the Continent & islands of N. America. To the Continent we send an amazing quantity of white stone ware & some of the finer kinds, but for the Islands we cannot make anything too rich & costly. This trade to our Colonies we are apprehensive of loseing in a few years as they have set on foot some Potwork there already, & have at this time an agent amongst us hireing a number of our hands for establishing new Pottworks in South Carolina, haveing got one of our insolvent Master Potters there to conduct them. Haveing material there equal if not superior to our own for carrying on that manufactorie, & as the necessaries of life & consequently the price of labour amongst us are daily upon the advance, I make no question but more will follow them & join their Brother Artists & Manufacturers of every Class who are from all quarters takeing a rapid flight indeed the same way! Whether this evil can be remedyed is out of our sphere to know but we cannot help apprehending such consequences from these emigrations as make us very uneasy for our trade, & our Posterity.

Your well known attention to the arts & Commerce of your Country encourages me to give you this trouble, – pardon my freedom & believe me with the greatest respect

Sir

Your very gratefull & most Obediant humble servant.

---

2   Anonymous (British): 'Ode to Trade' (1851)

The band of commerce was designed,
To associate all the branches of Mankind
And, if a boundless plenty be the robe,
Trade is the golden girdle of the globe.

---

3   Karl Marx (German): 'The Commodity' (1867)

The wealth of societies in which the capitalist mode of production prevails appears as an 'immense collection of commodities'; the individual commodity appears as its elementary form. Our investigation therefore begins with the analysis of the commodity.

The commodity is, first of all, an external object, a thing which through its qualities satisfies human needs of whatever kind. The nature of these needs, whether they arise, for example, from the stomach, or the imagination, makes no difference. Nor does it matter here how the thing satisfies man's need, whether directly as a means of subsistence, i.e. an object of consumption, or indirectly as a means of production . . .

The usefulness of a thing makes it a use-value. But this usefulness does not dangle in mid-air. It is conditioned by the physical properties of the commodity, and has no existence apart from the latter. It is therefore the physical body of the commodity itself, for instance, iron, corn, a diamond, which the use-value or useful thing. This property of a commodity is independent of the amount of labour required to appropriate its useful qualities. When examining use-values, we always assume we are dealing with definite quantities, such as dozens of watches, yards of linen, or tons of iron. The use-values of commodities provide the material for a special branch of knowledge, namely the commercial knowledge of commodities. Use-values

107

E

are only realised in use or in consumption. They constitute the material content of wealth, whatever its social form may be. In the form of the society to be considered here they are also the material bearers of . . . exchange-value.

Exchange-value appears first of all as the quantitative relation, the proportion, in which use-values of one kind exchange for use-values of another kind. This relation changes constantly with time and place. Hence exchange-value appears to be something accidental and purely relative, and consequently an intrinsic value, i.e. an exchange value that is inseparably connected with the commodity, inherent in it, seems a contradiction in terms.

---

4   Christopher Dresser (British): 'The Beautiful has a Commercial Value' (1873)

At the very outset we must recognise the fact that the beautiful has a commercial or money value. We may even say that art can lend to an object a value greater than that of the material of which it consists, even when the object be formed of precious matter, as of rare marbles, scarce woods, or silver or gold.

---

5   Emile Zola (French): 'The Department Store as a Harem' (c.1890)

Mme Guibal: "Isn't it just like a harem? And not expensive.'

---

6   Thorstein Veblen (American): 'Conspicuous Consumption' (1899)

The quasi-peaceable gentleman of leisure, then, not only consumes of the staff of life beyond the minimum required for subsistence and physical efficiency, but his consumption also undergoes a specialisation as regards the quality of the goods consumed. He consumes freely of the best, in food, drink, narcotics, shelter, services, ornaments, apparel, weapons and accoutrements, amusements, amulets, and idols or divinities. In the process of gradual amelioration which takes place in the articles of his consumption, the motive principal and the proximate aim of innovation is no doubt the higher efficiency of the improved and more elaborate products for personal comfort and well-being. But that does not remain the sole purpose of their consumption. The canon of reputability is at hand and seizes upon such innovations as are, according to its standard, fit to survive. Since the consumption of these more excellent goods is an evidence of wealth, it becomes honorific; and conversely, the failure to consume in due quantity and quality becomes a mark of inferiority and demerit.

This growth of punctilious discrimination as to qualitative excellence in eating, drinking etc., presently affects not only the manner of life, but also the training and intellectual activity of the gentleman of leisure. He is no longer simply the successful, aggressive male – the man of strength, resource, and intrepidity. In order to avoid stultification he must also cultivate his taste, for it now becomes incumbent on him to discriminate with some nicety between the noble and the ignoble in consumable goods. He becomes a connoisseur in creditable viands of various degrees of merit, in manly beverages and trinkets, in seemly apparel and architecture, in weapons, games, dances, and the narcotics. This cultivation of the aesthetic faculty requires time and application, and the demands made upon the gentleman in this direction therefore tend to change his life of leisure into a more or less arduous application to the business of learning how to live a life of ostensible leisure in a becoming way. Closely related to the requirement that the gentleman must consume freely and of the right kind of goods, there is the requirement that he must know how to consume them in a seemly manner. His life of leisure must be conducted in due form. Hence arise good manners in the way pointed out in an earlier chapter. High-bred manners and ways of living are items of conformity to the norm of conspicuous leisure and conspicuous consumption.

---

7 P. F. William Ryan (British): 'London's Department Stores' (1902)

'The stores' is a common phrase in the trivial common talk of everyday life. It is generally understood that at one of those comprehensive emporiums practically everything may be ordered. This is true to a certain extent only, for it must be remembered that there are 'stores' which cater for the humblest strata of the middle class. Those are naturally less ambitious in their aims than the establishments which supply the needs of the rich and comparatively rich. Without quitting the premises of one of these latter, with their acres of warerooms, their tireless 'lifts,' their well-drilled assistants, it is almost impossible to ask for anything which will not be promptly yours. Do you want a house built? You have but to give the necessary instructions. Would you like to decide upon your furniture? In a moment you will find yourself inspecting improvised drawing-rooms and dining-rooms, bedrooms and billiard-rooms, studies and kitchens.

Do you want your greenhouse equipped? From where you stand possibly you can see a tangle of shrubs and plants, and nestling amidst them the flowers of the season in full bloom. Do you love animals? Then visit the zoological department, and buy a monkey or a puppy, a kitten or a canary. A lion or a tiger may not be included in the stock on hand, but if your ambition lies in that direction your order will be booked and the stores van will soon deposit the exile from African veldt or Indian jungle at your doorstep. Your wife can purchase your daughter's trousseau in one room, while in another you obtain the impedimenta incidental to a shooting expedition. Pass through the 'lamp and glass' department. It reminds one somehow of a scene in a pantomime, for there are numerous lights though it is noonday, and the flood of colour is rich and dazzling. Next door are washing tubs and washing boards, pails, mangles, and ladders. Pots and pans are not far away. Move on, and you tread on a gorgeous carpet: all around are carpets stacked in huge rolls. One resembling a great green avenue is unfolded that a lady may judge of its effect. Turn in this direction, and you see silks glistening in glorious little multi-coloured billows, where they are strewn over a long counter for the satisfaction of likely purchasers. A few steps further, and the confectionery department is in sight. Here there are many ladies having lunch. Some are indulging in the trifles on which woman alone can live and thrive – and shop! Others are enjoying fare of the more substantial sort. Full recital of the resources of the 'stores' is impossible. When you have bought your medicines, your literature, your pictures, your saddlery, the latest bicycle and electric plant, flowers for the epergnes, bacon, eggs, and vegetables, fish, poultry, boots, and butter, you may, if you have time, step aside and sit for your photograph, having first made a special toilet, beginning with the bath and ending with the hairdresser and manicurist. Even then the 'stores' have not been fully explored!

8 Henry Ford (American): 'The Economic Logic of the Cheaper Motor Car' (c.1908)

The automobile of the past attained success in spite of its price because there were more than enough purchasers to take the limited output of the then new industry. Proportionately few could buy, but those few could keep the manufacturers busy, and price therefore, had no bearing on the sales. The automobile of the present is making good because the price has been reduced just enough to pass sufficient new purchasers to take care of the increased output. Supply and demand, not cost, has regulated the selling price of automobiles . . .

The automobile of the future must be enough better than the present car to beget confidence in the man of limited means and enough lower in price to insure sales for the enormously increased output. The car of the future, 'the car for the people', the car that any man can own, who can afford a horse and carriage, is coming sooner than most people expect . . .

A limited number of factories can supply all the demand for high-priced cars, but the market for a low-priced car is unlimited. The car of the future will be light as well as low in price. This means the substitution of quality for quantity, even to the use of materials not yet discovered.

9 Fernand Léger (French): 'The Shop-front' (1924)

Thus we come to *art in shop-fronts* which for some years has had a great importance. The street has become a permanent spectacle of ever-increasing intensity.

That the shop-front must be a spectacle has become a major source of anxiety to the retailer. A frantic rivalry prevails: *to have the best display in the neighbourhood* is a violent desire actuating our streets. Have you any doubt that such work is not accompanied by extreme care?

10 Eric Mendelsohn (German): 'The Client' (1925)

The client in all cases is a petty grocer, who only respects intelligence when it delivers the goods to him. He is only too glad to declare his respect for art, however, but only in order to get a thousand-pound pig for the price of a piglet. He is accustomed to regarding the vanity of the established artist as the most fruitful field for his own speculations.

We are indeed nothing other than the salesman for our own wares, and if we were . . . not hampered by our irrationality, we would surely take pride in outmanoeuvring them.

But this grain of the irrational always ruins our calculation, which without this unknown factor would make for a good, because simple, piece of business . . .

This hybrid position continually gives rise to the clouds of uneasiness and depression, of doubt and despair, and it is these which rob us of the facility of inspiration and the joy of our naive imagination.

---

11   Norman Bel Geddes (American): 'Three Things a Window Display Needs to Do' (1935)

Too many display windows are cluttered with accessory paraphernalia when they are not overloaded with merchandise. That window is a failure which does not do three things in succession: arrest the glance; focus the attention upon the merchandise; persuade the onlooker to desire it. The store window is a stage on which the merchandise is presented as the actors. The rules that apply to designing for the stage are in many ways true here. Keep the emphasis on the actor, for it is he who tells the story.

---

12   Pierre Chareau (French): 'Money' (1935)

Between architecture and men lies money: that all-powerful monster that needs to grow, grows to live, and grows by subjugating people to it.

An architect can only be approached with it acting as an intermediary. And he can only work for the benefit of man if there is money at his disposal.

But those who have money are not the kind of people the architect can represent. They are not the masses. They belong to a group whose function is to conserve money. They had needs once. All they need now is prudence.

They commissioned works of art.

Now they are afraid of them and can no longer inspire them.

They can feel the money moving out of their grasp. They want to keep it. They had their Art once. They believe the time has come to profit from it by exploiting it commercially. But their Art was made by individuals and thus is not 'commercializable'.

---

13 Eric Gill (British): 'Art and Business' (1940)

The result of Industrialism (factories and machines) has been to multiply the necessaries of life exceedingly and to reduce the number of things which we regard as beautiful. It has also greatly increased the number of salesmen, who do not make things but only sell them (with little knowledge). So we have the designer who designs what he never makes and the worker who minds the machine which makes what he never designs. And we have the salesman who neither designs things nor minds machines but is supposed to know what the public wants. But the public doesn't know what it wants, and it has no means of finding out. So people are dependent upon the salesman and the salesman is only concerned with what will sell. Saleability is his only criterion – if a thing sells it is good and if it won't sell it is bad – or at any rate, not worth making.

This is a bad state of affairs, as most people will admit. For though we have many more things than we used to have, few of them are really well made and none of them is worth keeping. They have none of the venerable or holy quality which things used to have – the quality which makes us treasure them and put them in museums. And so, though the first object of making things is to serve one another, we do not serve one another well. And we are forced to comfort ourselves with quantity because we cannot get quality.

Now there are all sorts of causes for this bad state of affairs, but we are not concerned with causes here. The point here is that one of the main reasons why things are bad is that the men who make them are not responsible. If you go to a shop to buy something it is generally impossible to find the person who made it. There isn't anyone. Nobody can be praised and nobody can be blamed. The whole system is quite impersonal. The workers only mind the machines. The machinemakers only take instructions from the designers. The designers take instructions from the salesmen. The salesmen are simply the servants of the investors. And the investors are only interested in dividends. You see it is a hopeless mess. So what?

Well, without going into the politics of the matter, or, deeper still, the religious causes of the trouble, there are some things which might be done. Everybody suspects advertisements, and everybody knows that the salesman as such is not a judge of what is good in itself. But everybody, just because he is human, prefers good quality to bad. How can we find good things? What guarantee can we obtain that things are well made and at a just price?

The first thing to do is, whenever possible, to buy things from the actual makers or from the shop where they are actually made. That is to say: The first thing is to re-establish the personal relationship between maker and buyer. The buyer knows the use of things and therefore he has the best reasons for knowing his needs. The maker knows how to make things – what else is he for? – and therefore he has the best reasons for claiming to be able to satisfy the needs of the buyer.

The shop is the place where the maker displays his goods, and it is the place where the buyer can most conveniently inspect them – it is the meeting place of maker and buyer. That is its proper function. The shopkeeper provides this meeting place. That is *his* function – he is the servant of both buyer and maker. If we could again establish shops where the goods for sale were made by the same firm and as far as possible on the same premises, and if the manufacturing side of the business were again given its proper primacy and responsibility – the selling side being honourably humble and subordinate – then we should be well on the way to the revival of the craftsmanship and beauty of design for which British manufacturers were formerly famous.

---

14   Vance Packard (American): 'Engineering' (1962)

The use of mass psychoanalysis to guide campaigns of persuasion has become the basis of a multi-million dollar industry. Professional persuaders have seized upon it in their groping for more effective ways to sell us their wares – whether products, ideas, attitudes, candidates, goals or states of mind. This depth approach to influencing our behaviour is being used in many fields and is employing a variety of ingenious techniques. It is being used most extensively to affect our daily acts of consumption. The sale to us of billions of dollars worth of US products is being significantly affected, if not revolutionised, by this approach, which is still only barely out of its infancy. Two-thirds of America's hundred largest advertisers have geared campaigns to this depth approach by using strategies inspired by what marketeers call 'motivation analysis'.

Meanwhile, many of the nation's leading public relations experts have been indoctrinating themselves in the lore of psychiatry and the social sciences in order to increase their skill at 'engineering' our consent to their propositions.

---

15   Raymonde Moulin (French): 'Living without Selling' (1968)

Twenty years before the May Revolution, the following state- ment was written by a liberal economist: 'The entire capitalist society functions regularly thanks to some social sectors that are not animated by the spirit of profit and the search for the greatest gain. When the high official, the magistrate, the artist, and intellectual become dominated by this spirit, society crum- bles and the entire economic order is threatened'. The existence of the work of art as merchandise, the dominant role assumed by the market in the organisation of artistic life, the subjection of artists to restrictions that are inherent in the logic of the economy, all this was inevitably contested in a far more radical way by the revolutionaries of May 1968. Could those who despise capitialist society, the consumer society, forgo such an appropriate occasion to emphasise the encroachment of fin- ancial monopolies on creative activity and to denounce the hypocrisy of an ideology that sacrifices art, glorifies artists, and portrays the relationship between the art lover and the work of art as a pure, disinterested love, while concealing the fact that works of art are the subject of commercial deals? The dignity that our society recognises in art constitutes one side of a system, of which the reverse is commercialisation in art.

---

16   W. F. Haug (German): 'Aesthetic Innovation' (1971)

In a society like the United States of America, a large part of the total demand depends on the need to replace a part of the stock of consumer durable goods as it wears out or is discarded. Since the way towards a total labour-saving society would amount to the abolition of capitalism, capital is now taking umbrage at the excessive durability of its products. One technique which answers this problem of particularly longer-lasting consumer durables like cars, electrical appliances, light bulbs and textiles, is to reduce the quality of the products. This technique has radically altered the standards of use-value in many areas of private consumption in favour of a shorter lifetime and lower resistance to wear.

The technique of reducing a commodity's useful life has been discussed under the concept of 'artificial obsolescence', which has been translated by the expression 'product senility'. The commodities enter the world with a kind of timing device which will trigger off their inner self-destruction within a calculated period. Another technique is that of reducing the quantity being sold in an unaltered guise. A compromise between qualitative obsolescence and quantitative reduction of a product is shown in the way cloth is becoming thinner, etc. Commodities particularly suitable for quantitative reduction are foodstuffs and similar articles for private consumption which are sold in filled, brand-named packets . . .

. . . As a rule, the reduction of use-value both in quality and quantity is compensated for by ornamentation. But even so, articles for use still last too long for capital's need for valorisation. The more radical technique seizes not only upon a product's objective use-value, in order to shorten its useful life in the sphere of consumption and generate further demand prematurely: this technique starts with the aesthetics of the commodity. By periodically redesigning a commodity's appearance, it reduces the use-lifetime of the specific commodity, whose models are already functioning in the sphere of consumption.

This technique, which we shall call aesthetic innovation, operates as follows: its full development and systematic application through the length and breadth of the commodity world, especially the sector for private consumption, requires the subordination of use-value to brand-name, thus in a sense ensuring the victory of the monopoly commodity, since every brand-name intends to set up an aesthetic monopoly.

Nonetheless, aesthetic innovation, like other such techniques, is not historically speaking an invention of monopoly capitalism, but it emerges regularly wherever the economic function, which is at its root, arises.

In the eighteenth century . . . aesthetic innovation was already a quite consciously employed technique. A decree passed in 1755 for the cotton industry of Saxony reads that for the good of the 'factory' – which here still meant craftshops, as production was still organised according to distributing firms (commodities were produced by individual proprietors for the capitalist wholesaler) – it was necessary that apart from the finer garments, the commodities themselves should be made to a new taste and design.

Note that the point is not the benefit of the buyers, as would be the case from the stand-point of use-value; rather, it is for the benefit of the entrepreneur, i.e. from the stand-point of exchange-value which is concerned with regenerating demand. Even though aesthetic innovation was not invented by mono- poly capitalism, it is only within this system that it achieves a crucial meaning, dominating production in all decisive branches of the consumer goods industry and playing a vital role in the capitalist organization of this industry. Never before was it manifested in such an aggressive manner. Like political slogans, posters in department-store windows announce the desires of capital, which command the customers, 'Out with the old in with the new!', for example, was a slogan recently used by a furniture chain.

---

17 Raymond Loewy (American): 'Industrial Design and the Marketplace' (1979)

About thirty years ago I once said that 'Industrial design keeps the customer happy, his client in the black, and the designer busy.' I still feel that this is a good maxim to keep in under- standing what we are about. It may seem facile, but one can infer from it, I believe, a concern for the society, for those who have the responsibility to initiate and produce, and for the pro- fession of industrial design to be understood and involved ...

Industrial design exists within the marketplace and helps define it. But I have always liked a phrase someone else once used in a slightly different context, 'the shaping of everyday life'. The idea of designing industrially without having the marketplace in mind would be both unethical and/or ineffective.

---

18 Deyan Sudjic (British): 'Cult Objects' (1985)

It's more difficult to analyse how a cult object is created than it is to identify one in action. Certain of them have the power to become the source of thinly coded messages, broadcasting to visitors what type of household they are in, or else they can pander to the obsessions of the household's members. Com- pare, for example, two different examples of such an apparently prosaic domestic object as the oven. Find an Aga in a British household, no matter how humble, and it will instantly place its owner as an aspirant to a very particular kind of wholesome rustic domesticity. It is the exact equivalent of parking a Volvo estate car outside the house, owning a Labrador, and baking your own bread. With its combination of heating and cooking functions, it is the earth goddess of suburbia; the last vestige of the hearth at the centre of the home. Its heavy, and antique enamelled outlines, and even heavier chambered doors, which swing shut with the ponderous majesty of a bank vault, contrive somehow to suggest the servant's hall of an Edwardian mansion. The problem for those who equip their homes with an Aga is that in reality it is none of these things, being originally a Swedish product, and named after the initials of the Svenska Akyiebolaget Gasacumulator, not the kind of mouthful that would go down too well in Finchley.

The diametric opposite of the Aga is the Neff, not exactly an object since it has to be built into a wall, but nevertheless, for a particular kind of home just as significant a purchase as the Aga. Once it had the same touch of exotic stylishness, coupled with modernity, as the Citroen DS, but now it's slipped back a little to become part of the prawn cocktail good life.

Cult objects aren't tied to any one of these extremes, but they all have special qualities over and above what one could be entitled to expect from the simple considerations of performing a function.

---

19   Penny Sparke (British): 'Like Janus' (1986)

My main thesis is that, within the framework of industrial capitalism which created it and which continues to dominate it in contemporary Western society, design is characterised by a dual alliance with both mass production and mass consumption and that these two phenomena have determined nearly all its manifestations. Like Janus, design looks in two directions at the same time: as a silent quality of all mass-produced goods it plays a generally unacknowledged but vital role in all our lives; as a named concept within the mass media it is, however, much more visible and generally recognised. In this latter guise design becomes an extension of marketing and advertising. The 'designer jeans' phenomenon, which persuades us to buy a product because it has been designed, is, culturally speaking, totally distinct from the activity of the anonymous designers within industry who resolve the problems of cost, appearance and use in consumer products.

---

20   Barbara Kruger (American): 'I Shop Therefore I Am' (1987)

I shop therefore I am.

---

21   James Woudhuysen (British): 'Teleshopping' (1988)

In Clearwater, Florida, the live TV show compere glances at a computer monitor off-stage. His eulogy for the sparkling rings and bracelets he has in close-up is, the monitor reveals, bringing sales of $700 a minute. In front of him 1,200 telephone opera-tors in soundproof cubicles take the calls from up to three million homes. Multiply that $700-a-minute figure by all the minutes in a day, and America's Home Shopping Network will rack up sales of hundreds of millions of dollars a year – on this, one of the three TV channels it runs coast-to-coast.

In White Plains, upstate New York, the top executives at Prodigy, a 700-strong subsidiary of IBM and Sears Roebuck, are optimistic. They launched a floppy disk and telephone gadget ('modem') which allows users of IBM or IBM-compatible ma-chines not just to shop for airline tickets and Polaroid cameras, but also to follow their favourite news, their local weather and – inevitably – the fortunes of their shares. The Prodigy package sells at $150 for half a year's usage; thereafter, the whole service costs but $9.95 a month to rent. Glistening ads, which fill much of the bottom part of every page you view, underwrite the prices.

These two examples cover the full gamut of buying from the privacy of your own home. Home Shopping Network is based on broadcast, and satellite television channels, price-slashing discounts and purchases made on impulse. You never know what will be up for sale next, and you can only get it while it's on the screen. HSN also provide viewers more with showbiz than genuine interactivity: you can phone in, live, to tell a nationwide audience how you just love that tiara, but, apart from using your touchpad telephone to confirm that you'll pay for it to arrive on your doorstep within four days (press 1 to go ahead, 2 for not to), the sense of being connected ends there.

By contrast with HSN, Prodigy caters for considered usage, and wires your PC up to impressive effect too. You can tab across a relatively primitive diagram of that Polaroid camera to have its various features highlighted and explained before you ask for a brochure – or the item itself – to be delivered. You can peruse every ad in more depth, though each decision to do so will be logged on a distant mainframe computer. Most important, you can key in questions about your waistline to Jane Fonda, or at least to her staff. They'll get back to you within seventy-two hours.

Every teleshopping system is different. Take France. There, one of the early acts of President Mitterand's regime was to distribute to the populace terminals and keyboards designed as a free, electronic substitute for telephone directories. More than three million Minitels now figure in homes and businesses as far-flung as France's overseas territories in the Indian Ocean.

---

22 Angela Partington (British): 'The Female Consumer of the 1950s' (1989)

The female consumer of the 1950s . . . was not the 'happy housewife heroine' of feminist mythology, passive and blissfully acquiring mass-produced goods and oblivious to her material conditions of existence. Even if the designed objects did represent patriarchal ideologies for designers and manufacturers, they were invested with other meanings and values by female consumers. Consumption was a form of consent to the position which was being allocated to women, but far from being a suspension of knowledge it was the basis of women's knowledge of their own economic and social position in postwar circumstances.

Although I am putting forward women's misappropriation of commodities as evidence of resistance, I am not suggesting that this was a form of spectacular or subcultural deviancy, understood as a withdrawal or refusal of consent. There was nothing self-consciously rebellious or romantically transgressional in this misappropriation. However, because it required consent it has remained largely unrecognised as resistance by feminists. Because women consumed readily and took pleasure in their consumption, they have been condemned as the owners of unraised consciousnesses; but it is precisely through consuming that feminine knowledge was articulated. Women paid 'lip-service' to legitimate notions of 'good taste' (responsible consumption) while their pleasures in consumption were inevitably 'improper' and irresponsible, because as a dominated group women could not isolate the practical functions of objects from the social contingencies and circumstances of everyday life.

23 Hester Matthewman (British): 'A Brief History of the Shopping Trolley' (1992)

'A trolley is a highly complex piece of equipment with huge dichotomies pulling it in different directions,' according to Donald Macdonald, Group Sales and Marketing Director for Clares Equipment Group, a leading wire-goods manufacturer. The company has made supermarket trolleys for more than 20 years. Being a trolley expert has certain disadvantages: 'At dinner parties, people are always onto you like a dose of salts with all sorts of complaints. There are so many different priorities which all have to be considered that people don't think of – safety, stability, capacity, maintenance, ergonomics, fitting through the checkout.'

Trolley design is a serious business. Another trolley manufacturer refused to say anything at all about his company's latest technical refinements, on the grounds that trolleys were often the subject of undue hilarity. 'It's not a topic that can be dealt with briefly, and it's not a humorous subject. I'm not prepared to talk to you,' he snapped.

The trolley was invented in 1937 by Oklahoma supermarket owner Sylvan Goldman. Known as the 'shopping cart' in the United States, it evolved from the wire hand-basket, when Goldman noticed that his customers stopped buying as their full baskets became too heavy to carry. As self-service shopping caught on, his trolleys became so popular that he had a seven-year waiting list for delivery by the end of the decade.

Fifty years later, Gene von Stein, vice-president of the US shopping-cart giant Unarco Commercial Products, hailed the trolley as 'a complex sociological phenomenon that has totally changed the commerce and culture of America and the world.' American trolleys can now be fitted with calculators and electronic store guides.

British shoppers made do with a primitive wooden frame on wheels that could support two baskets, until the shopping trolley arrived in the UK in 1950 at Sainsbury in Croydon. Since then, trolleys have changed very little.

American manufacturers have partially solved the perennial trolley-with-a-mind-of-its own problem, by fixing the two back wheels to keep their carts on the straight and narrow. However, this means that American shoppers have to keep strictly on track as they move round the shelves. According to Donald Macdonald, such a disciplined approach would not suit the impulsive British shopper. 'Have you ever pushed a trolley with fixed wheels at the front or rear? You can go in a straight line but you can't move sideways or get out of other people's way. If you want to fill your trolley with the pet-food that's across the way you can't do it. There are a lot of problems involved with going in a straight line.'

An average-sized supermarket has a fleet of around 250 trolleys, each costing 'up to £72' to replace, and 15 to 25 percent of supermarket rolling stock disappears every year.

One exasperated supermarket did eventually get a prosecution for stealing a trolley as far as crown court, only to have the case dismissed on a technicality. Because the woman concerned had put a pound in a coin slot to detach the trolley, she was deemed to have entered into a contract with the supermarket, despite the fact that when the judge asked her 'When did you gain possession of the trolley?' she replied: 'When I nicked it'.

As a report revealed last week, 7,500 unwary victims were hospitalised last year after tangling with shopping trolleys. Injuries ranging from fractures, concussion and bumped heads to severe bruising of shins and ankles. And this could be only the tip of the iceberg, warns a spokesman from the Royal Society for the Prevention of Accidents (RoSPA). 'Loads of people who get slight bruising, but still enough to hurt them, just don't bother to go to hospital.'

RoSPA admits that safety problems often come down to the user rather than the design of the trolley. 'Many trolley accidents are caused by people quite blatantly messing about. For instance, they use them as scooters.'

The new Health and Safety Executive guidelines on shopping trolleys recommend leaflets with the slogan 'Look out, there's a trolley about!' to highlight in-store dangers, and a spokesman offered the following advice to intrepid supermarket-goers: 'Be very aware of your surroundings. Don't go into the supermarket in a daze. You need to have your wits about you!'

RoSPA also hopes public-spirited shoppers will help to root out rogue trollies. 'If you start moving your trolley around and it's *not* going the way it should, i.e. *forward*, we would urge members of the public to make the situation known to the store management straightaway. They should be only too pleased to find you a replacement.'

6

THE HOME

The home is a key site for design. To a considerable extent over the past two centuries, people have inhabited domestic spaces designed for them by people they never met, and routinely used technologies they cannot understand. They have accommodated themselves to spaces and objects which were the embodiment of someone else's idea of the home, adjusting and appropriating the parts they couldn't assimilate pure into their own iconic range.

The home, of course, is not like a nest; it doesn't (and didn't) occur naturally, and people didn't come to it with a definitive idea of what it was. They had to be taught how a home should look, and, normally, their families gave them their first and most important lessons on it. These they might later drift away from, or overtly reject. It would be a mistake, however, to assume that when they rejected familial advice, people made completely individual choices when they created their home environment. The home has been subject to convention for centuries, and the usual design choices would certainly have been motivated in most cases by issues of class, rather than subjective value.

There are three types of quotation provided here. First, there are extracts from advice offered to householders from the 1850s through to the 1950s. Such advice became an entire industry in itself through the period. Second, there are a number of seminal sayings on the function of the house and home from leading thinkers. Finally, there are passages on different areas of the home, including home equipment. These are not exhaustive, but rather serve as exemplars, and where they are not typical, it is hoped at least that the reader will find them amusing. The chapter finishes in the early 1950s mainly because this seemed a point up to which one could characterise the literature reasonably well. The massive availability of primary material still in circulation after this point made the task of quotation seem somewhat pointless.

See also
Chapter 3 for technology as it relates to the home.

Chapter 5 for consumerism and the home
Chapter 8 for modernist ideas on housing and furnishings

---

1   Louis Simond (French-American): 'The Reason the English Keep a Commode Close By' (1815)

Drinking much and long leads to unavoidable consequences. Will it be credited, that, in a corner of the very dining room, there is a certain convenient piece of furniture, to be used by anybody who wants it. The operation is performed very deliberately and undisguisedly, as a matter of course, and occasions no interruption of the conversation. I once took the liberty to ask why this convenient article was not placed out of the room, in some adjoining closet; and was answered that, in former times, when good fellowship was more strictly enforced than in these degenerate days, it had been found that men of weak heads or stomachs took advantage of the opportunity to make their escape shamefully, before they were quite drunk; and it was to guard against such an enormity that this nice expedient had been invented.

---

2   'A Lady' (British): 'Observations for Use of the Mistress of the Family' (1851)

If our ancestors made domestic occupations too exclusively the aim of female education, it may be truly said that the present generation has fallen as unwisely into the contrary extreme. Young ladies of our time pride themselves upon knowing nothing whatever concerning those duties which most assuredly ought to be deemed essential in the mistress of the family, and taught as a branch of education. Generally speaking, there is a distaste among the educated classes of the female community of England to the details of house-keeping, and particularly to those connected with the kitchen, the consequence of which is, that dinners are seldom well arranged, or the most made of materials provided. It is indeed a very common, and very erroneous supposition, that attention to culinary affairs is unladylike, and beneath the dignity of a gentlewoman, yet there can be no question that elegance, comfort, social enjoyment, and, it may be added, health, materially depend upon attention to the table; and the prudent management of her family ought to be considered an important object amongst the duties of every lady when she marries.

There are comparatively few persons among the middle classes of society who can afford to keep professed cooks, their wages being too high and their methods too extravagant. In such cases a plain cook is alone attainable, who knows little beyond the commonest operations of the kitchen. The mistress ought therefore to make herself so far acquainted with cookery as to be competent to give proper directions for dressing a dinner, and having it properly dressed up.

Perhaps there are few occasions when the respectability of a man is more immediately felt, than the style of dinner to which he may accidentally bring home a visitor. Everyone ought to live according to his circumstances, and the meal of the trades-man ought not to emulate the entertainments of the higher classes; but if merely two or three dishes be well served, with proper accompaniments, the table linen clean, the small side-board neatly laid, and all that is necessary be at hand, the expectation of both the husband and the friend will be grati-fied, because no interruption of the domestic arrangements will disturb their social intercourse.

Hence, the *direction of a table* is no inconsiderable branch of a lady's concern, as it involves judgment in expenditure, respect-ability of appearance, and the comfort of her husband as well as of those who partake of their hospitality. Inattention is inexcus-able and should always be avoided for the lady's own sake, as it occasions a disagreeable degree of bustle and evident annoy-ance to herself, which is never observable in a well regulated establishment. In doing the honours of her table, the mode of carving is also important . . .

The mode of *covering the table* differs in taste. It is not the multiplicity of things, but the choice, the dressing, and the neat pleasing look of the whole, which give respectability to her who presides. The table should be furnished with more than the *necessary* quantity of plate, or plated ware, and glass, to afford a certain appearance of elegance; and if accompanied by a clean cloth and a neatly-dressed attendant, it will show that the habits of the family are those of gentility. For a small party, or a tête-à-tête, a dumb waiter is a convenient contrivance, as it partly saves the attendance of servants . . .

In most of the books which treat cookery, various bills of fare are given, which are never exactly followed. The mistress should give a moderate number of these dishes which are most in season. The cuts which are inserted in some of those lists put the soup in the middle of the table, where it should never be placed. For a small party a single lamp in the centre is sufficient;

but for a large number the room should be lighted with lamps hung over the table, and the centre occupied by a plateau of glass or plate, ornamented with flowers or figures.

The mistress of the family should never forget that the welfare and good management of the house depend upon the eye of the superior; and consequently, that nothing is too trifling for her notice, whereby waste may be avoided or order maintained. If she never had been accustomed, while single, to think of family management, let her not upon that account fear that she cannot attain it: she may consult others who are more experienced, and acquaint herself with necessary quantities, qualities and prices of several articles of family expenditure, in proportion to the number it consists of. The chief duties of life are within the reach of humble abilities, and she whose aim is to fulfil them will rarely ever fail to acquit herself well. United with, and perhaps crowning all, the virtues of the female character, is that of the well directed ductility of mind which occasionally bends its attention to the smaller objects of life, knowing them to be often scarcely less essential than the greater.

A minute account of the annual income and the times of payment should be taken in writing; likewise an estimate of the supposed amount of each article of expense; and those who are early accustomed to calculations on domestic articles will acquire so accurate a knowledge of what their establishment requires, as will enable them to keep the happy medium between prodigality and parsimony.

In proportioning the items of expenditure of a family, something should always be assigned for the use of the poor, which enables any pressing case of distress to be at once attended to, without a question 'whether it can be spared'. Much might be done for the poor if care were taken to keep a pan in which every bone and morsel of spare meat, vegetables, etc., were put: these might be stewed, the bones taken out, and a few peas added, making a meal, two or three times a week, for any deserving family, without increasing the family expenditure beyond a few pence.

Perhaps few branches of female education are more useful than great readiness in figures. Accounts should be regularly kept, and not the smallest article omitted to be entered . . .

It is very necessary for the mistress of the family to be informed of the prices and goodness of all the articles in common use, and of the best times, as well as places, for purchasing them . . . Though it is very disagreeable to question anyone's honesty, it is yet prudent to weigh meat, sugar, etc., when brought in . . .

. . . Respecting servants, there are a few things which cannot be too strongly urged: one is, never retain a cook who is not fond of her occupation . . . She also must possess a natural regard for cleanliness, or all the pains in the world will never render her cleanly: where dirty habits are manifested, dismissal should follow . . . As to wages, it is better to err on the liberal than the niggardly side . . .

An inventory of furniture, linen, and china should be kept, and the things examined by it thrice a year, or oftener if there be a change of servants: the articles used by servants should be entrusted to their care, with a list, as is done with plate. In articles not in common use, such as spare bedding, tickets of parchment, numbered and specifying to what they belong, should be sewed on each; and minor articles of daily use, such as household cloths and kitchen requisites, should be occasionally looked to . . .

In the purchase of glass and crockery ware, either the most customary patterns should be chosen, in order to secure their being easily matched when broken; or, if a scarce design be adopted, an extra quantity should be bought, to guard against the annoyance of the set being spoiled by breakage, which in the course of time must be expected to happen. There should likewise be plenty of common dishes, that the table set may not be used to putting away cold meat, etc. . . .

---

3   Shirley Hibberd (British): 'The Age of Toys' (1856)

An eminent author has called this the Age of Veneer, and another dignifies it with the title of the Age of Fustian. I shall take the privilege afforded me in this preface to call it the Age of Toys. We have nearly exhausted the means of morbid excitement, and are growing simpler, because purer in our tastes. Our rooms sparkle with the products of art, and our gardens with the curiosities of nature. Our conversation shapes itself to ennobling themes, and our pleasures take a tone from our improving moral sentiments, and acquire a poetic grace that reflects again upon both head and heart. The mark of our progress is seen in our love for toys, plant-cases, bird and bee-houses, fish-tanks, and garden ornaments,   they are the beads of our Rosary of homage to the Spirit of Beauty.

Happily in this country the Home of Taste is not merely ideal creation; our domestic life is a guarantee of our national greatness, and as long as we shall continue to surround that life with emblems and suggestions of higher things, so long will the highest teachings of knowledge, elegance, and virtue be attainable at the fireside. Our pleasures and pursuits have as powerful an influence on our national character as the precepts of sages at our seats of learning; and the simple toys that afford recreation for our hours of leisure may prove worthy advocates of morality and religion. In the contemplation of the wonders of nature, and the cultivation of domestic elegances, the intellect and moral nature must advance towards perfection, just as Ingomar and all his bandit savages are humanized by the presence among them of the chaste Parthenia.

---

4 C.L. Eastlake (British): 'The Fireplace' (1872)

Let us take a familiar example of household furniture by way of illustration. A coal-box, or scuttle, is intended to contain a very useful, but dirty, species of fuel. It is evident, looking to the weight of the substance which it is destined to hold, that iron or brass must be the best and most suitable material of which a coal-box could be made. It is also obvious that if it be invested with any ornamental character beyond that which may be afforded by its general form, such ornament should be of the simplest description, executed in colour of the soberest hues. But what is the coal-box of our day? Brass has been almost entirely discarded in its manufacture, and though iron is retained, it is lacquered over with delicate tints, and patterns of flowers, &c., utterly unsuitable in such a place. Nor is this all. Of late years *photographs* have been introduced as an appropriate decoration for the lid and sides. Could absurdity of design be carried farther? We might, with as much artistic propriety, make *papier-mâché* flower pots, and hang our chimney-pieces with Valenciennes.

Almost all the 'fashionable' shapes for fenders, grates, and fire-irons, are selected on a principle which utterly ignores the material of which they are made. The old type of fender in use about fifty years ago consisted of thin iron plates, perforated and framed between bars of brass or steel. It was not very graceful in design, certainly, but it was infinitely better art than the curvilinear and elaborate monstrosities which are produced in Birmingham and Sheffield at the present time. Moreover, it answered the purpose of protecting women's dress from contact with the fire much more effectually than they do.

In this and a hundred other cases the taste of the public and of the manufacturers has become vitiated from a false notion of what constitutes beauty of form. Every article of upholstery which has a curved outline, no matter of what kind the curve may be, or where it may be applied, is considered 'elegant'. Complexity of detail, whether in a good or bad style of ornament, is approved as 'rich' and with these two conditions of so-styled elegance and richness, the uneducated eye is satisfied. With regard to the special instance in question, it happens that as coal was not commonly burnt in English dwelling-houses before the close of the seventeenth century, the form of fender now in use was not invented until after the decline of decorative art. It has therefore never assumed a satisfactory form for ordinary sale. Some good examples, indeed, are occasionally to be met with at the mediaeval metal-workers'; but their present cost is, on an average, about three times that of other fenders. While such extravagant prices are kept up for articles which, if supplied in the ordinary way of trade, would be as cheap as anything else, it is impossible to expect a thorough reform in household taste.

---

5   N. M. Lowe (American): 'The Case for Double Glazing' (1876)

This brings up a very important subject, which we very much regret we cannot here make more than a passing allusion to, and that is the necessity in our Northern country of adopting a system of double windows for our dwelling-houses. We should be astonished if our inquiries in that direction led us to the discovery that 75% of the heat of our rooms, which is lost by our single windows in the winter-season, could be saved if these windows were provided with double sashes. During the cold weather, there will always be found, no matter how tightly or closely the sashes are fitted and protected with weather strips, a draught of cold air falling downward. This arises from the contact of the heated air with the cold glass, which renders the air colder and heavier, and causes it to fall. The air, at the same time, parts with a considerable proportion of its moisture by condensation upon the glass. The cold air thus formed falls to the floor, forming a layer of cold air, which surrounds the feet and legs, while the upper part of the body is enveloped in over-heated air. The layers of cold and warm air in an apartment *will not mix*. The warm air will not descend, and the cold air cannot go upward, except the one is deprived of its heat by radiation, and the other receives its heat by actual contact with a heated surface. This radical difference in the upper and the lower strata of atmosphere of the rooms, in which our people live during the cold season, is the prolific cause of most of the throat and lung diseases with which they are afflicted. Double windows to our houses, therefore, would not only be a great economy, as to fuel, but highly conducive to human longevity.

---

6   Joris-Karl Huysmans (French): 'How to Design a Bedroom' (1884)

There were in his opinion only two ways of arranging a bed-room; you could either make it a place for sensual pleasure . . . or else you could fix it out as a place of solitude. In the first case the Louis Quinze style was the choice for people of delicate sensibility . . . The eighteenth century, in fact, is the only age which has known how to envelop a woman in a wholly de-praved atmosphere, shaping the furniture on the model of her charms, imitating her passionate contortions and spasmodic convulsions in wood and copper . . . in his Paris house he had had a bedroom decorated in just this style . . . furnished with a great white bed which provides that added titillation.

---

7   May Morris (British): 'How to Make the Home Pretty' (1893)

Now with regard to a few practical hints on furnishing for a modest household: we cannot go through every detail of deco-rating and fitting, but I propose to glance at one room at least, and see what can be made of it. It is not necessary to say much here about the English sitting-room we read of in novels, 're-plete with every comfort and convenience.' The comfort and convenience is often found to consist of many superfluous yards of carpet and curtain, low easy-chairs into which the unwary fall as into a trap of feather-bed and cushions, a full *half more furniture than is needed,* a dismal twilight, and a certain dusty stuffiness and want of ventilation which is caused by the fear of *draughts,* those bugbears of the English housewife. So much for a certain ideal of home-comfort which has been greatly criticised of late years, and which one is glad to see gradually giving way to a healthier ideal, by which light and air are allowed more play, and superfluous furniture is banished.

I will presume that the room at which we are looking is in a house in London or suburban London, or in some other large and smoky town, closely surrounded by other dwellings, all more or less in need of more light and air than they get. I will also presume that there is a certain want of space in your apartments or house, and that sitting-room and dining-room are one. I know that to many people this seems nothing short of horror, and every effort and squeezing of bedroom space would be attempted to secure the necessary parlour or drawing-room; still many of us endure the privation with equanimity. To begin with, let us bear in mind that light and air being the great want among town-dwellers, to make the most of them every other consideration should be more or less subordinated. They have to be borne in mind in choosing wall-papers, selecting paint, arranging curtains, carpets, chairs and what not . . .

. . . The wall-covering, then, has first to be thought of; and, as our room is a very simple one, we have only a choice between an inexpensive machine-made wall-paper and a plain colouring or distemper. Of the two, I incline towards the former; for, unless it is proposed to cover up wall-space afterwards with a profusion of pictures or drawings, or otherwise break the space, one's eye tires of the broad flat display of colour, unbroken by folds, variety of texture, or any other play of light and shade. Still, the simpler the arrangement of wall-decoration, with the very humble materials at our command, the better. The plan of dividing a wall into three parts, with dado below the principal space, and frieze above it, is very handsome when treated with rich materials; panelled dado, hangings above, and plaster or painted frieze above that; but when mimicked in imitation wood-work, and by merely placing one paper above another of a different design, the result is pretentious and fussy without being effective. If for any reason distemper is chosen for your wall, the colour must be chosen with great care, otherwise you may find yourself burthened with some repulsive shade, which the local decorator in his anxiety to please will call for your benefit an 'art-colour'. As no brilliancy of tone can be obtained by this method, dark colours should be cautiously chosen, or even avoided; and really the safest and most inoffensive shade is a light silvery yet not *cold* green, if you can but hit it off. I have no great affection for upholstered 'nooks' and grimcracks that savour of the boudoir; but a simple way of breaking a bare wall is to fit up one corner of the room with a long low divan consisting of a plain wooden frame strung across with webbing (it can be speedily made by any one with a taste for carpentering), on which is laid a firm mattress covered with stuff or Indian matting, or, better still, a stout washing chintz.

The wall above and round the corner is hung with chintz or what not, to harmonize with the colour of the wall. The divan should be quite broad and low, otherwise it loses its character, and there should be plenty of bolsters and cushions.

---

8   Mary Jewry (British): 'The Mistress of a Family' (c.1894)

The Mistress of a family commands daily a small realm of which she is queen. Let her rule with justice, meekness and quietness. The most self-governed person will always be best . . . Good temper, patience, and a knowledge of domestic matters come first, . . . in the list of requirements for a model housewife.

After these, we will name *early rising*, which is very important.

A lady will find it best to give her servants orders for the day *before breakfast*, if convenient, and, to do this well, she must visit the larder herself early that she may judge what is required . . .

---

9   Mary Jewry (British): 'Food Consumption and Kitchen Equipment' (c.1894)

It is . . . essential that a housekeeper should know the average weekly consumption for food of each person in an ordinary family . . . For this purpose we subjoin a list of the usual allowances, which will of course vary very much from differing circumstances; but it will give a general idea on the subject:

Food for one person weekly
   Tea – two ounces
   Coffee – one quarter of a pound, for breakfasts
   Cocoa paste – one quarter of pound, for breakfasts
   Sugar – one half pound
   Cheese – one half pound
   Butter – one half pound
   Milk – one quart, varying with the taste of the family
   Bread – eight pounds for a woman, sixteen pounds for a man
      or boy
   Meat – six pounds
   Beer – one gallon for a woman, seven quarts to a man
   Potatoes – three and a half pounds

Of course this estimate of quantities must be modified greatly by the habits and tastes of the family, and by the fact of residence either in the town or the country. A large supply of vegetables, fish or puddings will greatly reduce the scale of meat; and making tea and coffee for numbers will reduce the amount of these articles. We merely give this general *idea* of quantity to guide, in a measure, the inexperienced housewife. We should have been thankful for such knowledge ourselves, as without it one invariably buys more than is actually needed for the consumption of the household.

Modern science has greatly aided the cook in the implements of her art, and in order to be able to recommend the newest and best cooking utensils, we have solicited and received the aid of some of the first manufacturing and furnishing ironmongers in London.

The more expensive list will seldom be required by persons of moderate income, but they may select from it with some profit some one or two articles . . .

Some of the recent inventions, such as Carson's Patent Salting Apparatus, Kent's Patent Soup Strainer and the Patent Mincing Machine, will be found to afford an immense saving of labour and of time; whilst the worst cook amongst 'general servants' can scarcely achieve the feat of spoiling the joint, if it be cooked in Captain Warren's Everybody's Pot.

Kitchen utensils absolutely required by a good cook
Set of 6 wrought iron sauce pans, 1 wrought iron stock pot, 1 bain-marie pan, 1 wrought iron tea kettle, 1 oval boiler, 1 digester, 1 sauce pan digester, 1 stewpan digester, 6 enamelled stewpans, 1 sauté pan, 1 French do., 1 potato steamer, 1 salamander and stand, 1 oval frying pan, 1 round do., 1 fluted gridiron, 1 bachelor's frying pan, 1 omelet pan, 1 omelette souffle pan, 1 braising pan, 1 preserving pan and spoon, 1 flour dredger, 1 sugar do., 1 brass kettle jack, 1 dripping pan and stand, 1 basting ladle, 1 wooden meat screen, 1 coffee mill, 1 meat chopper, 1 meat saw, 1 colander, 1 pestle and mortar, 2 gravy strainers, 1 bread grater, 2 sets of skewers, 1 fish slice, 1 egg slice and ladle, 1 pairs of steak tongs, 1 egg whisk, 1 beef fork, 1 French cook's knife, 1 steak beater, 1 fish kettle, 1 mackerel saucepan, 1 turbot kettle, 1 salmon and jack kettle, 1 pair of fish scissors, 1 double ranging gridiron, 1 sling toaster and trivet, 1 cheese toaster, 3 larding pins, 2 cook's knives, 1 mushroom mould, 1 star fritter mould, 1 scroll fritter mould, 1 vegetable cutter, or French vegetable cutter, 1 vegetable mould,

3 pudding moulds, 6 jelly moulds, 3 cake moulds, 2 wooden spoons, 1 mashed potato fork, 1 ice closet, 1 sugar spinner, 1 sugar mould, 1 toasting fork, 1 Carson's patent salting apparatus, 1 Kent's patent soup machine, 1 mincing machine, 1 weighing machine, 1 spice box, 1 herb stand, 1 box of paste cutters, 12 patty pans, 3 tart pans, 3 Dariol moulds, 1 marble slab, 1 rolling pin (American, with revolving handle), 1 paste jigger, 1 'piston' freezing machine.

The cost of the above would be £38–10 shillings.

The medium set
1 teakettle, 1 toasting fork, 1 bread grater, 1 wooden meat screen and bottle jack, 1 dripping pan and stand, 1 meat chopper, 1 colander, 3 block tin sauce pans, 5 iron sauce pans, 1 do. and steamer, 1 large boiling pot, 4 enamelled stewpans, 1 butter sauce pan, 1 stock pot, 1 fish and egg slice, 2 fish kettles, 1 flour dredge and pepper and salt do., 2 frying pans, 1 omelet pan, 1 double hanging gridiron, 1 salamander, 2 sets of skewers, 1 pair of steak tongs, 1 box of larding pins, 2 pudding moulds, 2 jelly do.'s, 1 rolling pin, 1 paste board, 1 paste jigger, 12 patty pans, 2 tart pans, 1 pan for Yorkshire pudding, 1 Warren's Everybody's Cooking Pot, 1 Warren's Everybody's Curry Pot, 1 spice box.

The cost of the above would be £10–15 shillings.

The small cottage set
1 Slack's Patent Digester, 1 tea kettle, 1 toasting fork, 1 bread grater, 1 tin meat screen and bottle jack, 1 set of skewers, 1 meat chopper, 1 block tin butter saucepan, 1 colander, 2 iron sauce pans, 2 iron stew pans, 1 enamelled saucepan, 1 iron boiling pot, 1 fish slice, 1 fish kettle, 1 flour dredger, 2 frying pans, 1 gridiron (hanging), 1 salt and pepper dredgers, 1 rolling pin, 1 pasteboard, 12 patty pans, 1 pan for Yorkshire puddings, 1 pair of scales, 1 spice box.

The cost of the above would be £4–5 shillings.

---

10   J. H. Elder-Duncan (British): 'The English Householder and l'Art Nouveau' (1911)

Another, and more recent movement of importance had its genesis in this country, but its serious results are almost entirely confined to the Continent. It arose from the determination of certain gifted architects and craftsmen to be free of past conventions in applied art; but this liberty, enjoyed here with circumspection and restraint, was embraced with such unwonted exuberance by the Continental craftsmen that the originators must have bitterly regretted their decision to dispense with the accepted canons of their art. The chaos in design has spread all over France, Germany, Austria and Italy, upon which countries the creed of 'L'Art Nouveau' lies heavily. There, all respect for natural limitations in the materials has been cast to the winds. Wood is cut as though it were a grainless and fibreless substance like cheese; metal is twisted into the most weird and unnatural shapes. Chairs appear as clumps of gnarled tree roots; twisted boughs conspire to form a bedstead; electroliers appear to be boxes suspended by innumerable strings; walls show trees with their roots in the skirting boards, and foliage on the ceiling; sea serpents chase each other round the walls, and entrance doors are guarded by appalling dragons. Nowhere is the purpose of an article frankly and honourably expressed. The electric lights must masquerade in pools under the eyes of a nymph, or in the glowing horseshoe upon a blacksmith's anvil; snakes twisted into ingenious knots for stair balusters threaten you as you ascend; the door knocker becomes a grinning satyr, and even the carpet casts malevolent eyes at you as you traverse it. In no case is this ghastly riot of form more marked than in Germany and Austria, where ingenious fancy, a craze for novelty, and a certain morbid strain in the Teutonic temperament have combined with the most unhappy results.

Fortunately, the English craftsmen and – to his honour be it said – the English householder, have set their faces against the threatened invasion, and comparatively little of this ephemeral rubbish is to be seen in our shops. Certain manifestations (largely the result of a mania for novelty) in modern English applied art have been dubbed 'L'Art Nouveau'; but the British form is severity itself beside that of the Continent, and, fortunately, does not appear to be making much headway. It is satisfactory, too, to note that English influence in the matter of good design, both in architecture and applied art, is beginning to be felt on the Continent, and even in Germany. Design, though still wild and thoughtless, appears to be assimilating some of the sobriety of the best English work.

---

11   R. Randal Phillips (British): 'The House' (1920)

Some people use their dining-rooms much more than their sitting rooms. There are some indeed who may perhaps speak with a certain superior air when talk is going as to cottage parlours that become cheerless domestic mausoleums, yet who use their sitting-rooms no more than the average parlour is used. On that fact might be based a strong argument for eliminating the sitting-room from the middle-class house and having instead one large living-room – large enough, indeed, to allow a dining-table to be set comfortably at one side of it, leaving plenty of space around for sitting, writing, or reading ...

... One uses the word sitting-room in preference to drawing-room as it implies a more reasonable outlook on domestic life. In the old days the with-drawing room was a place where the ladies used to withdraw, while the gentlemen settled down elsewhere, ultimately under the table. But in the modern contradiction of the term, 'drawing-room' has the smack of some rather artificial place for special occasions only, where every one is supposed to be on his best behaviour. The fallacy underlying this idea unfortunately still persists, and too often we find, in the drawing-room, chairs and other pieces of furniture that are not fitted to our use, chairs perhaps so eager to be delicate-looking that a heavy person sits down on them with trepidation lest their elegant legs should collapse in one awful moment; occasional tables, too, with hardly so much demand on their services as the name implies; and other things of the same kind. As however I am not setting out to say how a room should be furnished, we can pass this by with a bare reference. But it comes very properly within my scope to emphasize that no servantless house can ever be run with a minimum of trouble if rooms are filled with superfluous furniture, and ornaments are scattered about with a profusion at once baffling and exasperating to those who have to pick up each one of them when 'dusting.' The great thing after all is to have sensible rooms that look as though we really used them and enjoyed living in them, with furniture that meets our everyday requirements, and with just sufficient ornaments or other features of decoration that add an element of gaiety and refinement, while not entailing endless work in keeping the place in a reasonable condition of cleanliness.

---

12   Fred Campbell (British): 'An Ideal Installation' (1922)

The last few years have shown a wonderful increase in this country in the number of domestic labour-saving appliances, and many of them are becoming firmly established in our homes. The greatly advanced prices of the absolute necessities of life, such as food, clothing and coal, and the apparently increasing servant difficulties, are compelling our housewives to take a more practical interest in anything that helps to reduce either the work or the expense of running a house. The small establishment that can be easily handled by the woman of the house with the help of a day-girl, or by herself in an emergency, is the ideal dwelling of the future, at any rate for people whose purses are only moderately lined.

---

13 *Daily Mail* (Britain): 'A Home of Your Own for £880' (1922)

This is now possible owing to the reduction of building costs. Though not actual 'house-builders', we are 'home-builders' in every sense of the word, providing as we do those essential services which transform the mere house into a home.

The Heating, Lighting, Cooking, Washing and Sanitary Appliances will make a serious drain on your capital unless you avail yourself of expert assistance in their selection and installation.

Come to us for this assistance. We have been Building Specialists in every line for over half a century. It is undoubted economy to place yourself in our hands and by so doing avoid overlapping and unnecessary expenditure, through opening several accounts. We can regard your wants as a whole – save you money here, suggest an alternative there; leaving nothing to chance.

When we have supplied you with all your needs, your home will be a model of comfort, taste, dignity, and convenience. Your friends will congratulate you, and, the satisfactory results considered, you will be surprised at the small costs. And you will have a home that will last through the years – an Englishman's home. Why delay? Spring is here the building season, and time is flying. Get into touch with us now by a personal call if you can, or if not, write to us to-night for an appointment, a postcard to Dept. 272 is all that is needed:

Central Heating: efficiently installed keeps your home healthy and comfortable, saves fuel and furniture, pays for itself in time and labour saved.

Electric Lighting: should you require to generate your own electric light and power, we will install an efficient little plant which can easily be run by a lady . . .

Fireplaces and Stoves: 'the fireplace makes the room', and it is because we so thoroughly appreciate this home truth that we concentrate so intently on this line. The largest fireplace show-rooms in the Kingdom are at your disposal . . .

Bathroom and Sanitary Fittings: We will make your bathroom one of the most attractive apartments in your home, with an always-ready, hot-and-cold water supply, showers, sprays, towel drying rails etc. . . .

Kitchen Fittings: Not least important in the furnishing of the home comes the kitchen and its requisites. After all, the welfare of the household depends largely on the kitchen . . .

Door and Window Fittings: As in all things, 'it is the finishing touch which means so much', and the design and maintenance of your doors and windows are no exception . . . The door handles, finger-plates, and window fasteners will all be of artis-tic design, yet simple and secure in operation.

Fencing: The frame within which the picture is set is often as important as the picture itself. Yet how frequently one sees the appearance of an otherwise pretty homestead spoilt by untidy fences and clumsily repaired fencing . . . We will give your garden that really rustic appearance with Chestnut paling, made of the toughest, strongest native timber . . .

---

14 Le Corbusier (J. E. Jeanneret) (Swiss, resident in France): 'The House is a Machine for Living In' (1924)

The problem of the house has not yet been stated.

Nevertheless there do exist standards for the dwelling house.

Machinery contains within itself the factor of economy, which makes for selection.

The house is a machine for living in.

---

15 L. Mies van der Rohe (German): 'The Modern Home' (1927)

Today the factor of economy makes rationalisation and stand-ardisation imperative in rental housing. On the one hand, the increased complexity of our requirements demands flexibility. The future will have to reckon with both. For this purpose skeleton construction is the most suitable system. It makes possible rationalized building methods and allows the interior to be freely divided. If we regard kitchens and bathrooms, because of their plumbing, as a fixed core, then all other space may be partitioned by means of movable walls. This should, I believe, satisfy all normal requirements.

16 Alvar Aalto (Finnish): 'The Room' (1930)

The concept 'room' exists in a final 'proletarianized' form but continues to have the same meaning it had in the palaces from which it is a descendant. The living room in a peasant farmhouse – whose Finnish name *tupa* developed from the Lapp *Kota*, in Swedish *kata* – is a combination of different functions and was never, before its period of decline, combined with the concept 'room.'

In the city dwelling, on the other hand, the room continues to exist in an artificial manner, as an inheritance from palace architecture, in circumstances where it is really no longer appropriate. No family can live in one room, not even two, if they have children. But any family can live in an equivalent area if this area is divided up with particular attention to this family and its members' lives and activities. A dwelling is an area which should offer protected areas for meals, sleep, work, and play. These biodynamic functions should be taken as points of departure for the dwelling's internal division, not any outdated symmetrical axis or 'standard room' dictated by facade architecture.

17 Frank Lloyd Wright (American): 'The Decline of the Home' (1931)

To the homes of this country we must look for any beginning of the awakening of an artistic conscience which will change this parasitic condition to independent growth. The homes of the people will change before public buildings can possibly change.

18 Frank Lloyd Wright (American): 'The Cardboard House' (1931)

Any house is a far too complicated, clumsy, fussy, mechanical counterfeit of the human body. Electric wiring for nervous system, plumbing for bowels, heating system and fireplaces for arteries and heart, and windows for eyes, nose and lungs generally. The structure of the house, too, is a kind of cellular tissue stuck full of bones, complex now, as the confusion of Bedlam and all beside. The whole interior is a kind of stomach that attempts to digest objects – objects, 'objets d'art' maybe, but objects always. There the affected affliction sits, ever hungry – for ever more objects – or plethoric with over plenty. The whole

F

life of the average house, it seems, is a sort of indigestion. A body of ill repair, suffering indisposition – constant tinkering and doctoring to keep alive. It is a marvel, we its infestors do not go insane in it and with it. Perhaps it is a form of insanity we have put into it. Lucky we are able to get something else out of it, though we do seldom get out of it alive ourselves.

---

19 Estrid Ericson (Swedish): 'Estrid Ericson's Catechism' (1939)

A rented flat is not built for a particular individual, but if it has a good layout it will meet the demands which most people probably have more or less in common. The new types of flat differ from the earlier ones in that the rooms are a good deal less schematic. All rooms used to form an enfilade and they all used to be roughly the same size. The modern flat already derives character from its very layout, and so this makes it easy for us tenants to vary the interior design by simple means. The different rooms are characterised by their positions and sizes. Formerly, when all rooms were the same shape, they had to be furnished in a particular style or colour. But today there is no longer any need for a red room or a green room or a blue room.

One is always hearing people ask: What sort of wallpaper shall I have? What is the best – and loveliest – colour for the walls? Answer: White. It gives us complete liberty. In our white room we can include all the colours we need or want. Colourful textiles gives twice the pleasure when standing out against white. White also makes the room look larger, whereas dark walls make it crowded. It is a good idea to paint the doors the same shade of white as the walls, because in this way they will not be obtrusive, even if unsuitably positioned.

A flat must be sparsely furnished. Never forget that one needs free floor space to move about in. Nowadays we do not buy furniture purely for decoration. With rooms in the new flats getting smaller and smaller, we can only buy the furniture we know to be absolutely necessary. We must stop buying out of habit and in order to keep up with the Joneses. Let us take the example of a writing table. If you are furnishing a study, then the finest item of all is a writing table and it gets the best position in the room, which ought to have been used in a much more pleasant manner. Very often this writing table could be dispensed with and replaced by a secretaire or some such item of furniture which takes up less room and at the same time can be used for storage purposes. The same goes for many other items of furniture and other objects, such as nearly all the small articles on the writing table.

If we have budgeted a certain amount of money for fitting out the home, then first and foremost we have to make sure that everything purchased is of the best or at least sufficiently good quality. A chair, for example, can cost anything from 4 to 200 crowns. All these chairs serve their purpose and are perhaps equally durable. Birch is just as strong as palisander.

The acquisition of an armchair or bed is a different matter altogether. Here the material and workmanship make a big difference and only the very best will do. Where fabrics and lamps are concerned, simple things can be useful. The modern home, therefore, is a mixture of objects, some more expensive than others, which do not have to match. The main thing is not for the different items to match one another, to be old or new, or for the colours to form a single unit, the main thing, quite simply, is convenience and pleasantness.

Furniture must be light and easily movable and no larger than the occasion demands. Do not assume that a piece of furniture must always occupy the same position or has been made for a certain place. If furniture is of such a kind that it can be moved around as needed, one can make do with a much smaller number of pieces. Large, heavy items of furniture should be avoided. We no longer need big cupboards, because in the modern flat these are in-built. They fit together with wall and ceiling and form part of the architecture of the room. Not all dining chairs need be alike. And easy chairs must be differently shaped and offer different degrees of comfort.

It is a prejudice that all the furniture in a room must be of the same kind of woods. Usually it is far more gratifying to see several woods in the same room. The light, straight-backed chair must be made of hard, strong wood. The large table top must be of a wood with a stout structure which divides up the surface and makes it interesting. There are about 300 different kinds of wood and it is frequently impossible to say exactly which one is loveliest. Each has its own character, its particular colour and grain. The wood must be allowed to retain its natural colour, so as to do justice to its beauty. It must not be painted or stained, because then it will immediately lose its charm and in fact be reduced to insignificance, of whatever kind it may be. It is commonly supposed that there are great differences in the prices of different woods and that imitations are money-saving. This is not so. The price of a piece of furniture is mainly governed by its production cost; the material cost is relatively small. And sometimes an imitation can cost more than the genuine wooden article. The use of certain kinds of wood is, on the whole, a question of fashion, and a naturally treated wood can never lose its beauty.

Lamps have changed more than furniture through the ages. First came paraffin, then gas and, finally, electricity. Lamp design ought really to have changed no less radically. But light fittings are still being made, sold and bought with the old shapes, and designs are being retained which were intended for candles and gas, and have now been but poorly adapted to electric light. This is the case with chandeliers of crystal and bronze etc.

Electric light does not involve any danger of fire. This has a bearing on the design of light fittings. There is no need for heavy, rigid glass shades which were essential in the age of paraffin and gas. The electric light fitting can be made more flexible than the others. The light can be pointed upwards or downwards, or in whatever direction one pleases, and in this way the lighting of a room can be made full of variety. The table lamp belongs to the paraffin age. The ceiling lamp belongs to the gas age. The lamp of our own age – the age of electricity – is the standard lamp – movable and mobile. The ceiling lamp was always permanently attached to the ceiling, always in the middle of the room, and furniture had to be arranged in compliance with this suspended object. The table lamp often took up too much room on the table and was far from ideal for its true purpose. A relic of this type of lamp is the frequently occurring bedside lamp, which takes up most of the room on the bedside table and which it would be far more sensible to replace with a light on the wall behind the bed. The colours in a room are determined by the textiles. Fabrics, unlike furniture, do not have to last for a lifetime and so one has more liberty in choosing them. For just as it is wrong to choose a single type of wood for a room, it is equally wrong to use only the one fabric or one colour. And the time will soon come when we find constructed colour compositions just as ridiculous as we now do 'suites of furniture'. A planned, schematic colour scheme makes the room rigid and incapable of receiving a new colour. Suppose we suddenly fall for a painting which does not match the curtains!

We must never forget that we ought to have sufficient liberty in our homes not to have to refrain from something merely because it would jeopardise our aesthetic formalism. A home derives its personal imprint, not from a certain, contrived harmony of colour but from all the things gathered in the course of a lifetime. All the things one used to be fond of and is fond of now. Our homes are never complete; we spend the whole of our lives building them.

---

20 Robert W. Symonds (British): 'The Englishman's Home' (c.1946)

The English ideal is a house and garden, and this brought about the 'Garden City', from which developed the 'Garden Suburb', and the 'Housing Estate', i.e. the building of houses in an open development, which formed a new suburb or a new town. Many suburban Housing Estates, both large and small, were built between the wars.

After two World Wars, ideas on housing have been revolutionized. Plans for the re-building of war-scarred London and many of the bombed cities have been drawn up and await execution; also plans for new satellite towns. Legislation in the form of the Town Planning Act has been passed, which controls all types of housing and building, and new and widespread powers are now held by the authorities. Almost a new vocabulary has sprung up in connection with housing: planning, zoning, densities, decentralization, community centres, precinct, development charge.

Post-war housing has progressed badly, the main reason being the scarcity of timber. To solve the problem of housing, all types of materials – brick, concrete, steel, aluminium, asbestos – and all varieties of houses – temporary and permanent, prefabricated or factory-made of mass-produced units – have been tried out. Many have fallen by the way, whilst others have secured recognition.

From the post-war school of thought, it appears that the low-density house and the high-density flat are the two forms of housing that will prevail in Great Britain. The future housing suburb or satellite town will not consist of a drab row of uniformed houses (known as 'Council Houses') but will be planned to include a combination of houses and flats, both varying in size and oriented in site (i.e. windows opening upon as much sun as possible), with a community centre, schools, shopping and business centres, and open spaces. The density of the population of a new town will be so designed as to form a 'well-balanced community'. The future Englishman's home will be small, compact, and labour-saving.

21 Eunice Airey (British): 'Swedish "Knock-down" Furniture' (1947)

This new type of furniture called 'knock-down' or package furniture, is the contribution of the Swedish architect-designer Elias Svedberg towards a solution of his country's housing problem.

The furniture is so named because it is made in separate pieces which simply fit together. It can be packaged in boxes, and it needs just a screw driver and common sense to put it together.

The householder can experiment to his heart's content. He can achieve endless variations with shelves, cupboards, tables. He can buy more shelves to fit onto his bookcase as his library grows; he can expand a set of drawers into a sideboard; a single bed into a double bed; a cupboard into a wardrobe. Even the chairs and desk come to pieces and can be packed flat.

Thus precious space and transport are saved, and standardisation ensures that the average family can buy high quality furniture at cheap prices.

Like the rest of the world, Sweden has housing problems; in her case arising particularly from cramped room space. Sweden has sought to solve the problem by interesting the general public in modern design and higher living standards and by enlisting the practical aid of architects and designers. Educational courses have been arranged in towns and factories; exhibitions have toured the countryside, visiting remote villages.

The results have widely influenced the whole furnishing trades, and its effects can be traced even to such details as new trends in knife and spoon handles.

Svedberg's furniture is one of the most important results.

22 Frank Lloyd Wright (American): 'The New House on the Prairie' (c.1950)

First thing in building the new house, get rid of the attic, therefore the dormer. Get rid of the useless false heights below it. Next, get rid of the unwholesome basement, yes, absolutely in any house built on the prairie. Instead of lean, brick chimneys bristling up everywhere ... I could see the necessity for one chimney only. A broad generous one, or at most two. These kept low-down on gently sloping roofs or perhaps flat roofs. The big fireplace in the house below became now a place for a real fire. A real fireplace at that time was extraordinary. There were mantels instead. A mantle was a marble frame for a few coals in the grate. Or it was a piece of wooden furniture with fire stuck in it around the grate, the whole set up against the plastered, papered wall. Insult to comfort. So the *integral* fireplace became an important part of the building itself in the house. I was allowed to build out there on the prairie. It comforted me to see the fire burning deep in the solid masonry of the house itself. A feeling that came to stay . . .

Taking a human being for my scale, I brought the whole house down in height to fit a normal one – ergo 5' 8" tall, say. This is my own height. Believing in no other scale than the human being I broadened the mass out all I possibly could to bring it down into spaciousness. It has been said that were I three inches taller than 5' 8½" all my houses would have been quite different in proportion. Probably . . .

House walls were now started at the ground on a cement or stone water table that looked like a low platform under the building, and usually was. But the house walls were stepped at the second-storey window sill level to let the bedrooms come through in a continuous window series below the broad eaves of a gently sloping, overhanging roof . . .

In this new house the wall was beginning to go as an impediment to outside light and air and beauty. Walls had been a great fact about the box in which holes had to be punched. It was still this conception of a wall building which was with me when I designed the Winslow house. But after that my conception began to change . . .

My sense of 'wall' was no longer the side of a box. It was enclosure of space affording protection against storm or heat only when needed. But it was also to bring the outside world into the house and let the walls of the house go outside. In this sense I was working away at the wall as a wall and bringing it toward the function of a screen, as a means of opening up space, which, as control of building materials improved, would finally permit the free use of the whole space without affecting the soundness of structure.

And at this time I saw a house, primarily as viable interior space under simple shelter. I liked the sense of shelter in the look of the building. I still like it.

The house began to associate with the ground and became natural to its prairie site.

What I have just described was on the outside of the house. But it was all there, chiefly because of what had happened *inside*.

Dwellings of that period were cut up, advisedly and completely, with the grim determination that should go with any cutting process. The interiors consisted of boxes beside boxes or inside boxes, called rooms. All boxes were inside a complicated outside boxing. Each domestic function was properly box to box.

I declared the whole lower floor as one room, cutting off the kitchen as a laboratory, putting the servants' living and sleeping quarters next to the kitchen but semi-detached, on the ground floor. Then I screened various portions of the big room for certain domestic purposes like dining, reading and receiving callers.

There were no plans in existence like those at the time. But my clients were all pushed towards these ideas as helpful to a solution of a vexed servant problem. Series of unnecessary doors disappeared and no end of partitions. Both clients and servants liked the new freedom. The house became more free as space and more livable too. Interior spaciousness began to dawn.

Thus came an end to the cluttered house.

---

23 *The Woodworker* (British): 'Furnishing the Small House' (1954)

Key notes of the contemporary interior (how one detests the word but is there a better one?) are function and simplicity of design. This does not necessarily mean bareness or lack of comfort, or even the box-like character of two decades ago. Curves are natural and desirable. It means that the useful and aesthetic qualities of every piece in the home are carefully studied. Such a scheme although not cheap need not be unduly expensive and there is a considerable saving in irritation and work. These considerations are especially important when rooms are small such as in a modern council house. The idea of space should be emphasised and overcrowding avoided. Pattern is undesirable in the interior decoration and should be restrained in the soft furnishings.

Living Room – The lay-out [under consideration in this article] is that of a typical council house, with party wall to the adjoining house. Although family meals are usually served in the kitchen, facilities for meals should be available in the living room for festive occasions and for visitors.

A small dining table with chairs tucked beneath it [should be] within easy access of the door to the kitchen wherever it may be . . . The dining chairs with drop-in upholstered seats should be as small and light as possible.

A suggestion is also made for a small bureau chest which would make a useful sideboard, one top drawer having a loose lined tray for cutlery, the other being used for table linen.

Television is having increasing influence upon seating arrangements. Chairs are lighter, generally as units, smaller independent articles of furniture are eliminated . . . This enables chairs to be easily moved around for viewing. The conventional three-piece suite is an archaism today.

Low back chairs have a better appearance but higher backs . . . are preferred for head support. The seats are coil sprung and padded with loose cushions over. Loose coverings for backs and cushions which can be washed might be considered. The occasional fireside chair with low arms should find a place. This need not take the form shown and could be arranged with a removable work box beneath or inside a seat arranged to lift . . .

The coffee table is handy, the top forming a tray which if lined with cloth or baize underneath could be used for games. Many may prefer the usual standard lamp and shade, designs of which have appeared frequently in these pages, but the [preferred] type . . . has advantages, as the chromium plated rod carries an adjustable screened light to any height and angle. The leg base is of wood.

Mantelpieces are generally lower than formerly which makes it easy to provide useful flanking cupboards and bookshelves. Plate glass sliding doors may be fitted as convenient. If possible, a fitted carpet up to the skirting is better, adding to the spaciousness of the room. Where television is installed the curtain material should be somewhat heavier than usual and lightproof. Finally, employ pictures sparingly, having one good one rather than many poor. The backs should be removable with small wood or metal turn-buttons to facilitate cleaning and occasional changing of the picture . . .

Kitchen – A cabinet with a drop-down or pull-out working table is an essential feature of the modern house. This may be a built-in fixture . . . The table should be a folding type, preferably with drawers . . . Folding chairs or stacking stools could be used with it . . . The ironing board should be adjustable in height, clipping on to a caravan table. It is stored inside when not in use.

A useful addition to any kitchen is a round stool with a padded seat, covered with some washable material. There should be a supporting bar or bars for the feet and it would be advantageous to have a screw-type adjustable seat, enabling the housewife to raise or lower it at will and swivel around on it if needed. Linoleum is the best floor covering but hardboard might be considered if joints are carefully made. Curtain material should be bright, attractive and washable. Painted washable walls are the best.

Scullery – Sinks are still being fixed far too low, especially for taller women. If at all possible raise it to suit rather than to suffer perpetual backache. Fitments are easily made with sliding doors if not part of the house fittings . . .

Hall – Sometimes these are too small for anything excepting perhaps an umbrella and stick stand. A hall cupboard as shown is useful if there is room for it with a glove box and small mirror inside the door.

[At the end of this article the description of the bedroom was promised for a future issue, but this apparently did not appear.]

7

NATION, RACE AND ETHNICITY

This period saw peoples of different nations come together as they never had done before. The contact, we are forced to admit, has rarely been harmonious. Given the explosion of trade and industry, and the voraciousness of capital, it was always likely that exploitation would accompany the Europeans wherever they went. Similarly, outside the imperial sphere, the meeting of races has hardly been accomplished amicably. The rise of structured, politicised nationalism led, from the second half of the nineteenth century, to tensions which plunged much of the world into two wars.

The three terms used in the title of this chapter were chosen so as to suggest a differentiation between organised political structures (nation), between the discourses which surrounded what were considered to be separate groupings within the human race (race) and the idea of locale, where custom and region counted as factors in the distinguishing of peoples (ethnicity). Quotations related to all three mingle freely through the chapter. Perhaps the single most noticeable feature throughout is the insistence the writers have on differentiating the races they are dealing with. Sometimes this is done with a calm presumptiveness; at other times, we are subjected to an offensive arrogance; occasionally, we simply have to laugh at the logic in operation. All too often, there is a tragic intensity at work, which belies the quasi-objectivity of the language.

Discussion of race is usually couched in terms of archetypes. Writers describe other races collectively, and point, as proof of that race's homogeneity, to the archetypal characteristics they discern. Occasionally, when a race breaks out of the archetype-mould it has been appointed to, new explanations as to the constitution of that race have to be provided. In this regard, the Japanese have been a most troublesome race to the Europeans. Quotations record how attitudes toward the Japanese had to be consistently adjusted, as their cultural, economic and military status grew.

This was truly the age of Empire. The overseas empires created by the European nations yielded economic benefits which tipped over into, and eventually became completely synonymous with, political and cultural considerations. It is not possible to understand European culture in the nineteenth century in the absence of empire. To construct a cultural picture of Europe, and especially of Britain and France, without foregrounding imperial activity is to irrevocably distort it.

It follows from this that through the same period, empire has been one of the greatest influences on European design. This came from two directions. Most movements in design during the nineteenth century, were first of all aesthetically and iconographically transformed through design of other nations. Second and more important were the raw materials and the large, tame markets, which accounted for the very existence of the many designed commodities in the first place.

The quotations consist largely of a member of one race commenting on another, and fall into two types. In the first, European designers and critics acknowledge the qualities of design from various other nations. Some of these passages are basically formal analysis. Others are more complex, and try and offer explication as to what foreign design means, how it was made, and, most puzzlingly, how supposedly 'inferior' nations can produce superior design.

The second group is more broad, and offers writings which reveal the tenure of thought on race, ethnicity and nation. This includes writings on specific races, often by commentators on design, but not always. Towards the end of the chapter, some of the most important writers on cultural aspects of race over the past decade are cited.

See also
Chapter 1 for other aspects of the ornament debate
Chapter 8 for internationalism and the impact of modernism

---

1   **Prince Napoleon, Cousin to the Emperor Napoleon III (French): 'On the Origins of the Expositions Universelles and the Role of the French Character in them' (1855)**

Universal Exhibitions are a necessity of our times. Without bringing any prejudice to the nations, which are the basis of human organisation, they strengthen the generous influences that allow nations to live in harmony of feeling and interest . . .

What struck me once again about these great meetings was that from them springs the proof that modern society must walk towards freedom. When one examines the origin of the wealth they spread at our feet, one is able to witness that the industrial superiority of a nation depends above all on its morality and its individual spirit of initiative.

I insist on saying that the exposition was a French idea. As early as 1849 our Parliament made the proposal of organising an exposition, although England was the first to have one. This must be attributed to political events, to squeamish attitudes at home, as well as to a difference of genius between the two nations; we are best at conceiving an idea and they are best at putting it into practice. But the success of the London Exhibition was an exemplar for us; as soon as the Crystal Palace's doors were closed, from everywhere there was a demand for Paris to organise one as well. Your majesty wanted to satisfy this wish of public opinion and on March 8th 1853 the Universal Exhibition of products of industry was decided. As scheduled, it opened on May 1st 1855 and closed its doors on September 30th 1855.

Although France once again let herself be up-staged in the realisation of the ideas its genius produced, when she puts them into practice, she gives them a different character that elevates them and embellishes them . . .

---

2 John Connolly (British): 'The Ethnological Exhibitions of London' (1855)

There is scarcely a year in which, among the miscellaneous attractions of a London season, we do not find some exhibition illustrative of the varieties of mankind. But some of these are unsatisfactory, some deceptive, and all nearly unprofitable, because not rendered instructive, to the public.

The commercial relations of England afford such extensive opportunities of intercourse with all the races of men, that no country should be expected to prosecute the study of Ethnology with more success; and in no metropolis ought we to expect to find, from time to time, such instructive illustrations of all parts of this science as in London. Until very recently, however, the observations made in voyages and travels seem to have been considered interesting chiefly in proportion to their marvellous character; and specimens showing the progress made in arts or in science among rude people and in remote regions, and even the natives of such regions, when brought to our country, have been merely regarded as objects of curiosity or of unfruitful wonder, rather than as manifestations of human intellect and modifications of human development in various parts of the same globe, and illustrative of man's unwritten history and progress. The possible improvement of all the varieties, and the ultimate concentration of all the powers developed among them, in widely different situations and circumstances, upon some ulterior results in civilization, have scarcely occupied the mind of any who gazed on mere varieties of form, and colour, and inventive industry, as curious distinctions, inherent or permanent, and associated with no definite sequence.

The institution of the Ethnological Society only twelve years ago, (in 1843) and the interest it seems already to have imparted to ethnological inquiry, and its representation in a Section of the British Association for the Advancement of Science, afford every hope that our advantages will, in future, be turned to better account. In the mean time, however, very interesting specimens of the inhabitants of countries little known to us arrive nearly in every year, are exhibited for money for a time, are even invited for inspection in fashionable drawing-rooms among the novelties of the Spring, and depart: having gained small notice from the ethnologist, and excited no moral interest even among the most serious or the most philanthropic portion of our countrymen. They arrive in a state of barbarism, and without possessions or knowledge; and they depart from civilized communities equally ignorant and equally destitute.

Within the last seven or eight years, several groups of the natives of western, southern, and northern parts of the world have been exhibited; as, from North America, at least two groups; from South Africa, three; and from the arctic regions, one. Of the second group of asserted American aborigines, Ioways and Ogibbeways, the genuineness of a portion appeared doubtful; yet of both groups the greater number were unquestionable natives of a wild land, whose unmitigated shouts and exciting war-dances bore the stamp of fierce reality.

---

3   Owen Jones (British): 'Ornament of Savage Tribes' (1856)

From the universal testimony of travellers it would appear, that there is scarcely a people, in however an early state of civilization, with whom the desire for ornament is not a strong instinct. The desire is absent in none, and grows and increases with all in the ratio of their progress in civilization. Man appears everywhere impressed with the beauties of Nature which surround him, and seeks to imitate to the extent of his power the works of the Creator.

Man's earliest ambition is to create. To this feeling must be ascribed the tattooing of the human face and body, resorted to by the savage to increase the expression by which he seeks to strike terror in his enemies or rivals, or to create what appears to him a new beauty. As we advance higher, from the decoration of the rude tent or wigwam to the sublime works of a Phidias or Praxiteles, the same feeling is everywhere apparent: the highest ambition is still to create, to stamp on this earth the impress of an individual mind.

---

4   R.H. Soden-Smith (British): 'Art-instinct' (1867)

It is notable that the absence of art-beauty in these homely objects is most conspicuous among nations claiming to be the highest according to the present scale of civilization. The people whom we are content to regard as semi-civilized – Oriental nations, tribes of Northern Africa, races from distant parts of the Russian Empire – show an understanding of colour, at least, which, renders their otherwise rude household goods models for the skillful European to study and strive to imitate. Art is thus not instinctive among Western nations. The objects that minister to the daily needs and conveniences of common life are for the most part wanting – and it is a lamentable want – in every quality that can give pleasure to the eye.

The entire household furniture, carpets, fittings, articles of daily use, complete clothing for young and old, may be selected . . . and yet not one object found which ministers in the smallest degree to that art instinct which is gratified by the commonest productions of Oriental workmanship . . .

Among Oriental nations what may be called an instinct of art-feeling guides their work conspicuously in colour, and to a lesser degree in other sources of beauty. It is not so among the most civilized of Western nations – not so in France, any more than elsewhere.

Where manufacture has triumphed in rapidity, certainty, and cheapness of production, the results are usually astonishing examples of the power of making common and really useful objects hideous.

Finally, it is obvious that if Great Britain is to continue competing successfully with her continental rivals in the supply of articles which surround the daily lives of millions, and which represent a trade encompassing the whole globe, her manufactures must bring to bear on their business higher qualities than are commonly deemed necessary for money-making; qualities, some of which at least must necessarily be sought beyond their own body – inventive capacity, knowledge and practice of art, wide acquaintance with new materials, and scientific skill to make them available.

---

5 **Jacob Falke (British): 'The Excellence of Chinese Design'
(1870)**

Yet nevertheless, this eastern Asiatic Art, when examined with that critical eye which can discern the wheat from the chaff, and which does not look to it for that which it does not possess, but only regards its peculiar beauties and excellencies; nevertheless, I say, it offers sufficient artistic peculiarities to merit, for their sake, the consideration of the friends of Art of the present day, and to be a useful adjunct to any Museum or institution devoted to that practical aesthetic object, the elevation of taste and of modern Art-Industry. It is from this point of view that we would proceed in the present article, to glance at Chinese and Japanese Art, its peculiarities, its beauties and its excellencies.

It is commonly supposed that those qualities which are at all worthy of consideration for modern Art-Industry consist solely in special workmanship, as for example, the excellence, solidity and lustre of the lackerwork and polish to which our artists cannot in any degree approach. But so exclusive an opinion is assuredly a mistake; the artistic works of the Chinese and Japanese – by which we intend the productions of Art-Industry, and not their pictures or purely plastic works – have positive aesthetic peculiarities which demand recognition. We must only take care not to look upon the object as a faultless piece of work according to aesthetic principles, as pure in form, design and ornamentation; we must consider that this or that determinate creation, this or that determinate figure was partly owing to their histories and tradition, partly to their civil and religious laws, under pressure of which the artist was obliged to bend. We must conceive of these works from the point of view of decoration, we must try them by the effect which they produce as a whole, and by the way in which they harmonise with other works of Art. We may then go further and shall find much that is charming and attractive in the details and peculiar structure of their creations, if only we do not expect these advantages in the very first object that meets our eye.

Consider under this decorative point of view, those artistic productions of eastern Asia, even the most modern and the most common, never appear without harmony in their coloristic effect, never glaring and hard in their tints, a defect which till of late, and even now is so general in modern Art-Industry. The newer Chinese works may often be liable to the reproach of paleness and feebleness of color, which however is not always a defect, but the composition is always correct, and the effect pleasant to the eye. This is a quality which deserves to be well considered by the Art-Industry of the present day, and which in its time the *Rococo* well understood how to turn to advantage. But if we separate the really good from the common and poor, which the Chinese, as a rule, sent to us as good enough for 'the Barbarians', and if we fix our attention especially on the more ancient objects of Art, to whatever branch they may belong, we shall be obliged to acknowledge their positive excellencies. Instead of that mere harmony which appears frequently to be a purely negative excellence, we shall come upon effects of color which are most admirable, full of glow and depth, quiet and sober, yet still rich and elegant which would do honor to any time and any style of Art, and which are highly to be recommended for study and imitation. We shall find also a quantity of originally shaped vessels which just as they are, or perhaps with only and slight alterations, would be suitable for modern use, and even satisfy a delicate perception of form, and lastly, even in ornamentation, in the conventionalising of the flowers, for example, as found in the more ancient works, we shall discover motives which may be useful for decorators of the present day. We put on one side the workmanship which is partly lost even to the Chinese themselves, but which might be most advantageously revived.

6   Charles Darwin (British): 'Natural Selection amongst Peoples' (1871)

All that we know about savages, or may infer from their traditions and from old monuments, the history of which is quite forgotten by the present inhabitants, show that from the remotest times successful tribes have supplanted other tribes. Relics of ancient or forgotten tribes have been discovered throughout the civilised regions of the earth, on the wild plains of America, and on the isolated islands in the Pacific Ocean. At the present day civilised nations are everywhere supplanting barbarous nations, excepting where the climate opposes a deadly barrier; and they succeed mainly, though not exclusively, through their arts, which are the products of the intellect. It is, therefore, highly probable that with mankind, the intellectual faculties have been gradually perfected through natural selection; and this conclusion is sufficient for our purpose. Undoubtedly it would have been very interesting to have traced the development of each separate faculty from the state in which it exists in lower animals to that in which it exists in man; but neither my ability nor knowledge permit the attempt.

---

7   Jules Bourgoin (French): 'Arabic Art and the Orient' (1873)

For any understanding of Arabic art it is necessary to follow and to study the growth of the Arab conquest throughout the world, that is to say in every territory of this vast region of the planet extending from India to southern Europe and including a major part of Persia, India, western Asia, Turkey, Spain and its annexes.

With the information available to us today it is difficult to define the precise role played by the Arab race in this blossoming of the arts in the Orient. The Arab conquest engulfed so many different peoples of such diverse racial origins, it took root in so many diverse regions in which had previously flourished the colossal civilizations of India, Assyria, Persia and of Greco-Roman antiquity, that it is difficult to know how much influence should be attributed to the conquest and how much is residual to the vanquished countries. However, we should notice that the monumental constructions erected since the advent of Islam are in perfect correlation with the monuments surviving from previous civilizations.

All the conquering Arabs overrunning the world to the rallying cry of the Prophet, and for eight centuries imposing their activity on the planet, were in no way barbarians; they knew a lot about the world around them and, conquerors or conquered, they shared that particular tempering of spirit which so profoundly distinguishes the Asiatic from the European; they shared the same or, at least analogous principles. The conquest was also very rapid, extending within only a few centuries from the Far East to the south of Europe.

Arabic art is essentially decorative and deals in surfaces; but where monuments had been built using substantially large basic materials, Arab civilizations employed the same means. This is what happened in India, Egypt and western Asia. In Persia on the other hand, where architecture consisted principally of revetment, Persian Islamic art reveals the use of small-scale materials such as bricks, faced with plaster or faience. In Spain and in Africa Moorish architecture is all of one piece and considerably lacks – a point which is important to note – the wealth of architectural construction inherent in most other systems. Moorish architecture is an architecture of decoration, which renders it inferior, and this is why we should not judge the art of the Orient in terms of what we understand about Moorish or African countries.

From all this, we can begin to understand the importance of the milieu. If one considers the paucity of artistic activity among the original semitic or 'semiticized' races, how distant these races are from a sensibility of nature and an ability to interpret it, we must recognize that we are in the presence of a singular civilization.

It is important, therefore, in consideration of the arts in Arabian civilization, to disregard the rather defined idea we have of art itself. By this we mean the expression of intellectual beauty, be it poetic, plastic or musical. Our aesthetic is wholly inappropriate in these concerns, and it would be a mistake to attempt to apply it. Neither should we expect to find in the history of Eastern art an equivalent to the rigorous linkage between different phases that exists in Western art. The Orient is the native soil of all art, as it is of all religion, and the incessant communication between all Asiatics has led to such a diffusion of different manifestations of the activities of these industrious peoples that it is extremely difficult to decipher what is attributable to whom. In all examples of art from the Orient we can trace infinitely diverse influences: we could say that Oriental art is a syncretism of elements such as Byzantine, Persian, Indian, Moorish etc. which combine to form the complex tapestry of Arabic art.

But this is not the place to examine these questions in depth; let us set aside these generalities and approach a subject which is of great importance in Oriental art: interlace, this decorative element, originally invented by the Greeks of the Lower Empire, was adopted by the Orientals who extended and developed it with infinite craft. This process was extremely important: wherever in the world there is evidence of Arab conquests, in India, western Asia, in Africa and Spain, we find this decorative element, and in every edifice it plays such an important role that we could, at least provisionally, consider it as a major characteristic of Arabic art.

Taking the word art in its abstract sense, we could consider

Arabic art as a decorative system based entirely on order and geometric form, borrowing little or nothing from the observation of nature; that is to say an art complete in itself, deprived of natural symbolism and idealist significance. The inspiration is abstract and in the execution the plastic has no place. Obviously, this definition is incomplete and too absolute; nevertheless it expresses the truth of the matter well enough. In fact, by its very exaggeration it serves to emphasize the special objective we have in mind, namely an understanding of the importance of geometric information in this decorative art.

---

8   **Christopher Dresser (British): 'Contact with Europeans Unfortunately Brings about a Deterioration of Eastern Art' (1873)**

In order that you acquire the power of perceiving art-merit as quickly as possible, you must study those works in which examples of bad taste are rarely met with, you must at first consider art-objects from India, Persia, China, and Japan, as well as examples of ancient art from Egypt and Greece. But in selecting modern works from the East, choose those which are not altogether new if possible.

During the last ten years the art-works of Japan have deteriorated to a lamentable extent. Contact with Europeans unfortunately brings about the deterioration of Eastern art: in order that the European demand be met, quantity is produced and quality disregarded, for we cavil respecting price, and yet by thus creating a demand for inferior work we raise the price even of that which is comparatively bad, and soon have to pay for the coarser wares a price for which superior articles could at first be procured.

But this should be noted: that the commonest wares which we receive from Japan and India are never utterly bad in art. Inharmonious colouring does not appear to be produced by these nations, and the same may be said of Persia and China, and to an extent of Morocco and Algeria, the only exceptions being where European influence has been long continued. In selecting examples for study you may almost rely upon the beauty of all works from China, Japan, Persia, and India, which have not been produced under European influence.

A notable example of the deteriorating influence of European taste (perhaps chiefly English taste) upon Eastern art is apparent if we examine old carved sandalwood boxes from India, and those which are now sent to us from the same country; the quiet, unobtrusive consistency of the ornament by which it is sought only to enrich a properly constructed box was not sufficiently attractive to suit European (or English ?) taste. The ornament must be more pronounced and in higher relief, and the entire work must be more attractive – more vulgarly attractive I might say, and thus the exquisite refinement of the older works is sacrificed to the wants of a rich but vulgar people, whose taste for art is infinitely below that of their conquered brethren, from whom they learn the principles of a beautiful art but slowly, while they do much to destroy the refinement of art-taste which the workmen of our Eastern empire appear to inherit. Study the works of the Eastern nations in conjunction with the remarks which I made in my first chapter, and then consider the numerous objects left to us by the early Egyptians and Greeks, and bear in mind while viewing them what we have said on Egyptian and Greek art, and after having learnt to understand the merits of Persian, Japanese, Indian, and Chinese art, and of that of the ancient Egyptians and Greeks, you may commence to consider other styles, taking up the study of Italian and Renaissance art in its various forms last of all; for in these styles, or dialects of a style if I may thus speak, there is so much that is false in structure, false in representation, untruth-ful in expression, and pictorial rather than ornamental in effect, that a very complete acquaintance with ornamental art is neces-sary in order that all the defects of these styles be apparent, and in order that the student avoid falling into the error of regarding a pictorial effect as the result of a true style of ornamental art.

9   G. L. M. Birdwood (British): 'Progress and the Aryan Race'
     (1878)

Everywhere the keen, bright, energetic Aryan race excited other races to a higher civilization, and only the civilizations in which the Aryan element is pure or predominant have proved progres-sive; those in which it was overwhelmed by the Turanian races having always been unprogressive, as in India, Egypt and Assyria.

10   The Earl of Kimberley, Secretary of State for India (British):
     'The Calamity of the Introduction of Our Taste into Eastern
     Arts' (1886)

I have often been struck with the calamity of the introduction of our taste into Eastern Arts and manufactures, for their taste is far better than ours, although we have no doubt engineering knowledge and skill, and the command of capital; and I cannot conceive of any advantage greater than the two countries brought together.

11 Rush C. Hawkins (American): 'The Artistic Character of the Latin Races' (1889)

That there is in the human race such an intangible quality as the art instinct there can be no reasonable doubt; and that it has been more marked and strongly developed among the northern people, is also indisputable. If the history of art proves one thing more than another, it is the value of this instinct in the development of painting, sculpture, and architecture among the southern races. To the influence of the Greeks, and, in later times, the great era of the Italian Renaissance, is the Northern part of the civilised world indebted for much that is good in its achievement. But in no country has that double influence taken such deep root and retained such vigorous life as in France; in no other has it produced such far reaching and beneficial re-sults. In that country it has kept alive a natural love for the artistic, which even in these materialistic days of steam and iron, adorns every phase of national life.

12 Oscar Wilde (Attributed) (Irish): 'America' (c.1890)

America is the only nation to have gone from barbarity to decadence without going through civilization.

13 F. Edward Hulme (British): 'The Universal and Relative Nature of Ornament' (1894)

Even in the Neolithic days, when our prehistoric ancestors, the men of the stone period, were chipping flints and chisels, the soft clay of their rude vessels afforded opportunity for orna-ment, and in the whole field of ethnographic research no tribe is found so low in the scale of humanity as to yield no illustra-tion of this love for decoration. The claims of religion and of war are ordinarily paramount, and it is to these two directions that we most naturally look for illustrations of decoration . . .

To man the simple formula, 'Let us eat and drink, for tomorrow we die', is not enough for his needs. It may suffice for the lower animals; but even the lowest savage is a man made in the image of God, and the dark recesses of his mind are lit up with aspirations that mere animalism will not satisfy. In the simplest zig-zags on the pottery dug out of some prehistoric barrow or the choicest examples of the ceramic art of Hellas, we alike see the desire to create forms of beauty, and the difference between the carved prow of a South Sea canoe and the sculptures of the shrine of Athene Parthenos is only a difference of degree and not of kind. That we may not ourselves think a given thing beautiful is beside the mark. We have been educated on other lines and have had other opportunities, and the only fair way to view a thing that appears to us rude, archaic, barbarous, is not to estimate it from our own prepossessions at all, but to frankly see in it the endeavours of a man whose environment was in every possible way different from our own, to attain to some ideal of beauty in his mind. Judged by this common-sense principle, the efforts of every age and of every race are of interest, and all fall naturally into their appointed place in the history and development of ornament.

---

14   F. Edward Hulme (British): 'The Japanese Love of Art' (1894)

The love of art appears to be ingrained in the Japanese. In that beautiful country, life passes under easier and more graceful conditions than in these islands of the West. The cruel tyranny of fashion and the senseless cry after novelty are unknown, and in their place is the changeless law of love and beauty for its own sake. The government, sharing the national passion for beauty in nature and in art, plants seats just at those spots in its public gardens where the view is perfect of Fujiyama or of the sea, or of some strange wooded hills, and it is common along the by-roads to find official notices telling you where to stop for the best prospect, or how to find the best clump of plum or cherry blossom. In the same spirit the peasant and the artisan, when the wife sets a flowering plant on the tansu, looks upon it almost in the light of a good meal, and might grudge money for fish or rice rather than for that.

15 Siegfried Bing (German, resident in France): 'American Culture' (1895)

The entire past of American culture is . . . comprised of a series of spurts forward. One day the desire mounts to break away from the banality of everyday life. But instead of progressing gradually, in accordance with general laws, the thrusts follow one another, at broken intervals, attempting to move, without transition, from the most rudimentary mores to the most extreme refinements. Aspirations go astray through inexperience, ending in the false glitter of intemperate luxury. This efflorescence has taken place in such a hasty and impetuous way that some observers have compared its results to the products of an overheated greenhouse – an apt comparison in many cases. But one very important point is thus missed: the rich exuberance of forced flowers has hidden the unobtrusive growth of a few young shoots breaking through the earth with fresh charm, which promise, when they bloom, the evolution of a new strain.

Is this a sign of sudden metamorphosis of the arts in America? Will this nation now produce a pure and harmonious art? Alas, the creative spirit, already rare in those surroundings wrought by ancient civilizations, must remain still more so in this vast, barely cleared land. But however timidly America may take the first step in a new direction, we can safely predict that the last steps will always lead to some result or solution of supreme brilliance.

16 Richard Glazier (British): 'The Ornament of Oceania' (1899)

The ornamentation of the people of the Pacific Isles is full of interest, and is remarkable for the evolution and perfecting of an ornamental style by a primitive people, with myths and traditions purely local, and in no way influenced by other nations. It is a style of ornament full of meaning and symbolism, yet simple in detail and arrangement, not founded upon the beautiful vegetation and flora of their islands, but upon abstract forms derived from the human figure, and arranged with a pleasing geometrical precision remarkable for a primitive people.

The ornamental art of these people may be broadly divided into provinces, each with its distinct ornamental characteristics and traditions, New Zealand showing the highest development and Australia the lowest in the ornament of Polynesia and Melanesia.

162

Much of the ornament is purely linear, consisting of parallel and zig-zag lines; that of Australia consists almost entirely of these lines incised in the ground and occasionally filled in with colour. In New Guinea a higher development is reached, the ornament, of straight and curved lines, being carved in flat relief. In the province of Tonga-Samoa, the surface is divided into small fields, and the linear ornament runs in a different direction on each of the fields. The Hervey and Austral Islands are distinguished by their remarkable adaptations of the human female figure, the illustrations given here showing the original type and its ornamental development. These examples, to-gether with the circular eye pattern, form the elements of the Hervey province, of which the Heape collection contains many fine examples. In the Solomon Island the linear ornament is occasionally interspersed with an inlay of angular pieces of mother of pearl. The New Zealand province is distinguished by its skillful pieced carving, the beauty of its spiral forms adapted from the human figure, and the constant use of the border here given. No preliminary design was used, nor was the pattern outlined upon the object of the decoration. It was, so to speak, evolved from the artist's head as he worked, much as a musician improvises at the piano. This art, once general, now appears to be falling rapidly into oblivion.

---

17 Alex M. Thompson (British): 'A Comparison between the English and French Worker' (1900)

It is really astounding that a strip of sea, not half the width of the stretch of land between London and Brighton, should be able to make such a difference. Is not the commercial and social intercourse between the two countries constant and reciprocal as the ebb and flow of a great tide? Have we not in the very heart of London a French Soho? Has not Paris, even in its hottest seasons, its frigidly English Quartier de St Honore? Has it not its seventeen thousand English residents always with it? Is it not blessed with its pickpockets and bookmakers all exclusively English? And from Boulogne all the way to Dinard in the summer time do not the restless, roving Britishers actually outnumber, and outstare, too, the resident sons and daughters of Gaul?

Eh bien, alors? How does it make itself that such curious national differences still subsist – the difference, for instance, between the flaring gin palace and the artistic Montmartre cafe;

between English prudery and French moral *sans-gene*; between London solidity and Parisian effervescence? . . .

. . . What a difference between these workmen and ours! The universal blue and white blouse is not conducive to smartness of aspect, yet he looks very alert, this Monsieur Jacques Bonhomme, and has an air of getting more fun out of life than Mister John Smith. If you become acquainted with him, you will find that he could sing amorous ditties and drinking songs, dance quadrilles, and make love before he had a hair on his lip; that he is inclined to gaiety and revolutions as a duck to water, and has infinitely more vigour, vivacity, and – yes, perhaps, vanity than his even Christian in Europe.

And how he does enjoy himself! See him on Sunday; what dinners he consumes with his family at the suburban restaurant! what good places they occupy at the theatre, and what pleasant drives they take in open carriages! How does he do it on his wages? Perhaps the fact that he never seems to get drunk may have something to do with it.

Incidentally, one would not regard him as likely ever to die of over-work. Observe this group of road-menders. Though the traffic seethe and roar about them, they chip-chip in a leisurely and unconcerned manner which is delightfully soothing to the nerves. But look you now: suddenly, *crenom de nom!* a heap of paving stones shows signs of collapse. Instantly – or thereabouts – the men spring to their feet, and strike attitudes of dismay. For half an hour – or thereabouts – they attitudinise, gesticulate, and scream altogether, in token of fear lest that heap of stones should fall. But not a man of them puts his hand to the heap to prevent the stones from falling.

Yet these Parisian workmen can do things. As a class they are quick, sensitive, innately artistic in all their perceptions, particularly as to details and finish, and though given to inordinate desire for originality of effect, their products, however showy or bizarre, are never unsightly. Behold the evidences of their taste and skill in the public buildings and shop windows. Their work does not show the rigidity, the ponderosity, the solidity which their English rival's products display; but you may take it that wherever effect depends on taste, the comparison is against us.

---

18   Paul Gauguin (French): 'The Character of the Danes' (1903)

I hate Denmark – its climate and its inhabitants – profoundly.

Oh, there are some good things in Denmark, that is undeniable. In Denmark they do a lot for education, science, and especially medicine. The hospital in Copenhagen can be considered one of the handsomest establishments of its kind, because of its size and above all for its cleanliness, which is first-class.

Let's pay that much tribute to them, especially since aside from that I can't see any but negative things. I beg your pardon, I was about to forget one thing: the houses are admirably built and equipped either to keep out the cold or for ventilation in the summer, and the city is pretty. I must also add that receptions in Denmark are generally held in the dining room, where one eats admirably. That's something anyhow, and it helps to pass the time. But don't let yourself be too bored by this monotonous kind of conversation: 'You, a powerful country, must find that we are far behind. We are so small. What do you think of Copenhagen, our museum, etc.? It's nothing very much.' All this is said so that you will say exactly the opposite; and you say it, of course, out of politeness

. . . I must say that in Denmark the system of getting engaged is a good thing in that it doesn't commit you to anything (people change fiances the way they change handkerchiefs), and, in addition, it has every appearance of love, liberty, and morality. You are engaged; so you can go out for a walk – even go travelling – the mantle of engagement covers everything. You can fool around with 'going-almost-all-the-way-but-not-quite,' which has the advantage, for both parties, of teaching them not to be careless and get into trouble. With each engagement the bird loses a lot of little feathers that grow back without anybody noticing. Very practical, the Danes.

---

19 Hermann Muthesius (German): 'The English House' (1904-5)

English domestic architecture today is an amalgamation of the revived tradition of old rural architecture and of the modern Arts and Crafts movement. But let me repeat once more that the modern English artistic movement has no trace of those fanciful, superfluous, and often affected ideas with which a part of the new continental movement is still engaged. Far from this, it tends more towards the primitive and the rustic; and here it fits particularly well with the type of traditional rural house. Moreover this outcome is perfectly to the taste of the Englishman for whom there is nothing better than plain simplicity, who finds the unspoilt original poetically attractive because it appeals to his rural tendencies and who finds random fanciful extravagances at their most obnoxious when he has to live daily surrounded by them. The Englishman in his house wants peace. A tidy coziness, fully developed comfort, that is what is important to him. A minimum of 'forms' and a maximum of peaceful, comfortable and yet lively atmosphere, that is what he aims for. His unalterable preference is for the rural and the rustic. Such accord seems to him to be a link with beloved Mother Nature, to whom, despite all higher cultures, the English nation has remained more faithful than any other people. And today's house is proof of this. The way in which it is situated far back from the road, surrounded by flower gardens, the way it opens itself behind broad, luxuriant lawns which exude the fresh vigour and calm of nature, the way in which its broadly spreading mass is more expressive of protection and shelter than for striving for pomp and architectonic deployment, the way in which it lies far away hidden from all civilisation and demands from the inhabitants the daily sacrifice of covering great distances (which they willingly undertake out of love), the way in which it fits so admirably into surrounding Nature in the happiness of its colouring and the solidity of its form: in all these ways it stands there today as cultural proof of the healthy tendencies of a nation which amid all its wealth and advances in civilisation has retained to a remarkable degree its appreciation of what is natural. Urban civilisation, with its destructive influences, with its senseless haste and press, with its hothouse stimulation of those impulses toward vanity which are latent in man, with its elevation of the refined, the nervous the abnormal, to unnatural proportions, all this has had practically no harmful effect on the English nation.

---

20   George Trumbull Ladd (American): 'On the Business Morals of Japan' (1908)

The one charge against the Japanese which is most loudly and frequently made, and which the friends who respect and admire them have most difficulty in answering, involves their conduct in commercial relations with other nations. Now that, having twice triumphed in foreign wars, they are entering in a larger way upon the rivalries of trade with foreigners, this charge has become more than ever emphatic and impressive. It is claimed that they do not keep promises; that they have scanty regard for the sacredness of the contract; that their commodities are not up to the sample; that engagements with them to furnish labor or its products are lightly rewarded; and that the pledged word is *not* in their case, as it is in the case of other nations of first-class commercial standing, equal to a bond. Especially are they deficient in the nobility which swears to its own hurt and changes not. In brief, at the very time that this gifted and ambitious people is eager to turn all its energies in the direction of economical development, it finds itself handicapped with the reputation of being deficient in the most essential economic virtues.

More than anywhere else, perhaps, in the civilized world this charge is aggressive, insistent, and bitter in spirit, on our own Pacific Coast. It is just now the custom there, moreover, to accentuate it by contrasting the commercial virtues and excel-lencies of the Chinese with the vices and failures in business morals of the Japanese. To this particular example of the general complaint there is indeed a comic as well as a serious side. The voice, clamorous and depreciative of everything from China, which rose to the heavens from San Francisco as its center has scarcely died out of our ears; the tales of insulting and brutal treatment of the 'pig-tailed' Oriental have only of late failed to enliven the papers of the entire Pacific coast. And these things were contemporaneous with words of respect and admiration for those wonderful neighbours of the Chinese, who were ready to cut their hair and their clothes, and to change their habits in business and in art, to adapt them to Western notions of what is civilized and respectable. But now the tables, in this part of the world at least, seem turned with a vengeance. What profound change in racial characteristics has so quickly taken place? Has the ancient and hitherto slow-moving dragon of China all at once taken wings and soared aloft toward heights scarcely yet attained by those of us who have a longer and more varied experience in the arts of 'high-fliers' in trade; while the Rising Sun has suffered a decline to the horizon above which the honesty, truthfulness, and fair dealing of Great Britain, Ger-many, and the United States are still so plainly to be seen? This is a question which deserves investigation as to facts, and, if possible, their explanation in case the facts can be discovered.

How much of the truth, then, is there in the charge that the business morals of the Japanese are of a relatively low order not only when compared with the greater commercial nations on the Western world, but even with their neighbor in the Orient, the Chinese?

. . . In accounting for this evil reputation, something – in certain cases much – is to be allowed for failure on both sides to understand each other's languages and methods of doing business. Moreover, if China and Japan were to exchange compliments with the Western World in regard to the conduct of business intercourse, they could tell tales of exaction, fraud, debased goods, and 'junk' of varied kinds palmed off upon the 'heathen' which would quite outmatch the most extravagant stories of the same kind told by the San Francisco and Seattle dealer, or the Chicago and New York importer of Oriental wares. That the cheating fell somehow within the lines of a contract – shrewdly worded to fit the case, and in a foreign language – naturally fails altogether to appease the anger or to apologize for the wrong. Besides, business dealings, carried on and consummated usually through foreign agents in the treaty or other ports, are by no means a sure and complete test, or perfect revelation, of the spirit of honesty, truthfulness, and fair-dealing which characterizes a nation at large. Neither is the jinrikisha-man or a keeper of a bazaar where foreigners buy cheap truck in Yokohama, more worthy to defame an entire nation than the 'cabby,' or the shopkeeper on the Strand or Fifth Avenue, in London or New York.

After all just apologies are made, however, we are forced back to the confession that the Japanese commercial classes, with whom foreigners have hitherto come into contact, have not the same high standard of business honor which characterizes the same classes in the United States or in northern Europe, or even in the treaty ports of China. What, now, is the explanation of this difference? The first and most profound reason is historical. It was during the Tokugawa period, for two hundred and fifty years previous to the expedition of Commodore Perry, that Japan was consolidating those social factors and aptitudes which have made possible its remarkable and unique career of the development during the last half-century. During this period the 'man of honor' would not, and could not, engage in business. There were, indeed, many honorable men in all the different trades and forms of business life. And the history of the period shows a little known but surprisingly skillful and elaborate organization of such affairs in 'Old Japan'. Still, it is true that until very recently 'men of honor', men who had the ideal of knightly character before them and who thought, above everything else, of attaining and maintaining this ideal, would not stoop to make their motive or main business in life the gaining of wealth. They despised rather than sought the making of money. The shopkeeper, with the innkeeper, the maker of sake, the Buddhist monk, and the peasant, belonged to a lower order – not so low, indeed, as the actor, but still quite distinctly apart from the samurai, or knightly gentlemen, whose rule of life was the *bushido*. To this day the more old-fashioned of the upper-class families in Japan, even where they are not able to disregard, not to say despise, the business classes, feel grieved and somewhat degraded by the intermarriage with them of a son or daughter.

It has been these samurai, and their sons and now their grandsons, who have chiefly made the 'New Japan'. From them have come the great statesmen and warriors – and the modern world has not known greater – who went abroad to observe, investigate, and study; and who returned to fill all the important and responsible government positions in education, in the army and navy, and in the most exacting forms of civil service. Of late years, but only of late years, they have turned themselves to business and to the economical development of their country. So that now the men of honor are going into those pursuits and forms of service their very title formerly forbade their undertaking; and not only so, but the sons of the classes formerly counted of the lower, and lowest, are being carefully educated in the ways, and in the accepted morals, of the modern business world. All this is rapidly changing, and has indeed already profoundly modified, the character of the business morals of Japan.

There is one particular, however, which demands a special consideration, if we would understand the Far East; and this is the standing and the value of the *contract* in modern business morals. Before instruction and experience, the Oriental does not appreciate, as do we, this business device. And, indeed, why should he? The Confucian ethic, as it reached its development in Japan, – and in Japan it was that it produced a higher type of manhood than in Korea or in China, – emphasized the principle of loyalty, or personal fidelity, as the leading principle of morality. Get, then, a true Japanese, high or low, old-fashioned or new-fashioned, committed to you loyally, in friendship or under a pledge of personal fidelity, and there is no other man on the face of the earth whom you may trust more implicitly, and to the death if need be, than him. But, as I have already said, it requires education and experience to make the same man understand why he should be faithful to a form of words which he has perhaps not thoroughly comprehended at the beginning; or when circumstances, known, it may be, by the other contracting party as likely to occur, but not possibly or easily foreseen by him, have quite unexpectedly rendered the keeping of the contract greatly to his hurt.

---

21 Dr Jacobus X (French): 'Analogy between the Industry and Habits of Prehistoric Times and those of Contemporary Savages' (1908)

A considerable analogy exists between the industry and manner of life of prehistorical savages on the one hand and of contemporary savages on the other. These similarities, which are often very striking, have been noticed by Lubbock in England and by Hamy in France, and had already been pointed out by Jussien, the naturalist, in 1723. The resemblances are in fact numerous and curious, and their number increases in proportion to the advance of prehistorical archaeology.

Letourneau enumerates a certain number of them, such as lance-heads made of obsidian stone axes, arrows, etc. of contemporary savages identical with those of their prehistoric ancestors. It is the same with the cups for grinding up colours, with the chiefs' staffs of command, with the mode of obtaining fire by striking a flint against a lump of ferruginous pyrites, with engravings and drawings upon the bones of large animals, with the manufacture of pieces of rude pottery, and, among savages who are unacquainted with the art of making burnt pottery, with the habit of boiling water by throwing into it red-hot stones, etc.

The Tasmanian and Australian aborigines are or were still in the broken-stone age, and a number of American tribes have not passed the shaped-stone age. The New Caledonians and Polynesians had reached the polished-stone period. The latter, however, were still ignorant of pottery, while the Papuans and Guaranis are ceramists and, like our ancestors of the polished-stone period, entrust their women with the task of moulding the clay by hand, without a potter's wheel.

The progress of the wild races is slow: thus, though the sea is the principal source of the food supply for the populations of Melanesia, many of them have not as yet discovered the use of the hook, which does not appear to have been thought of in Europe until the end of the polished-stone period . . .

It is not only in his habits that the savage of the present day resembles prehistoric man. Like him he possesses the greater part of the inferior anatomical characteristics. The most frequent of these characteristics are, – tibias shaped like the blade of a sabre, persistence of the Olecranian Fozamen, Pragnathism, diminished size of the cranium, thickness of its walls, existence of superciliary swellings, simplicity of intracranial cerebral impressions, wisdom teeth with five roots, like the jaw-bone of the Naulette, etc. The cranian evidence should not be appealed to without reserve. There are, in fact, savages with short heads and savages with elongated heads. It is however impossible to help remarking that dolichocephaly is a characteristic both of our quaternary ancestors and of the majority of the very belated races of our own times.

From all these analogies, which sometimes go as far as identity, Letourneau draws this conclusion: 'Inferior, contemporary races, generally speaking, are a reproduction of primitive humanity; prehistorical times live again under our own eyes, and the antiquity of the past is resuscitated in the antiquity of the present. Some human types, better endowed than the rest, have evoluted and gained more and more ground in the struggle for existence. These favoured races have thriven; their representatives have multiplied; they have created complex civilizations and formed a kind of abyss between themselves and the races which have remained stationary, or at least have only evoluted with the millenary slowness of the earliest ages. Man, gradually growing civilized, has come to despise and too often to exterminate the retarded human races, but no less are the latter living portraits of his ancestors.'

22 Government Official (British): 'The Striking Similarity between the Japanese and our Own People' (1910)

One curious similarity runs through the whole, that is, the striking similitude between the Japs and our own people. This resemblance manifests itself in manner, physical stamp, and the shape of the head. To anyone acquainted with the principles of phrenology the resemblance is very marked. This last point is indicated by the large proportion of the brain in front of and above the ear. These structural conditions are distinctive indications of considerable mental power, and are emphasised by the portraits of some of the most highly placed representatives. Taken as a whole, they constitute a good augury for the growth of sympathy between the East and the West.

G

---

23   Government Official (French): 'The Simple Taste of the English' (1912)

The English are excessively nationalistic and look, as far as possible, to their own country for their produce . . . Looking at their gross national product and their current resources, they feel they don't need to look abroad for products of art, which they are unable themselves to create. Their simple taste and their rationale of comfort harmonises well with the things they make in their vast factories, and it is this which explains the regrettable decline in exports [from France to Britain] over the past five years.

---

24   Clive Bell (British): 'Negro Sculpture' (c.1914)

Negro art has been treated with absurd contempt, we are all inclined now to overpraise it; and because I mean to keep my head shall doubtless by my best friends be called a fool. Judging from the available data – no great stock, by the way – I should say that Negro art was entitled to a place amongst the great schools, but that it was no match for the greatest. With the greatest I would compare it. I would compare it with the art of the supreme Chinese periods (from Han to Sung), with archaic Greek, with Byzantine, with Mahommedan, which, for archaeological purposes, begins under the Sassanians a hundred years and more before the birth of the prophet; I would compare it with Roman-esque and early Italian (from Giotto to Raffael); but I would place it below all these. On the other hand, when I consider the whole corpus of black art known to us, and compare it with Assyrian, Roman, Indian, true Gothic (not Romanesque, that is to say), or late Renaissance it seems to me that the blacks have the best of it. And, on the whole, I should be inclined to place West and Central African art at any rate on a level with Egyptian. Such sweeping classifications, however, are not to be taken too seriously. All I want to say is that, though the capital achievements of the greatest schools do seem to me to have an absolute superiority over anything Negro I have seen, yet the finest black sculpture is so rich in artistic qualities that it is entitled to a place beside them.

I write thinking mainly of sculpture, because it was an exhibition of sculpture that set me off. It should be remembered, however, that perhaps the most perfect achievements of these savages are to be found amongst their textiles and basket-work.

Here their exquisite taste and sense of quality and their unsur-
passed gift for filling a space are seen to greatest advantage,
while their shortcomings lie almost hid. But it is their sculpture
which, at the moment, excites us most, and by it they may fairly
be judged. Exquisiteness of quality is its most attractive characteristic. Touch one of these African figures and it will remind
you of the rarest Chinese porcelain. What delicacy in the artist's
sense of relief and modelling is here implied! What tireless
industry and patience! Run your hand over a limb, or a torso, or,
better still, over some wooden vessel; there is no flaw, no break
in the continuity of the surface; the thing is alive from end to
end. And this extraordinary sense of quality seems to be universal amongst them. I think I never saw a genuine nigger object
that was vulgar – except, of course, things made quite recently
under European direction. This is a delicious virtue, but it is a
precarious one. It is precarious because it is not self-conscious:
because it has not been reached by the intelligent understanding of an artist, but springs from the instinctive taste of primitive people. I have seen an Oxfordshire labourer work himself
beautifully a handle for his hoe, in the true spirit of a savage
and an artist, admiring and envying all the time the lifeless
machine-made article hanging, out of his reach, in the village
shop. The savage gift is precarious because it is unconscious.
Once let the black or the peasant become acquainted with the
showy utensils of industrialism, or with cheap, realistic painting and sculpture, and, having no critical sense wherewith to
protect himself, he will be bowled over for a certainty. He will
admire; he will imitate; he will be undone.

At the root of this lack of artistic selfconsciousnesss lies the
defect which accounts for the essential inferiority of Negro to
the very greatest art. Savages lack self-conciousness and the
critical sense because they lack intelligence. And because they
lack intelligence they are incapable of profound conceptions.
Beauty, taste, quality, and skill, all are here; but profundity of
vision is not. And because they cannot grasp complicated ideas
they fail generally to create organic wholes. One of the chief
characteristics of the very greatest artists is this power of creating wholes which, as wholes, are of infinitely greater value than
the sum of their parts. That, it seems to me, is what savage
artists generally fail to do.

Also, they lack originality. I do not forget that Negro sculptors have had to work in a very strict convention. They have
been making figures of tribal gods and fetishes, and have been
obliged meticulously to respect the tradition. But were not

European Primitives and Buddhists similarly bound, and did they not contrive to circumvent their doctrinal limitations? That the African artists seem hardly to have attempted to conceive the figure afresh for themselves and realize in wood a personal vision does, I think, imply a definite want of creative imagination. Just how serious a defect you will hold this to be will depend on the degree of importance you attach to complete self-expression. Savage artists seem to express themselves in details. You must seek their personality in the quality of their relief, their modulation of surface, their handling of material, and their choice of ornament. Seek, and you will be handsomely rewarded; in these things the niggers have never been surpassed. Only when you begin to look for that passionate affirmation of a personal vision which we Europeans, at any rate, expect to find in the greatest art will you run the risk of being disappointed. It will be then, if ever, that you will be tempted to think that these exquisitely gifted black artists are perhaps as much like birds building their nests as men expressing their profoundest emotions.

---

25 Hugh Kennedy (Irish): 'The Design of the Great Seal of Saorstat Eireann' (1924)

The State needs a Seal, and, inasmuch as its sealed instruments must frequently speak abroad, as for instance to proclaim the authority of a specially empowered representative, its seal must be distinctive in character; while, as it declares an Act of State, it must be cast in a fitting dignity of design. So soon as the Saorstat attained the status of international recognition, it became necessary for the Government to provide the paraphernalia, without which this Cinderella of the world politic become *debutante* could not maintain her proper position in the Society of her Sister Nations, and very important among these paraphernalia was the Great Seal.

The Seal of the Saorstat must be individual and characteristic, at once recognisable as of Ireland, and it must be dignified and worthy to speak for an ancient nation. There are several emblems commonly associated with our people, some indeed through tawdry sentiment and sickly verse, but one stands out and is recognised everywhere, whether mute in subjection or ringing out a note of hope in liberty, as the symbol of our country. It was not necessary then to seek out a device. The harp has been and is the National device and symbol of Ireland, and every design of a seal for the Saorstat must start from that fact.

Modern European national devices, coats of arms, and flags are largely the product of the curious and quite artificial science of Heraldry, a body of quaint laws, regarded as very imperative by the archaically-minded persons who choose to bend the knee to their authority, Norman and feudal in their development. The Ireland of the Gael, however, throws back to ancient chivalry of its own, and the Government of the Saorstat felt that there was no compelling reason for bending the design of the Seal of State to the strange code and jargon which had no historical root in this country. Indeed, had the Government acted otherwise, they should first have scrapped the tricolour which had been the flag of our fight for freedom during three-quarters of a century, for it shocks the Heralds by flouting one of the fundamental laws of their code.

The decision then was to take the harp as the National symbol and set it in a frame of characteristic but sympathetic Irish design.

But there are harps and harps, and when it was decided that the harp should be the centre-piece of the design, it still remained to select the type of harp which should be enshrined. A poem of Moore's and a painting by Maclise have thrown a certain glamour or romance around the bastard design of a harp which the British Heralds inserted in the British Royal Arms, and which has often been displayed on green flags and blue flags and otherwise as if it were the legitimate emblem of Eire. Earlier British Heralds had used another conventionalised type of harp, ornamented with a lion's head, somewhat after the pattern of the Hathor with which we have become familiar in pictures of the tomb of Tutankhamen. This harp is embroidered on tabards of the seventeenth century. These and other designs which were submitted to the Government were rejected in favour of the so-called Brian Boru harp which, in antiquity, in history, and in strength and loveliness stands on a plane by itself.

---

26 John Ryan (British): 'Japanese Methods' (1928)

How do the Japanese do it? The Japanese are steadily reducing the number of standard cloths, a method which has proved very successful in other trades, reducing costs. I will give you a few quotations. 'The great strength of the cotton industry in Japan is to a large extent due to the close connection that exists between the various interests involved, i.e., the importers of raw cotton, the spinners and weavers, and exporters of piece-goods, whilst another important factor also making for strength is the fact that these interests are very largely concentrated in a relatively small number of powerful firms.'

'Unless Lancashire is prepared to cater for the bulk of business on lines similar to the Japanese, it must be content with the mere fringe of the luxury end of the trade. In order to recapture the large bulk of trade, Lancashire must adopt measures of bulk production and distribution.'

---

27 André Demaison (French): 'A Visit to the French International Colonial Exposition, Paris' (1931)

I am certain, from the first steps and until the end of this visit – which will require time and frequent stops – you will go from one surprise to another. But here you will not find the exploitation of the baser instincts of a vulgar public. Merely the name of the man who presides at the destinies of this exposition is proof of its uncontested grandeur. Marshal Lyautey, and Governor General Olivier and all their collaborators, have considered you, dear Visitor, as a man of good taste. No monstrosities of the side-show; no improper dances; no fake exoticism, such has discredited other colonial expositions. Instead, a realistic reconstitution of tropical life, with all its true picturesqueness and color. Here will be more diversions than you ever dreamed of. In addition, colonial attractions of quality, fetes both night and day, the splendour of which will astonish, will bring repose, will give spice to the more serious aspects of the exposition.

If you are a manufacturer or a business man, annoyed daily by problems of a commercial nature, the Exposition will present for you an inventory, as complete as possible, of the resources offered for your activity.

Are you an artist? Here you will find new lines, new colors, new sonorities. On several occasions during French history, persons and objects coming from exotic countries have greatly influenced our fashions, our art, our literature. Here, direct contact with these bewitching realities will provoke in your homeland, you who see and who think, unaccustomed resonances.

Are you a worker? an artisan? a farmer? a skilled mechanic? Whether you work in a shop or in the field, this spectacle will show you that other men, different from you, and far, far away, also work and suffer and succeed, just like you, although their labor be dissimilar. You will recognize the raw material which passes every day through your hands, the material which comes from secret and sumptuous forests, from endless plains, from high mountains the existence of which you never suspected.

This communion of work, of work from day to day across vast spaces, will create a current of human solidarity which will not be, dear Visitor, one of the least of the effects of this exposition.

And you, young men, young women? For you, the exposition presents a grandiose lesson. It enlarges the moral and material horizon which satisfied your parents but which is too small for your aspirations. How, in effect, can you disinterest yourself of the life of our colonies, you who find the world with its wealth just big enough for your ambition? Trade between our far-away territories and France surpass 17 billion francs each year, out of a 36 billion total. With better methods, which will be suggested to you during your visits, this figure will shortly be still greater. There is a place for everybody at one end or the other of this chain. Each increase in the material relations between our colonies and France corresponds to greater security as regard foreign markets. A man is strong? isn't he? when he has many friends? When a man possesses his own field and garden, doesn't he get better prices elsewhere?

But, material advantages, although necessary to man, are not everything. Thanks to our protection, note this well, millions of men, women and children have been delivered from the nightmare of slavery and death. Do not forget that, before the arrival of the Frenchman in African territories, might ruled right, woman was only a beast of burden, children practically nothing at all. Even where we found the remains of an antique civilization built on outworn principles and antiquated forms of government, what miraculous transformations we have effected! The system of justice was venal, the state of war was chronic, the populations annihilated by famine and sickness. Commerce was limited to insignificant barters, the government was anti-foreign and ruled by red tape, while the fate of the poor was lamentable.

Today, the manner of life of these peoples is much closer to our own standards than you imagine. Gaze upon our achievements! Regard these peoples! Listen to their songs, taste their national dishes which they offer you at a bargain price. Verily, peoples do not speak to each other only by word of mouth; impressions are not all due to the eyesight .

In truth, it is the evolution of these peoples that you will follow, the rungs in the ladder leading to higher and better things. All the documents which capture your attention . . . well, I can't enumerate them here. Five volumes, like the present guide, would be insufficient. Further, each colony, each private exhibitor, adds to the information about French colonization methods. I merely hope to initiate you, by reason and sentiment, in new manifestations of exotic life, to their so varied forms.

You will understand, of course, that the heroic period of colonization is over. The patient and efficient construction of new countries requires new qualities other than warfare. At the present hour, to colonize means: *to engage in the commerce of ideas and things, not with beings burdened with moral and physical misery, but with well-to-do persons, who are free and happy.*

A bit of advice. As you behold strange things, foreign to you, do not laugh either at customs or at men which you do not understand. The teasing, ill-considered laughter of certain Frenchmen has created more enemies for us than cruel defeats or onerous treaties. The ideas of other men are frequently your own, but expressed in different fashion. Think on it! May the highest joy animate you, dear Visitor, and may it follow you after your visits.

On entering the exposition, I can give you no better password than that coined by Marshal Lyautey, the great Frenchman of such high human conceptions: 'In this exposition, you must find – with the lessons of the past instruction for the present – above all lessons for the future. I desire visitors to leave this exposition, resolved to live and do for France – always better, always greater, wider, and more supple.'

---

28 Adolf Hitler (German): 'Greeks and Romans Suddenly Stand Close to Teutons' (1933)

It is therefore no surprise that each politically historical epoch searches in its art for the link with a period of equally heroic past. Greeks suddenly stand close to Teutons . . . Because it is better to imitate the good things than it is to produce new bad things, the intuitive creations of the people under consideration can without doubt fulfil the educational and leading mission as a style today.

**29   Gordon Russell (British): 'The English and Industrial Design'
(1946)**

[I]ndustrial design has lagged behind. Those of us who have
been pioneering in this field have mostly been doing a job
singularly like a corporal and two men trying to push a steam-
roller into the foothills of the Himalayas. Before it is possible to
formulate a workable scheme for improving this curious state of
affairs it is essential to know something of the background
which has led to it. Some Englishmen take it for granted and
discuss it as being relatively of small importance. 'We are hard-
headed practical people' they say. 'We do things – important
things, like building bridges or aeroplanes. Can you beat our
best motor-cars? We've never been any good at trying to play at
being long-haired artists, or musicians. It isn't our role in life at
all, and never was!'

But if we look back a few centuries we see that this isn't true
at all. English architecture, especially domestic architecture,
reached an astonishingly high level in the seventeenth and
eighteenth centuries. And so did all the things that go into
houses; clocks, furniture, chintzes, table glass, pottery. Our
towns were not only beautiful, but workable. Our general level
was high and it was high in design, in workmanship and in
material. Progress was sustained and reached an ever-widening
circle of people.

Then came the nineteenth century, and between the years
1830 and 1880 a great and serious decline in many standards set
in, accompanied by an astonishing volume of money wealth for
some people, a general rise for many and great poverty for a few.
It was quite natural that William Morris, poet artist, social
reformer, should ascribe this to the introduction of machinery.
The misuse of the machine was at the bottom of it: the fact that
the machine made it possible to make so much money that
people seemed to forget that the most important products of
industry, that is, men and goods, existed.

This was a nightmare from which we are awakening, and our
only consolation is that our mistakes, as industrial pioneers, are
writ plain for all to see and we hope, to profit by. For it must be
obvious that a system which does not offer men a full life
cannot be a good system. How can it hope to produce goods of
high quality, if it takes no account of men? This is a social
problem. Good design – which is an integral part of quality, as
important as good workmanship and good material – is an
outward and visible sign of a good standard of living, a real

179

standard of living, not just so much wages a week. It will not grow out of an unjust system. Sweated labour, scamped workmanship, lying advertisements, bad conditions generally do not provide the soil out of which good industrial design can grow. We must get fundamental conditions right first.

I think it cannot be said too often or too strongly that it is not just a matter of paying for good design instead of bad design. You cannot decide to make the change and then do it all overnight, for it presupposes a fresh approach to the problem. Good design is not just a sales stunt, which can be run for a bit and then dropped if figures begin to fall off. I believe most sincerely that it is necessary – or perhaps I should say it will be very soon – if sales are going to be maintained. But that is not its justification, which is, quite bluntly, that you cannot live a really civilized life without it.

In England the eighteenth century made goods beautifully in small quantities, the nineteenth century made goods in large quantities, our century must show that it is possible to make goods beautifully in large quantities.

---

30   Richard J. Neutra (American): 'Three Points of Un-Americanism' (1952)

Americans, we know, can be divided into two types; the ones who think that they are as good as anyone else, and those others who think that they are better than everybody else. We, who are living here in the Home of the Brave, have not all desirable recognition for our absolute superiority over the rest of the world; in fact some ignorant foreigners cling to some prejudicial doubts about the subject. However this may be, there is really no doubt that we are quite *de facto* living in the home of an industrial technology which in output is leading the world (God knows where!). And that has quite a bearing, of course, on the architect and architecture. Even those who hate us – and lots of people seem to do it with gusto – admit that we are living in the shadow of a hectic industrial know-how. They also admit that we have another speciality. We have, in the lower portion of Manhattan, a short and rather narrow street, walled off by sky-high buildings which is verily recognized all over the world as the main prop of our propaganda, and world finance. Finance naturally has also a great deal to do with the situation of our American architecture because construction costs money.

Ours is a time when American and Un-American attitudes are widely discussed. And so we should like to state three points of Un-Americanism to set us off properly from the foreigners who try to build. First of all, it is – in normal times – very Un-American to have any shortage of materials. Second, a lack of equipment is very Un-American. Rather, we have all the gadgets in the world, from those for bulldozing the hills and bullying the landscape, to those for electrically grinding the garbage and flushing it out of our mentioned miracle kitchens. And third, of course, it is very Un-American not to be financed, not to have means.

All these things are not so common in other countries. We here are not exemplary in living without ample means like these British and those Italians, who put up with a severe shortage of materials, with a lack of equipment. We wouldn't have any famous know-how, in such a case. But usually we don't have to. As a rule we have had all those things to roll in. Yet with all these means, it must be admitted to somewhat surprised visitors, that we have not exactly solved our own situation or broadly achieved the good life.

---

31 Wilbur Zelinsky (American): 'American Culture' (1973)

It would be difficult to imagine a culture more efficiently programmed for expediting progress towards the most advanced technologies and socio-economic organisations . . . There is an irresistable urge to achieve – and proclaim – the quantifiably superlative – the biggest, the highest, costliest, loudest or fastest, frequently without any dollar and cents justification.

---

32 Edward W. Said (American): 'Orientalism' (1978)

By Orientalism I mean several things, all of them, in my opinion, interdependent. The most readily accepted designation for Orientalism is an academic one, and indeed the label still serves in a number of academic institutions. Anyone who teaches, writes about, or researches the Orient – and this applies whether the person is an anthropologist, sociologist, historian, or philologist – either in its specific or its general aspects, is an Orientalist, and what he or she does is Orientalism. Compared with *Oriental studies* or *area studies* it is true that the term *Orientalism* is less preferred by specialists today, both because it is too vague and general and because it connotes the high-handed executive attitude of nineteenth-century and early-twentieth-century European colonialism. Nevertheless books are written and congresses held with 'the Orient' as their main focus, with the Orientalist in his new or old guise as their main authority. The point is that even if it does not survive as it once did, Orientalism lives on academically through its doctrines and theses about the Orient and the Oriental.

Related to this academic tradition, whose fortunes, transmigrations, specializations, and transmissions are in part the subject of this study, is a more general meaning of Orientalism. Orientalism is a style of thought based upon an ontological and epistemological distinction made between 'the Orient' and (most of the time) 'the Occident.' Thus a very large mass of writers, among whom are poets, novelists, philosophers, political theorists, economists, and imperial administrators, have accepted the basic distinction between East and West as the starting point for elaborate theories, epics, novels, social descriptions, and political accounts concerning the Orient, its people, customs, 'mind,' destiny, and so on. *This* Orientalism can accommodate Aeschylus, say, and Victor Hugo, Dante and Karl Marx. A little later in this introduction I shall deal with the methodological problems one encounters in so broadly construed a 'field' as this.

The interchange between the academic and the more or less imaginative meanings of Orientalism is a constant one, and since the late eighteenth century there has been a considerable, quite disciplined – perhaps even regulated – traffic between the two. Here I come to the third meaning of Orientalism, which is something more historically and materially defined than either of the other two. Taking the late eighteenth century as a very roughly defined starting point Orientalism can be discussed and analyzed as the corporate institution for dealing with the Orient – dealing with it by making statements about it, authorizing views of it, describing it, by teaching it, settling it, ruling over it: in short, Orientalism as a Western style for dominating, restructuring, and having authority over the Orient. I have found it useful here to employ Michel Foucault's notion of a discourse, as described by him in *The Archaeology of Knowledge* and in *Discipline and Punish,* to identify Orientalism. My contention is that without examining Orientalism as a discourse one cannot possibly understand the enormously systematic discipline by which European culture was able to manage – and even produce – the Orient politically, sociologically, militarily, ideologically, scientifically, and imaginatively during the post-Enlightenment period. Moreover, so authoritative a position did Orientalism have that I believe no one writing, thinking, or acting on the Orient could do so without taking account of the limitations on thought and action imposed by Orientalism. In brief, because of Orientalism the Orient was not (and is not) a free subject of thought or action. This is not to say that Orientalism unilaterally determines what can be said about the Orient, but that it is the whole network of interests inevitably brought to bear on (and therefore always involved in) any occasion when that peculiar entity 'the Orient' is in question. How this happens is what this book tries to demonstrate. It also tries to show that European culture gained in strength and identity by setting itself off against the Orient as a sort of surrogate and even underground self.

---

33   Martin J. Weiner (American): 'The English and Progress' (1981)

For a long time the English have not felt comfortable with 'progress'. As one social analyst has perceived, 'progress' is a word that in England has come to possess a curiously ambiguous emotive power. 'It connotes tendencies we accept, even formally approve, yet of which we are privately suspicious.' It is a historic irony that the nation that gave birth to the Industrial Revolution, and exported it throughout the world, should have become embarrassed at the measure of its success. The English nation even became ill at ease enough with its prodigal progeny to deny its legitimacy by adopting a conception of Englishness that virtually excluded industrialism.

This suspicion of material and technological development and this symbolic exclusion of industrialism were intimately related in Britain. They appeared in the course of the Industrial Revolution, but instead of fading away when the new society established itself, they persisted and indeed were extended and strengthened. In later years of Victoria's reign they came to form a complex, entrenched cultural syndrome, pervading 'educated opinion'. The idealisation of material growth and technical innovation that had been emerging received a check, and was more and more pushed back by the contrary ideals of stability, tranquillity, closeness to the past, and 'nonmaterialism'. An 'English way of life' was defined and widely accepted; it stressed nonindustrial, noninnovative and nonmaterial qualities, best encapsulated in rustic imagery – 'England is the country', in Stanley Baldwin's phrase (by this time already a cliché). This countryside of the mind was everything industrial society was not – ancient, slow-moving, stable, cozy and 'spiritual'. The English genius, it declared, was (despite appearances) not economical or technical, but social and spiritual; it did not lie in inventing, producing or selling, but in preserving, harmonising and moralising. The English character was not naturally progressive, but conservative; its greatest task – and achievement – lay in taming and 'civilising' the dangerous engines of progress it had unwittingly unleashed.

---

34 Martin Bernal (British): 'The Invention of the Aryan Model' (1987)

These volumes are concerned with two models of Greek history: one viewing Greece as essentially European or Aryan, and the other seeing it as Levantine, on the periphery of the Egyptian and Semitic cultural area. I call them the 'Aryan' and the 'Ancient' models. The 'Ancient' model was conventional amongst Greeks in the Classical and Hellenistic ages. According to it, Greek culture had arisen as the result of colonisation, around 1500 B.C., by Egyptians and Phoenicians who had civilised the native inhabitants. Furthermore, Greeks had continued to borrow heavily from near Eastern cultures . . .

If I am right in urging the overthrow of the Aryan Model and its replacement by the revised ancient one, it will be necessary not only to rethink the fundamental bases of 'Western Civilization', but also to recognise the penetration of racism and 'continental chauvinism' into all our historiography, or philosophy of writing. The Ancient Model had no major 'internal' deficiencies, or weaknesses in explanatory power. It was overthrown for external reasons. For eighteenth and nineteenth century Romantics and racists it was simply intolerable for Greece, which was seen not merely as the epitome of Europe but also as its pure childhood, to have been the result of the mixture of native Europeans and colonising Africans and Semites. Therefore the Ancient Model had to be overthrown and replaced by something more acceptable.

35 Javier Mariscal (Spanish): 'The Spanish, the Arabs, the Americans' (c.1990)

The concept is of the Arabs having conquered Spain in a single battle, but it wasn't really like that. It was more at the level of the village people who changed their way of life very slowly under the influence of really very few people of the Arab race. To say that the Arabs conquered Spain would be like saying that the Americans had invaded us in the late twentieth century. Of course we are being Americanised. Like all countries, we have Madonna, we have supermarkets and Fords, motorways and Coca-Cola, but it's much more complex than calling it 'an invasion'. It's a question of people taking on elements of different cultures that seem attractive, and adopting them as their own.

8

THE MODERN MOVEMENT

Had this volume been compiled twenty years ago, it is likely that this chapter, much expanded, would have comprised the entire volume. For much of the century, modernism has dominated the literature on design, just as it has throughout the visual arts. There are reasons for this. Many of the most interesting ideas on design come to us from modernists; modernism provides us with a wide selection of named designers, who fit nicely into movements and who are broadly researchable in the same way that practitioners in the fine arts are. Modernism has its heart in architectural practice, which has long had established academic mechanisms. And modernism, for academics brought up in universities and colleges of art and design, *looks* better in the formal sense.

At this point in time, the historian's brief has rightly expanded well beyond the Modern Movement. But we should not underplay the enormous impact that it has indeed had on the manufactured environment. During the 1920s, when Le Corbusier was writing his most vibrant modernist texts, one would have had to search the suburbs of Paris to find a single example of modernist building. The situation wasn't much different on the eve of the Second World War. But between 1945 and 1975, there was hardly a building erected in Europe or America of any size which did not display the stylistic and technical mannerisms of the Modern Movement. Whether the pioneer modernists approved of these buildings or not, the success of the style can not be doubted; it is the most prolific of all time.

The movement fared less well in design areas other than architecture, but, nevertheless, large numbers of significant examples of it have peppered the commodity market for decades. The interesting feature in this regard however, is the extent to which modernism as a *concept* dominated to a far greater extent than modernism as an *actual design idiom*. Indeed, between 1945 and 1975, there was barely a 'modernism' debate at all with regard to products, so powerful and complacent did modernist design reformers become in the field of discussion. In terms of bought and sold goods in the actual marketplace however, populism and historicism never lost their grip. Most urban and suburban homes in Europe and America never really accepted the pure and simple sleekness of the Modern Movement. In this sense, the rise of the postmodern, plurality lobby, rather than creating a new opposition to modernism, gave voice (and theory) to what was, in effect, an ongoing, silent consensus.

The passages quoted here in the first part of the chapter are typical examples of modernist principles and ideas. The later part of the chapter contains two things: first, passages which attempt to sum up what exactly modernism was in a context broader than design, and, second, are anti-modernist passages which typify the attack it came under from the 1970s onwards.

See also
Chapter 1 for discussion of decoration and modernism
Chapter 2 for the moral and political background to modernism
Chapter 3 for modernism and technology
Chapter 5 for attitudes to consumption
Chapter 6 for modernism and the home
Chapter 7: for Design from countries outside Europe and America
Chapter 9 for modernist aesthetics

---

1   Siegfried Bing (German, resident in France): 'Art Nouveau' (1902)

It was evident that the future of this new-born movement was in great danger. The only way to save it from total collapse was to endeavor to make it follow a fixed direction, carefully marked out; to keep it within the bounds of sobriety and good sense, avoiding the extravagances of exuberant imaginations and relying for its salvation upon these two fundamental rules. *Each article to be strictly adapted to its proper purpose; harmonies to be sought for in lines and color.* It was necessary to resist the mad idea of throwing off all associations with the past, and to proclaim that, on the contrary, everything produced by your predecessors is an example for us, not, assuredly, for its form to be servilely copied, but in order that the spirit which animated the authors should give us inspiration. Things which we call ancient were supremely modern at the time they were made. To none of our ancestors would it have occurred to look backward for the purpose of repeating what artists of former periods had invented to suit the habits and customs of their own day; but neither would he have tried to do anything more than take up the work at the point where his predecessor had left it, and in his turn develop it logically to meet the general spirit of the age in which he was living.

There was only one way in which these theories could be put into practice – namely, by having the articles made under my personal direction, and securing the assistance of such artists as seemed best disposed to carry out my ideas. The thousand ill-assorted things that I had collected together in a haphazard way gave place, little by little, to articles produced in my own workshops, according to the following program, to the exclusion of all other considerations. Thoroughly impregnate oneself anew with the old French tradition; try to pick up the thread of that tradition, with all its grace, elegance, sound logic and purity, and give it new developments, just as if the thread had not been broken for nearly a century; strive to realize what our distant predecessors would do if they were alive to-day – that is, enrich the old patrimony with a spirit of modernness, bearing in mind the eternal law which ordains that everything which fails to keep progressing is doomed to perish.

Far be it from me to imagine that nothing good can be produced except in the way which I conceive to be the right one. In the wide field now open each of us can sow his seed according to the fruits he wishes to gather. The only danger lies in the growth of rank weeds, impudently thrusting themselves to the front and choking the tender young plants just springing up. By 'rank weeds' I mean all those crude imitations, shaped without regard to the most elementary rules of logic and given the name of 'Art Nouveau'; all that parasitic vegetation which, as yet, prevents hesitating spirits from seeing that the time has come for us to shake off our foolish inertia, and that there is now no longer any reason why our decorative arts should not recover their full freedom of expansion and flourish as gloriously as they did in former times.

2   Alfredo Melani (Italian): 'The New Art' (1902)

New Art requires consciences that are free, artists who think and who warm themselves by beauty's blaze. Therefore it puts copyists to flight and welcomes those souls who are trusting and strong. One has to be strong to resist, and it is necessary, nowadays, to resist: to resist the inroads of the opposition, who strive to defeat us on every front. Nor do I deny that there are men of worth among our adversaries, for there are. And I have heard New Art decried for being limited and narrow in its aspirations and for harboring the germs of decadence. The floral! they say to us, why always the floral? It is as ancient as the world. Agreed. It is not necessary to go far afield. The Duomo in Milan is full of leaves and flowers, but it is not New Art; and this, the Gothic feeling for flowers and leaves, is not the modern taste, neither this nor that. I can understand that Ruskin, the 'ethereal Ruskin,' as Carlyle called him, did feel the poetry of flowers and championed it; I am aware that William Morris designed splendid floral compositions; but that is a personal event, not New Art, or rather, not all of New Art. Even you readers also love and draw flowers, and for this?

Gentlemen, New Art is not all floral; as a matter of fact, Van de Velde, one of the apostles of modern beauty, does what is the contrary of floral, the linear; and the French, those bizarre wits, with a very effective turn of phrase, described the new style of the Belgian Van de Velde, also cultivated in Germany and Austria, as *l'art à coups de fouet*, whiplash art. Think of a whip when it cracks; it produces agitated, sinewy, serpentine lines: the lines of Van de Velde's art.

So, I have made clear to you, two forms of New Art: the floral and the linear. You find me another one, and I will be happy to express my satisfaction.

This, finally, will show you that New Art, which is based on freedom, welcomes all artists who build their productions on their own personalities.

---

3   P. Janak (Czech): 'Cubist-Applied Art' (1911-12)

Formerly art was used to create a cushion, a jewel, and so on. Now creative art expresses itself in the conception of a teapot, a tray, etc. It is important that art should consciously move towards the form itself in order that new ideas about forms and the relationships between them can be discovered, and so that the value and regularity of the form can be ascertained by trying out variations of it in differing environments; realizing a particular form in one material is not enough: the form – the substance of stylistic composition must be reduced to its essentials, to an abstraction which is then valid in all materials (timber, glass, stone, and so on) having the ability by means of its shape, to overcome all these substances.

In this way creative activity in the applied arts is helping to resolve architectural problems: it works over and supplements the experiences gained in architecture; architecture expresses plastically certain large wholes and complicated intersections of energies, while a candlestick, a bowl, or a teapot provide opportunities for resolving, on a small scale, similar problems taking into account shape, size, etc. which make it possible to realize our Cubist opinion concerning mass and its volume.

---

4   F. T. Marinetti (Italian): 'Initial Manifesto of Futurism' (1912)

1. We shall sing the love of danger, the habit of energy and boldness.

2. The essential elements of our poetry shall be courage, daring, and rebellion.

3. Literature has hitherto glorified thoughtful immobility, ecstasy and sleep; we shall extol aggressive movement, feverish insomnia, the double quick step, the somersault, the box on the ear, the fisticuff.

4. We declare that the world's splendour has been enriched by a new beauty; the beauty of speed. A racing motor-car, its frame adorned with great pipes, like snakes with explosive breath . . . a roaring motor-car, which looks as though running on shrapnel, is more beautiful than the VICTORY OF SAMOTHRACE.

5. We shall sing of the man at the steering wheel, whose ideal stem transfixes the Earth, rushing over the circuit of her orbit.

6. The poet must give himself with frenzy, with splendour and with lavishness, in order to increase the enthusiastic fervour of the primordial elements.

7. There is no more beauty except in strife. No masterpiece without aggressiveness. Poetry must be a violent onslaught upon the unknown forces, to command them to bow before man.

8. We stand upon the extreme promontory of the centuries! . . . Why should we look behind us, when we have to break in the mysterious portals of the Impossible? Time and Space died yesterday. Already we live in the absolute, since we have already created speed, eternal and ever-present.

9. We wish to glorify War – the only health giver of the world – militarism, patriotism, the destructive arm of the Anarchist, the beautiful Ideas that kill, the contempt for woman.

10. We wish to destroy the museums, the libraries, to fight against moralism, feminism and all opportunistic and utilitarian meannesses.

11. We shall sing of the great crowds in the excitement of labour, pleasure or rebellion; of the multi-coloured and polyphonic surf of revolutions in modern capital cities; of the nocturnal vibration of arsenals and workshops beneath their violent electric moons; of the greedy stations swallowing smoking snakes; of factories suspended from the clouds by their strings of smoke; of bridges leaping like gymnasts over the diabolical cutlery of sunbathed rivers; of adventurous liners scenting the horizon; of broad chested locomotives prancing on the rails, like huge steel horses bridled with long tubes; and of the gliding flight of aeroplanes, the sound of whose screw is like the flapping of flags and the applause of an enthusiastic crowd.

It is in Italy that we launch this manifesto of violence, destructive and incendiary, by which we this day found Futurism, because we would deliver Italy from its canker of professors, archaeologists, cicerones and antiquaries.

---

5 Paul Scheerbart (German): 'Glass Architecture' (1914)

If we wish to raise our culture to a higher level, we are forced for better or for worse to transform our architecture. And this will be possible only if we remove the enclosed quality from the spaces within which we live. This can be done only through the introduction of glass architecture that lets sunlight and the light of the Moon and stars into our rooms not merely through a few windows, but simultaneously through the greatest possible number of walls that are made entirely of glass – coloured glass. The new environment that we shall thereby create must bring with it a new culture.

---

6 Lyonel Feininger (American, resident in Germany 1887-1937): 'Opposition to the Bauhaus' (1919)

So much has to be attended to in a day, so much to be talked over with Gropius, the works of the students to be inspected – by the way, I have another pupil. At my studio door now my name testifies to my presence. When I got in this morning, there were about a dozen young people goggling at my card. Funny conditions prevail. The school is crowded with male and female students who are all doing more or less as they please. An undercurrent of individualism is strongly evident. The intrigue against Gropius is becoming very pointed and naturally also against myself. The city government is thrown into a ferment. It would almost seem as if they were willing to make an end of us by refusing us subsidies. This evening there will be a meeting of our antagonists, and they have announced a fight at daggers drawn. These now are the 'protectors of the Fatherland,' the Pan-Germans! And although our affair concerns art only, they are dragging party politics into it. The mere fact of having changed the name of the art school to 'Bauhaus' has been enough to enrage them. The guilds are also afraid of us, of impending rivalry in their field of crafts, and are moving in closed ranks against Gropius. The director of the museum in Erfurt, on the other hand, is on the side of Gropius and myself. He is expected to talk this evening at the meeting, to tell them some things plainly, and stand up for *Sturm* expressionism in his speech.

---

7 **Theo van Doesburg (Dutch): 'De Stijl Manifesto: Towards a Newly Shaped World' (1921)**

The creation of a new world has commenced. Capitalists are deceivers and so are the Socialists. The former want to possess, and so do the latter. The former seek to swallow large amounts of money, large numbers of human beings and many steaks; The latter wish to swallow the former. Which is worse? Will either succeed?

We do not care in the least.

We know just one thing; only the exponents of the new spirit are sincere. Their wish is solely to give. Gratuitously. They arise among all nations, among all countries. They do not boast in deceiving phrases. They do not call each other 'brother', 'maestro' or 'partisan'. Theirs is the language of the mind, and in this manner they understand each other.

The creators of a new mentality for our time do not found sects, churches or schools.

In the old world spiritual concentration (Christ) and material concentration (Capitalism), *property,* represented the axes around which everyone rotated. *Today, however, the spiritual concentration has been dispersed.* Yet exponents of the new creative mind are linked together through a common inner life.

There is no escape for Europe. Spiritual concentration and property, intellectual and materialism individualism, were the basis of the old Europe. It has imprisoned itself within those ideas, and it cannot liberate itself. The situation is fatal. We are watching this situation quietly; even if it were within our power to intervene, we would not. We do not desire to prolong the life of this old prostitute.

A new Europe already is arising thanks to us. The first, second and third Socialist Internationals constituted ridiculous nonsense; they were merely words. The International of the Mind is an inner experience which cannot be translated into words. It does not consist of a torrent of vocables but of plastic creative acts and inner or intellectual force, which thus creates a newly shaped world.

We do not summon the various nations to 'unite' or to 'join us'. *We do not incite nations to anything. We know that everybody who joins us belongs to the new. The spiritual substance of the new world will be modelled by them alone. Create!*

---

8   **Theo van Doesburg (Dutch): 'Towards collective Construction' (1923)**

We must understand that art and life are no longer separate domains. The idea that art is *an illusion divorced* from real life must therefore be abandoned. The word 'Art' means nothing to us. We demand that it be replaced by the *construction of our environment according to creative laws* derived from well defined principles. These laws, which are akin to those of economics, mathematics, engineering, hygiene, and so forth, encourage a new plastic unity. In order to define the interrelationships among these laws, it is necessary to understand and to define them. Until now, the human creative domain and its constructive laws have never been studied *in a scientific manner.*

These laws cannot be produced by the imagination; they exist. One discovers them only through cooperative effort and from experience.

The basis for such experience derives from a knowledge of the elementary and universal means of expression, which allows one to find a method of organising them into a new harmony. The basis of this harmony derives from a knowledge of the contrasts or, rather, of a complexity of contrasts such as discord and many orders, which render visible our whole environment. This multiplicity of contrasts produces strong tensions, which, due to the interaction of mutual suppression, create balance and rest.

An equilibrium of tensions is the essence of the new constructive unity. This is why we demand the practical application or demonstration of this constructive unity in the real world.

Our era is hostile to every subjective speculation in art, science, technology and elsewhere. The modern spirit which already controls modern life almost completely is opposed to brutal spontaneity (lyricism), to domination by nature and to schoolwork and other such artistic cuisine.

---

9 **Le Corbusier (C.E. Jeanneret) (Swiss, resident in France) 'A Great Epoch has Begun' (1923)**

A great epoch has begun.
There exists a new spirit.

---

10 **Government Official (French): 'The General Conditions of Entry, Paris Exposition Universelle 1925' (1924)**

Works admitted to the Exhibition must be those of modern inspiration and of genuine originality, executed and presented by artists, artisans, manufacturers, model makers and publishers, in keeping with the demands of modern decorative and industrial art. Copies, imitations and counterfeits of antique styles are rigorously excluded.

The following may not be exhibited in any circumstances:-

(1) Pictures, statues or works that do not strictly conform to a decorative whole.

(2) Technical or manufacturing processes – unless they are intended to be exhibited in the instructional group.

(3) Sketches or rough models. The exhibits must be completed articles capable of being executed either singly or in a limited number or in any quantities. Such exhibits should either form in themselves a complete whole and be as ready for use or they should constitute the principal parts of an ensemble, but in the latter case they should be presented in such a state as to show undeniably their artistic character. Certain exceptions will be made in favour of exhibits destined for the instructional group. Exhibits should be accompanied by the names of the artists, designers and those of publishers or manufacturers.

11 Eileen Gray (Irish, resident in France): 'Steel Tubing, Standardisation' (c.1925)

Steel tubing, as conceived and used by avant-garde architects . . . [is] . . . expensive, fragile, and cold. . . .

The practice of employing uniform and standardised models is . . . contrary to good taste, even to good sense.

12 Henry Van de Velde (Belgian): 'The Formation of Modern Design' (1929)

The new movement which manifested itself in the last decade of the last century in the sphere of different art disciplines was followed by developments in architecture brought about by a violent and irrepressible reaction against ugliness.

Never had public taste been so revolted and affronted as it was in the last half of the nineteenth century. This ugliness was the result of constant repetition, less and less intelligent, less and less perfect reproductions of earlier styles, and a complete lack of control over the imagination.

The two great apostles of the new movement were John Ruskin and William Morris. A combination of the oratorial skills of Ruskin and the inspired works of William Morris brought about the lurch into the twentieth century. Ruskin spoke out against the highness of the nineteenth century whilst Morris's work took the art world by surprise.

Both were dedicated to the revival of the Gothic. The world found itself on the threshold of the twentieth century. There had been astonishing political and social developments brought about by the advent of the machine and the factory; the two pillars of industry and the new regime of production. To dream of reviving the Gothic on the threshold of the twentieth century!

Nowadays we ask ourselves how two such exceptionally intelligent men could have devoted themselves to such an illusion and how they could have recruited so many followers.

But there is an explanation. The revival of what, in effect, was the Gothic style, – repudiated up until this century, already having given way to the styles of the Renaissance – Ruskin and Morris saw the revival of the Gothic as the way forward for the world of art. To understand why this movement, dedicated after all to the past, enjoyed such success, one must understand the forces and the tensions bubbling under the surface of all walks of life – no century had ever witnessed such an upheaval.

The movement can be explained by seeing it as an improbable combination of the conservatism of Ruskin and the emergent socialism of William Morris. Ruskin saw a return to the Middle Ages as the only way of preventing the invasion of the machine and industry, the factory with its glowering chimneys, its railways and railroads; Morris exalted the Middle Ages as the time of the dignity of the craftsman which he wanted to recapture at all costs, even if it meant a revolution.

The whole movement looked forward to the twentieth century and the development of a completely new style.

This would not have been accomplished without some decisive intervention.

A group of English innovators virtually without genius accomplished a miracle.

It seemed as if the 'Arts and Crafts' movement didn't share the dream of Ruskin and Morris and their return to the Gothic style. Not least the architect Baillie Scott, not least the illustrator Walter Craine, not least the silversmith Ashbee, not least the maker of electric light fittings Benson, not least the glassblower, Powell. They were involved in a far less ambitious project; that of the creation of a new movement in architecture, furniture design and extremely simple objects; healthily conceived above and beyond the imitation of other styles.

The repercussions of such an undertaking were considerable.

Around 1894 without grandiose gestures, without great declarations, this group drove through the gates through which one could escape. The group were known across the continent – a stampede of like-minded individuals inspired by the regaining of a lost liberty, by the joy of having shaken off the nightmare of the imitation of styles, no longer accepting anything that smacked of imitation in any way or anything which might threaten their new found freedom. Everything a celebration of the escape from ugliness. I can only compare this liberation to the salvation of spring after a long, hard winter. This springtime took everyone by surprise. At the same moment of rebirth, we felt the comfort of having conquered a melancholy apathy; to be relieved of the burden which each winter imposes upon us.

And we had endured a long and tragic winter; an interminable winter during the course of which we believed we were about to die of disgust engendered in us by the ugliness of everything in our view.

We could have sustained ourselves, after all, with simple things, healthily conceived, charming; but this would have been a constraint on our liberty. So many hidden forces of creation were wanting to reveal themselves. And in most countries, artists were appearing who were demanding the right to create new styles; that is to say, shapes and ornaments liberated from the constraints of imitation of any kind. This involved Serrusier in Belgium, followed by the architects, Hanckar, Horta, van Rijsselberghe and myself; in Holland, Berlage; Otto Wagner and his disciples Olbrich and Hoffmann, in Austria; in Germany: Obrist, Endell, Riemerschmidt and Pankock; and in their wake, Behrens and others. Plumet, Selmersheim, Majorelle in France . . . Sarinen in Finland, and plenty of others besides.

By the end of the century, there was a legion of pioneers in a new style; each one fighting for their corner in their own country. Few were more motivated by circumstance than myself; forced by destiny to leave our own country to become the disciple of an idea.

Despite everything that life had in store for me I would not have changed anything. My life has been full; some failures, some victories – too many wonderful memories for me to feel bitter or ungrateful about my fate.

---

13 Charlotte Perriand (French): 'Wood or Metal' (1929)

Metal plays the same part in furniture as cement has done in architecture.

It is a Revolution.

The Future will favour materials which best solve the problems propounded by the new man:

I understand by the New Man the type of individual who keeps pace with scientific thought, who understands his age and lives it: the Aeroplane, the Ocean Liner and the Motor are at his service; Sport gives him health; His House is his resting place.

What is his house to be?

Hygiene must be considered first: soap and water. Tidiness: standard cupboards with partitions for these. Rest: resting machines for ease and pleasant repose. Beds: armchairs: chaises longues: Office chairs and tables: Stools, some high and some low: Folding chairs. The French word for furniture, *meubles*, comes from the Latin *mobilis*: meaning things that can be moved about. The only things that come into this category are chairs and tables.

We have stated the problem; now we must solve it . . .

Material now in use and material that ought to be used
Wood: a vegetable substance, in its very nature bound to decay, it is susceptible to the action of damp in the air. 'Central heating dries the air and warps the wood.' Since the war, we do not get dry wood any more: it is dried by artificial means, and inadequately.
Plywood: Composition wood:
    These should be used for panels, mounted on a metal framework, and allowing for 'play'.
Metal: a homogeneous material of which certain alloys are liable to be affected by acids in the air:
In that case protection is afforded by oxidising, or by application of paint, Duco, etc. ...
Cupboards of beaten sheet iron:
For chairs, metal 'bicycle' tubes:
A bicycle weighs only 10 to 12 kilograms. The minimum of weight, the maximum of strength.
Autogenous welding.
This process opens a vast field of practical possibilities.
The ratio between the weight necessary to ensure against breakage and the conditions of construction, in other words, the coefficient of security, would be about 6 in the case of metal, 10 in the case of wood. To be of the same solidity the wood would have to be 14 times as thick as metal:

Thrust
Compression } 14 times more in wood than in steel
Flexion

Technical conclusions
The Eiffel Tower could never have been made of Wood.
Metal is superior to wood; reasons?
The power of resistance in metal itself;
Because it allows of mass production in the factory (lessens amount of labour required).
Because by means of the different methods of manufacture it opens out new vistas; new opportunities of design;
Because the protective coatings against toxic agencies not only lower the cost of upkeep, but have a considerable *Aesthetic* value.
Metal plays the same part in furniture as cement has done in architecture.
It is a revolution

Aesthetics of metal
Aluminium varnish, Duco, Parkerisation, Paint, all provide variety in the treatment of metal.

If we use metal in conjunction with leather for chairs, with marble slabs, glass and india-rubber for tables, floor-coverings, cement, vegetable substances, we get a range of wonderful combinations and new aesthetic effects.
Unity in Architecture and yet again *Poetry*

A new lyric beauty, regenerated by mathematical science; Has produced a new kind of man who can love with fervour; Orly's 'Avion Voisin', a photograph of the Mediterranean, and 'Ombres Blanches'.

Even Mont Cervin is restored to a place of honour.

As for the public
Operation Theatres: Clinics, Hospitals:
Improve physical and moral health, Nothing extraneous.
Fashion: Look at the shops (which serve the public taste).
They make metalised wood;
They make imitation oak of metal;
They have even planned a chair made of plywood, metal and india-rubber to imitate marble.
Long live Commerce
The Man of the XXth Century
An intruder? Yes, he is, when surrounded by antique furniture, and No, in the setting of the new Interior.
Sport, indispensable for a healthy life in a mechanical age
Modern mentality also suggests:
Transparency, reds, blues,
The brilliance of coloured paint, That chairs are for sitting on,
That cupboards are for holding our belongings,
Space, light,
The joy of creating and of living . . .
in this century of ours.
Brightness, Loyalty, Liberty in thinking and acting.
WE MUST KEEP MORALLY AND PHYSICALLY FIT
Bad luck for those who do not.

---

14   L. Mies van der Rohe (German): 'The New Era' (c.1930)

The new era is a fact: it exists, irrespective of our 'yes' or 'no'. Yet it is neither better nor worse than any other era. It is pure datum, in itself without value content. Therefore I will not try to define it or clarify its basic structure.

Let us not give undue importance to mechanization and standardization.

Let us accept changed economic and social conditions as a fact.

All these take their blind and fateful course.

One thing will be decisive: the way we assert ourselves in the face of circumstance.

Here the problems of the spirit begin. The important question to ask is not 'what' but 'how'. What goods we produce or what tools we use are not questions of spiritual value.

How the question of skyscrapers versus low buildings is settled, whether we build of steel and glass, are unimportant questions from the point of view of spirit.

Whether we tend to centralization or decentralization in city planning is a practical question, not a question of value.

Yet it is just the question of value that is decisive.

We must set up new values, fix our ultimate goals so that we may establish standards.

For what is right and significant for any era – including the new era – is this: to give the spirit the opportunity for existence.

---

15 Sir Harold Wernher (British): 'Progress: The Swedish Contribution' (1930)

In times of industrial depression it is natural to survey conditions existing in other countries, and to attempt to solve the problem by studying the situation elsewhere.

Attention is naturally focused upon Sweden, for here is a country from which much can be learnt. In the first place, they are holding in Stockholm an exhibition of outstanding merit, and, secondly, in spite of the conditions referred to there are here proportionately less unemployed than in any other country in Europe. This is all the more remarkable in view of the fact that during the depression of 1922 they had 163,000 unemployed on their hands. Let us then investigate the reasons which may have led to this result.

The French Revolution, and later the World War, affected Sweden less directly than the belligerent countries; in fact it is true to say that whilst we have been striving for supremacy in the battle field, she has been consolidating her position along well planned social lines. Just as in the past she led the way in constitutional monarchy and the emancipation of women, so today she is tackling every problem in a modern spirit, from the development of a Hospital Air Service for outlying districts to research work in connection with radium. What has led to this social, industrial and agricultural development, and to the mass production of these days? Surely it is to be found in the wealth of modern inventions which can be traced to Sweden.

She was amongst the first to appreciate the important part electricity would play in modern industry, and the magnificent hydro-electric plants, particularly that at Trollhattan, will stand as a memorial to national foresight. But this is not all, for, in finance, mass production, architecture and modern art the Swedes excel, and, in addition, they have had the courage to blend the old with the new. Take for example the Royal Palace, a masterpiece of Nicodemus Tessin, yet how perfectly the New City Hall by Ostberg harmonizes with it. Make an inspection of the most modern factories, and you will see mass products turned out with the precision and beauty of a silversmith. How, then, have these results been achieved in a country with a national population smaller than the City of London (a further million and a half are located in the United States of America). Primarily the Swedes are out to learn. Better education for himself and his children is the goal that every workman sets himself to reach. The results of this can now be seen at the Stockholm Exhibition of Modern Industrial and Decorative Arts where, as the title implies, mass production has invited the aid of the artist, and a happy combination of the two has been created. We are apt to look upon mass production as an abortion of the twentieth century. At one glance the exhibition will quickly dispel this impression.

The Swedes are definitely adapting themselves to modern ideas, and have created not only dwellings but their equipment, such as furniture, glass, etc., all peculiarly modern, yet at a reasonable price, and though the articles are mass products, they are nevertheless pleasing to look at and delightful to live with.

We, here, have not been slow to learn from others in the past. Let us not be too late in adapting ourselves to these new conditions, and in following where Sweden is leading.

16 Norman Bel Geddes (American): 'The Development of the Modern Style' (1932)

Many persons are under the impression that the progressive changes in design, commonly referred to as the modern style, which is rapidly changing our environment for the better, is the result of an impetus that has developed within the past five years. This impetus has been underway for the past two generations. A graph-line would show its regular progress, with the single exception of the interval immediately affected by the World War. Only now have examples of this new expression accumulated in sufficient quantity to make themselves felt in various parts of the world. This is particularly true of the building media, architecture, sculpture, engineering.

This expression, the so-called modern style, was not the result of an attempt to be different nor was it a decorative movement. Serious people, whether they are artists or business men, do not think in such terms. It was a development that came as the result of fundamental thinking in terms of purpose, form and color.

17 Walter Gropius (German): 'The Bauhaus Course' (1935)

The best kind of practical teaching is the old system of free apprenticeship to a master-craftsman, which was devoid of any scholastic taint. Those old master-craftsmen possessed practical and formal skill in equal measure. But as they no longer exist it is impossible to revive voluntary apprenticeship. All we can substitute for it is a synthetic method of bringing practical and formal influences to bear on the pupil simultaneously by combining the teaching of first-rate technicians with that of artists of outstanding merit. A dual education of this kind would enable the coming generation to achieve the reunion of all forms of creative work and become the architects of a new civilisation. That was why we made it a rule in the *Bauhaus* that every pupil and apprentice had to be taught throughout by two masters working in the closest collaboration with each other; and that no pupil or apprentice could be excused from attending the classes of either. The Practical Instruction was the most important part of our preparation for collective work, and also the most effective way of combating arty-crafty tendencies.

Believing the machine to be our modern medium of design we sought to come to terms with it. But it would have been madness to turn over gifted pupils to the tender mercies of industry without any training in craftsmanship in the fond hope of thereby restoring 'the lost chord' between the artist and the world of work. Such idealism could only have resulted in their being overwhelmed by the narrow materialism and one-sided outlook of the modern factory. Since craftsmanship concentrates the whole sequence of manufacture in one and the same man's hands it would provide a nearer approximation to their intellectual status, and therefore offer them a better kind of practical training. Yet division of labour can no more be abandoned than the machine itself. If the spread of machinery has, in fact, destroyed the old basic unity of a nation's production the cause lies neither in the machine nor in its logical consequence of functionally differentiated processes of fabrication, but in the predominantly materialistic mentality of our age and the defective and unreal articulation of the individual to the community. The *Bauhaus* was anything but a school of arts and crafts, if only because a deliberate return to something of that kind would have meant simply putting back the clock. For now, as ever, man goes on improving his tools in order to spare himself more and more physical toil and increase his leisure proportionately.

The Practical Instruction was intended to prepare the pupil for work on standardisation. Starting with the simplest tools and methods he gradually acquired the necessary understanding and skill for more complicated ones, which culminated in the application of machinery. But at no stage was he allowed to lose the formative thread of an organic process of production as the factory-worker inevitably does. Intimate contact between the various *Bauhaus* workshops and those of industrial concerns were deliberately cultivated as being of mutual advantage. In the latter he obtained a superior degree of technical knowledge, and also learned the hard lesson that commercial insistence on the full utilisation of time and plant was something which has to be taken directly into account by the modern designer. That respect for stern realities which is one of the strongest bonds between workers engaged on a common task speedily dissipated the misty aestheticism of the academies.

After three years practical training the apprentice had to execute a design of his own before, and to the satisfaction of, a panel of master-craftsmen for his Journeyman's Certificate. Any pupil in possession of this certificate could present himself for the Bauhaus Apprenticeship Examination, which demanded a much higher standard of proficiency (particularly in regard to

H

individual aptitude for design) than the Journeyman's Certificate of Craftsmanship.

Thus our pupils' intellectual education proceeded hand in hand with their practical training. Instead of receiving arbitrary and subjective ideas of design they had objective tuition in the basic laws of form and colour, and the primary condition of the elements of each, which enabled them to acquire the necessary mental equipment to give tangible shape to their own creative instincts. Only those who have been taught how to grasp the comprehensive coherence of a larger design, and incorporate original work of their own as an integral part of it, are ripe for active cooperation in building. What is called 'the freedom of the artist' does not imply the unlimited command of a wide variety of different techniques and media, but simply his ability to design freely within the preordained limits imposed by any one of them. Even today a knowledge of counterpoint is essential for a musical composer. That is the solitary example of the theoretic basis every one of the arts formerly possessed but all the others have lost: something, in fact, which the designer must rediscover for himself. But though theory is in no sense a ready-made formula for a work of art it certainly remains the most important prerequisite of collective design. For since theory represents the impersonal cumulative experience of successive generations it offers a solid foundation on which a resolute band of fellow-workers can rear a higher embodiment of creative unity than the individual artist. Accordingly the *Bauhaus* had to assist in preparing the ground for an eventual reorganisation of the whole field of design along these lines – without which its ultimate goal would needs remain unattainable.

The sort of collaboration we aimed at was not simply a matter of pooling knowledge and talents. A building designed by one man and carried out for him by a number of purely executant associates cannot hope to achieve more than superficial unity. Our ideal was that what each collaborator contributed to the common task should be something he had devised as well as wrought himself. In cooperation of this kind formal unity must be maintained, and this can only be done by a recurrent reiteration of the proportions of the *motif* dominating the whole in each of its component parts. Every collaborator therefore needs to have a clear realisation of the comprehensive master design, and the reasons for its adoption.

18 Roy Lichenstein (American): 'This Insane Kind of Logic' (1967)

It's the thirties architecture that I'm really familiar with, and not the art, most of which I think doesn't really exist as painting. It exists as architectural decor, as jewelry design, and interiors – things like that. The architects and designers of the 1930's apparently – and I'm second guessing them – believed in the logic of geometry and in simplicity. Their art is composed of repeated forms, zig-zag marks, repeated lines in a row, or decreasing or increasing spaces, and arcs described by a compass. It seems that the compass, T-square, and triangle dictated their art. It was an art of the plan; circles are bisected exactly in the middle, the page is exactly divided diagonally, and there's all this insane kind of logic – insane because it has no particular place in sensually determined art. There's no reason why it can't be geometric, but there's no reason why it should.

19 Oriol Bohigas (Spanish): 'Against Despotic Design' (1969)

We no longer consider the possibility of a 'total design', neither do we believe, in accordance with Tomas Maldonado, in a simple addition of objects or 'well designed' conjunctions coming out of a 'well designed' world, because we are now aware of the fact that this is also the method of all despotisms that often attempt to create such a world in which one expresses the formal order of objects and one ignores, on the other hand, the disorder of men.

20 Berthold Lubetkin (Russian): 'The Vernacular and the Formation of Modern Russian Art' (1971)

The profound changes that Russia underwent at the end of the 19th century, the agony of a primitive rural economy, and the birth-pangs of a modern industrial state were accompanied by a violent crisis of conscience and an intellectual turmoil without parallel in European history. The dominant concern was the appearance on the historical scene of an urban middle class – the harbinger of advancing capitalism as a well-defined, strongly entrenched and rapidly growing force. Perplexed by the scope and rapidity of this change, the members of the progressive intelligentsia experienced the situation in terms of sheer disruption and proceeded to express it in art, to conceptualise it in philosophy, and embody it in programmes of political action. In a last desperate attempt to stem the rising tide of this demon-ridden world, the intelligentsia assumed that the horrors of industrial capitalism could be averted, or at least by-passed, by escaping into the sagas of the legendary past.

Thus started a frantic search for a specific Russian identity, an attempt to re-establish the idealised traditional social harmony in the face of the dreaded advance of foreign industrial capital. Striving to establish historical continuity, countless saturine young men in their homespun shirts, without combs or toothbrushes, descended in droves upon the patriarchal villages to seek enlightenment and inspiration at the fountainhead of popular wisdom among the simple, frugal little folk, the traditional guardians of the Russian conscience. But the real world of perishable mujiks, the rude world of horny hands, met them with hostility, suspicion, derision, and a stone wall of incomprehension. As a result of this encounter, their extravagant hopes and expectations lay in a heap of ruins. It was indeed too late. The bucolic villages were mortgaged. The howling wolves of the steppes had been shot and the fairy tales were over; the golden cockerels and the diamond-studded peacocks were changed into black two-headed eagles.

In Paris the shareholders of the Credit Lyonnais were foreclosing the fisheries of Lake Baikal and taking over the concessions of the Barnaoul forests and the Lena goldfields, seated around green baize under a resplendent still-life by Cézanne, while from the White Sea in the north to the Black Sea in the south an army of tramps, stragglers and vagabonds were swept into the ditches, where they remained on a voluntary basis, brooding, doomed and dry-eyed. It was indeed too late in the day; the attempts to escape from the present into the past led inexorably to the confrontation with the future.

It would be wrong, however, to write off all this experience as a gigantic failure and dismiss it as an irrelevant incident with consequences soon to be forgotten. On the contrary. although it failed in all its political objectives, the cultural consequences were immense. In philosophy it marks the decisive retreat from romanticism, from Fichte, Herder and Schelling, which were the dominant trends in Russia from 1825 on. The long-cherished view that ideas, principles and value-judgements spun, as it were, out of the mind in the seclusion of academic garrets, conceived or revealed in the cloud-land of the absolute, the notion that such independent ideas could chart the future course of history, was refuted. Instead, the conviction grew that man changes history by changing his physical environment and that, only as a consequence of this change, he adapts his thoughts and ways to the new situation. In other words, we do not live as we think, but we think as we live. Or, to put it in more general terms, ideas are products of man, and not man the product of ideas. This is a fundamental tenet of Marxist philosophy; as Marx himself said, it is standing Hegelian philosophy on its head.

The fiasco of the populists and the Slavophiles to which I referred before had equally ominous consequences in art. I have no hesitation in stating that it marks the birth of modern Russian art inasmuch as the passionate interest in popular culture tapped immense resources of native art which had hitherto been almost completely unnoticed and neglected. Unlike in most European countries, the vigorous primitivism was still alive in Russia, not yet stifled under successive layers of quaintness and sentimentality, and not yet buried under the ashes of the Industrial Revolution. How can one understand the music of Stravinsky or Shostakovich, the poetry of Chlebnikov or Yessenin, without taking into account the stimulus of Populism, the absorption into the mainstream of Russian art of a whole profusion of harmonies, dialects and local idioms? How are we to account for the revival of interest in sculpture without reference to the river barges, which the Volga boatmen used to cover with carvings during the long leisurely drift downstream to the Caspian sea?

Undoubtedly, among the most significant influences that affected the future development of painting were the popular prints called Lubki, a product of rural artisans which found great popularity in the countryside and were used for decoration, sometimes covering entire walls like wallpaper. Their primary purpose was to communicate visually with a semi-literate population on current events. They were distributed at markets and country fairs, among milling crowds, performing bears and goitrous cripples, and they conveyed the urgent messages of actuality, illuminating everyday events with the directness and insistence of a tom-tom: the joys and perils of garrison life; the glory of the volunteer Fire Brigade; sobbing widows and cashiered hussars; the scourge of the tax-collection; forests torn asunder by railways; and ravines filled with the victims of cholera epidemics. The impact of this imagery upon such early modern artists as Goncharova, Larionov and Burliuk is unmistakable, both in choice of subjects and in visual technique. Even Mayakovsky's work after the Revolution, his hand-painted posters, the decorated trains sent off to the front with laconic messages to the troops, show the closest links with this vigorous tradition.

And then there were the ikons and they do not need any introduction from me: strange, yet familiar; simple, yet intricate; sombre, and glowing; serene and frantic at the same time. Right up to 1912 these masterpieces of folk art were regarded purely as ritual objects, private attributes of worship, and their artistic secular significance was largely ignored, considered not only irrelevant but even irreverent. They were hung in dark corners, these dumb witnesses of everyday life, harbouring cockroaches in the warmth of the tallow candles. Then, as a result of the search for national identity that followed the pilgrimage to the land, to which I referred earlier on, the first public exhibition of ikons took place in 1912. All of a sudden the sheer splendour of this art burst on us like a revelation, summing up the entire course of Russian art. Some were 13th century ones from Novgorod; some 15th century, produced by the monks of the Novodevichi Monastery; others baroque ones of the 17th century Moscow school of Stroganov. But some had been made only yesterday by the village signwriter or some itinerant craftsman, and they combined centuries-old traditions with authentic inventiveness and originality, saying what no-one had dared to say before. Some depicted the mysteries of earthly life on densely-painted boards. Some were studded with semi-precious stones or had inserts of silver representing draperies, mantles or scrolls. The surface of some was entirely covered with metal sheet, leaving only cut-outs for the wrinkled face of the Pantocrator or his remote fingers folded in prayer. Sometimes dragons with the faces of billygoats were devouring swaddled corpses, set in a shimmering golden heaven.

In our attempts to trace the origins of modern art we are often guilty of a schematic over-simplification that distorts the very object of our enquiry. In our anxiety to find a common parentage we ascend the stream of time until, in the distance, we see nimble Picasso. I am therefore often amused to hear the opinion that Tatlin started to experiment with three-dimensional montages and reliefs after he met Picasso in Paris. Unfortunately, I cannot accept such a comforting version since Tatlin himself told me on several occasions how, inspired by the ikons, he started to drill his boards, mount metal rings, screws and bells on them, marking and scoring his backgrounds, gluing on beads, mirror and tinsel – aiming at a shimmering, dangling and sonorous composition which, already at that time, he called 'Compositions'. 'If it was not for the ikons', he used to say, 'I should have remained preoccupied with water-drips, sponges, rags and watercolours.'

Let me attempt to sum up what I have said up to now. I have tried to show that the origins of modern art in Russia differ substantially from those in the West though at a later stage, inevitably, the differences became blurred, the outlines crossed, in spite of the great divide of the war and Revolution. Due to the time-lag in development between East and West Europe, in Russia modern art grew organically out of folk art traditions which were identified and revived by the politically motivated and radical populist movement. In Russia my point of view must be rejected as heresy, since they persist in regarding modern art as a scourge and a visitation, imported by rootless cosmopolitan agents. Naturally, any view according to which Russian modern art is firmly rooted in indigenous popular tradition is anathema. Yet I persist in my view. Indeed, if I am wrong, how are we to explain the hostile reception given to Marinetti by the Russian avant-garde on his visit to Moscow in 1913? He was speaking about speed, engines, battleships, the benefits of tourism, of fist-fights and smashing furniture; while we were drinking tea around the samovar, thinking of honey, dusty roads and accordions floating high over the telegraph wires, above the silver birches and the meadows. At this stage I would like to emphasise again that Russian modern art bristles with social and political implications at all stages of its development. For that matter, all art does; but in Russia all the links in the chain of causality are particularly easy to trace. Even a deliberate renunciation on the artists' part of any political involvement is no less a social and political posture than its acceptance. One can, of course, speak of non committed artists, but not of non-committed art. At any rate, to the radical Russian intelligentsia this was a self-evident truism, needing no further elaboration after the collapse of the 'art for art's sake' movement.

---

21   Angela Carter (British): 'Universality' (1978)

The notion of a universality of human experience is a confidence trick and the notion of a universality of female experience is a clever confidence trick.

22 Susan Sontag (American): 'On Modernism' (1979)

The Romantics thought of great art as a species of heroism, a breaking through or going beyond. Following them, adepts of the modern demanded of masterpieces that they be, in each case, an extreme case – terminal or prophetic, or both. Walter Benjamin was making a characteristic modernist judgment when he observed (writing about Proust): 'All great works of literature found a genre or dissolve one.' However rich in precursors, the truly great work must seem to break with an old order and really is a devastating if salutary move. Such a work extends the reach of art but also complicates and burdens the enterprise of art with new, self-conscious standards. It both excites and paralyses the imagination.

23 Marshall Berman (American): 'Modernity, Yesterday, Today and Tomorrow' (1983)

There is a mode of vital experience – experience of space and time, of the self and others, of life's possibilities and perils – that is shared by men and women all over the world today. I will call this body of experience 'modernity.' To be modern is to find ourselves in an environment that promises us adventure, power, joy, growth, transformation of ourselves and the world – and, at the same time, that threatens to destroy everything we have, everything we know, everything we are. Modern environments and experiences cut across all boundaries of geography and ethnicity, of class and nationality, of religion and ideology: in this sense, modernity can be said to unite all mankind. But it is a paradoxical unity, a unity of disunity: it pours us all into a maelstrom of perpetual disintegration and renewal, of struggle and contradiction, of ambiguity and anguish. To be modern is to be part of a universe in which, as Marx said, 'all that is solid melts into air.'

People who find themselves in the midst of this maelstrom are apt to feel that they are the first ones, and maybe the only ones, to be going through it; this feeling has engendered numerous nostalgic myths of pre-modern Paradise Lost. In fact, however, great and ever-increasing numbers of people have been going through it for close to five hundred years. Although most of these people have probably experienced modernity as a radical threat to all their history and traditions, it has, in the course of five centuries, developed a rich history and a plenitude of traditions of its own. I want to explore and chart these traditions, to understand the ways in which they can nourish and enrich our own modernity, and the ways in which they may obscure or impoverish our sense of what modernity is and what it can be.

The maelstrom of modern life has been fed from many sources: great discoveries in the physical sciences, changing our images of the universe and our place in it; the industrialization of production, which transforms scientific knowledge into technology, creates new human environments and destroys old ones, speeds up the whole tempo of life, generates new forms of corporate power and class struggle; immense demographic upheavals, severing millions of people from their ancestral habitats, hurtling them halfway across the world into new lives; rapid and often cataclysmic urban growth; systems of mass communication, dynamic in their development, enveloping and binding together the most diverse people and societies; increasingly powerful national states, bureaucratically structured and operated, constantly striving to expand their powers; mass social movements of people, and peoples, challenging their political and economic rulers, striving to gain some control over their lives; finally, bearing and driving all these people and institutions along, an ever-expanding, drastically fluctuating capitalist world market. In the twentieth century, the social processes that bring this maelstrom into being, and keep it in a state of perpetual becoming, have come to be called 'modernization.' These world-historical processes have nourished an amazing variety of visions and ideas that aim to make men and women the subjects as well as the objects of modernization, to give them the power to change the world that is changing them, to make their way through the maelstrom and make it their own. Over the past century, these visions and values have come to be loosely grouped together under the name of 'modernism.'

---

24   **Peter Fuller (British): 'Modernism is in Crisis' (1983)**

'Functionalism' . . . is waning. Modernism is in crisis. Western culture is undergoing an upheaval of taste, an apparent shift in its sensibility, or 'structure of feeling'. Profound changes are affecting almost every area of artistic activity.

25   Gillian Naylor (British): 'Assessing the Bauhaus' (1985)

In spite of Gropius's efforts to emphasise the plurality and
continued relevance of approaches represented by the individuals teaching at the Bauhaus, the school's achievements must be
related to the social and political context that created it. It
marked the culmination in the industrialising nations of Western Europe of more than half a century's attempts at social
engineering through design reform. Its strengths, as well as its
weakness, lay in the fact that it aimed to change the world
through the discovery and application of 'universal' laws in art,
architecture and design. Such Utopian concepts were, of course,
not confined to the Bauhaus in the 1920's and 30's; they are
also found in Dutch, Russian, Scandinavian and British theory.
The pathos of such idealism has been revealed by subsequent
events. The fact that the school was destroyed by Fascism may
have enhanced its credibility in post-War Europe and the
United States, but its ideal of universality was a myth and a
mirage, shattered by war, politics and the demands of a consumer society. Today no designer or design organisation could
or would contemplate universal solutions to the problems of
design for the real world. We are still in search of a theory, social
commitment is still elusive, so we indulge in our fantasies,
ironies and pastiche, which are more comforting (and more
profitable) than that 'respect for stern realities' that Gropius
demanded from architecture and design.

26   Malcolm Bradbury and James McFarlane (British): 'Modern-
      ism: A Cataclystic Upheaval' (1990)

Cultural seismology – the attempt to record the shifts and
displacements of sensibility that regularly occur in the history
of art and literature and thought – habitually distinguishes
three separate orders of magnitude. At one end of the scale are
those tremors of fashion that seem to come and go in rhythm
with the changing generations, the decade being the right unit
for measuring the curves that run from the first shock to peak
activity and on to the dying rumbles of derivative *Epigonentum*.
To a second order of magnitude belong those larger displacements whose effects go deeper and last longer, forming those
extended periods of style and sensibility which are usefully
measured in centuries. This leaves a third category for those
overwhelming dislocations, those cataclysmic upheavals of cul-

ture, those fundamental convulsions of the creative human spirit that seem to topple even the most solid and substantial of our beliefs and assumptions, leave great areas of the past in ruins (noble ruins, we tell ourselves for reassurance), question an entire civilization or culture, and stimulate frenzied rebuilding. That the twentieth century brought us a new art is undeniable, and it is the purpose of this volume to explore some of its crucial manifestations. But we have also increasingly come to believe that this new art comes from, or is, an upheaval of the third and cataclysmic order.

9

THE AESTHETIC DIMENSION

The last two centuries have seen an expansion and a profession-alisation of the practice of aesthetic discourse. Thinkers have pondered, and ponder still, on the constituent parts of what might simply be termed 'beauty'. Design has been a site of intense aesthetic debate throughout our period, and was the dominant debating ground through much of the nineteenth century.

Commentators on, and practitioners of, design have long had a desire to place formal values on an objective footing. The idea that the qualities one admires in an object are no more than one's subjective whim, or, worse, are no more than an indication of one's social class, have proved unacceptable to many. The search for explications and justifications of significance for objects has been an ongoing one. There is an inherent desire of many involved in the visual arts to be able to point to timelessness and universality as being the key features in a disinterested aesthetic system. Plato has always been more the aesthete's friend than Heraclitus. So far the desire has not been quenched.

The passages in this chapter are here because of their ambition to define clearly what exactly is going on either in the designed object, the design process, or the consumer, from a cognitive point of view before any other. Perhaps aesthetics, and philosophy in general, is no more than an attempt to provide definitions.

Several ranges of question are addressed. First, there are discussions of the constituent qualities of the creation and the reception processes, such as the role of colour, space, simplicity and imagination in creation, and taste, empathy and pleasure in reception. Second, there are definitions of what design (and art in general) is. Lastly, the chapter presents a number of seminal aesthetic positions and methods. The reader may notice that some of the later passages directly address issues raised in earlier ones, usually with a commitment to refutation.

See also
Chapter 1 for the role of decoration
Chapter 2 for aesthetics and morality

Chapter 6 for beauty in the home
Chapter 7 for non-European design
Chapter 8 for modernist aesthetics

1 Immanuel Kant (German): 'Genius' (1790)

Genius is the talent . . . which gives the rule to art. Since talent, as an innate productive faculty of the artist, belongs itself to nature, we may put it this way: *Genius* is the innate mental aptitude . . . *through which* nature gives the rule to art.

Every one is agreed on the point of the complete opposition between genius and the *spirit of imitation*. Now since learning is nothing but imitation, the greatest ability, or aptness as a pupil, is still, as such, not equivalent to genius. Even though a man weaves his own thoughts or fancies, instead of merely taking in what others have thought, and even though he go so far as to bring fresh gains to art and science, this does not afford a valid reason for calling such a man of *brains*, and often great brains, a *genius*.

2 James Carter (British): 'Definitions of Taste' (1834)

The word *taste* is used figuratively, to denote that power or operation of the human mind by which it perceives and enjoys whatever is beautiful or sublime in nature or art.

. . . We observe however, that, although there is a general agreement as to the propriety of thus using the word *taste*, there is considerable difference of opinion respecting the nature of the faculty so called, which, consequently, has been variously defined; it may therefore, be proper to notice some of the principal definitions that have been given.

Among those who have never thought much upon the subject, the common definition of taste is, that 'it is the faculty by which we perceive beauty', and with this vague statement they are satisfied. Our chief concern however, is with the definitions given by such as have studied the subject more closely, and of these we shall first notice that given by Montesquieu, who says that 'taste is a power or faculty of discovering with quickness and precision, the degree of pleasure which everything ought to give to man', upon which it has been remarked, that 'there are many things which both do, (and ought to) give pleasure to man, which cannot with any propriety, be called objects of taste.'

Another French author affirms, that taste is 'the talent of discovering in the productions of art those qualities which ought to please sensible and feeling minds', which definition is said to be 'more appropriate to the art of criticism, (which depends chiefly upon the exercise of the judgment) than to the faculty of taste,' which faculty is certainly possessed and exercised to a considerable extent by many, who are but little acquainted with the works of art, but, who are, nevertheless, capable of perceiving the beauty or sublimity of natural objects. Such persons, therefore, are found to be susceptible of powerful feelings when called to witness the more magnificent and impressive phenomena of nature, and are able to give a fair account of the sources of their emotions, while the most accurate description or delineation of the same objects, is regarded by them with comparative indifference. I must, however, pass on to notice some other definitions, and shall do so as briefly as I can.

Mr Addison, in treating of the pleasures connected with taste, calls them 'the pleasures of the imagination.' Dr Blair defines taste to be 'the power of receiving pleasure from the beauties of nature and art.' Mr Dugald Stewart affirms, that, 'it is not a simple and original faculty, but, a power gradually formed by experience and observation.' Mr Burke has admitted the inutility of any definition, and says that he has 'no great opinion' of this 'celebrated remedy for the cure of the disorder' which arises from the use of figurative terms, when the things which we understand by those terms are not productive of any 'simple and determinate idea in mind.' 'For when,' says he, 'we define, we seem in danger of circumscribing nature, within the bounds of our own notions, which we often take up by hazard, or embrace on trust, or form out of a limited and partial consideration of the object before us, instead of extending our ideas to take in all that nature comprehends, according to her manner of combining.' He goes on to say, that 'we are limited in our enquiry by the strict laws to which we have submitted at our setting out.' And further, that 'a definition may be very exact, and yet go but a very little way towards informing us of the nature of the thing defined.' Yet, after all, in order to prevent disputes, he says that he means 'by the word, taste, no more than that faculty, or those faculties, of the mind which are affected with, or which form a judgment of, the works of imagination and the elegant arts.'

To the foregoing definitions I shall add only the following, which I met with in a manuscript note, in which taste is said to be 'a susceptibility with regard to every thing that affects the imagination.' This is, perhaps, as good an explanation of the term as any of the preceding; but, after all that has been done in the way of definition, we can derive but little information from this source, and shall, perhaps, be obliged to agree with Mr Burke, when he says, that, 'let the virtue of a definition be what it will,' yet, 'in the order of things, it seems rather to follow than to precede inquiry, of which, it ought to be considered as the result.'

3   E. E. Viollet-le-duc (French): 'Style' (c.1854-69)

Style. There is style and there are styles. The styles are the characters which allow one to distinguish the schools and the periods. The architectural styles of the Greeks, the Romans, and the Byzantines, Romanesque and Gothic are different in a way that it is easy to classify the monuments of each of those different arts. But it would have been truer to say: the Greek form, the Romanesque form, the Gothic form, and not to use for those terms, the word style, but as everyone uses the word style, Greek style, Roman style etc. have been admitted.

It is not what it is all about. In several entries of the dictionary, we underline the differences in style that enable one to classify the works of the Middle Ages, either by period or by school.

So, we are only going to talk about style because styles do not belong to Art considered as a conception of the spirit. In the same way as there is only art, there is only style. So, what is style? It is, in a work of art, the manifestation of an ideal established on a principle.

Style can be as well understood as a mode of life; that is to say, appropriation of a form from art to object. In consequence there are absolute style and the related style. The former dominates every conception and the latter is changed according to the destination of the object. The style that is appropriate to a church should not appropriate to a private home; but a house can let one see the mark of an expression in art (such as a temple or a barrack) totally independent from the object and belonging to the artist or rather the principle he took up as a creative device: that is style.

4   Gottfried Semper (German): 'Let Materials Have Their own
     Say' (1883)

Let materials have their own say, undisguised, in the shape, the
proportions, most suited to them by experience and science . . .
Wood should appear wood, iron, iron.

5   Charles Rennie Mackintosh (British): 'Creative Imagination'
     (1902)

The focus of the true art of our country, of the world, is being
gradually but surely accepted – and that focus will eventually
prove to be the work of the individual worker – will prove to be
the emancipation of all artists from the stupid forms of education
– which stifles the intellect paralyzes the ambition and kills
emotion. And as you are careful and anxious about the art you
yourself produce – as each new achievement gives you pleasure
and happiness – as you are jealous of every thought you think – so
also be jealous and happy in your seeking for, and assisting in the
encouragement of each youth of promise in your world – any
youth whose work may – no matter how slightly – suggest
promise of further things – like the first flowers of spring – who
may be likened to the seeds and bulbs which if carefully nurtured
and tended may grow to be beautiful things – whereas if neglected or discouraged their ultimate worth may be lost to the
world for ever. Each spadeful of earth carelessly thrown away –
may contain the germs of the most beautiful flower the world has
yet seen – and each year's group of students may contain a new
Heaven born genius – What is – in an artist the most important –
the essential faculty – The artist may have a very rich psychic
organisation – an easy grasp and a clear eye for essentials – a great
variety of aptitudes – but that which characterizes him above all
else – and determines his vocation is – the exceptional development of the imaginative faculties – especially the imagination
that creates – not only the imagination that represents – The
power which the artist possesses of representing objects to himself explains the hallucinating character of his work – the poetry
which pervades them – and their tendency towards symbolism –
But the creative imagination is far more important.

6   Theodor Lipps (German): 'Empathy' (1905)

There are three types, or, more precisely, three directions of
enjoyment. First of all, I enjoy a thing or a sensuous object
distinct from myself, for example, the taste of a fruit. Second, I
enjoy myself, for example, my power or my skill; I am proud of
a deed in which I have exhibited such power or skill. Between
these two possibilities lies a third which uniquely combines the
other two: I enjoy myself in a sensuous object distinct from
myself. This type is that of aesthetic enjoyment. It is objectified
self-enjoyment.

That I enjoy myself in a sensuous object presupposes that in
it I have, or find, or feel myself. Here we encounter the basic
idea of present-day aesthetics, the concept of Empathy.

7   Clive Bell (British): 'Significant Form' (1914)

All sensitive people agree that there is a peculiar emotion provoked by works of art. I do not mean, of course, that all works
provoke the same emotion. On the contrary, every work produces a different emotion. But all these emotions are recognis-
ably the same in kind; so far, at any rate, the best opinion is on
my side. That there is a particular kind of emotion provoked by
works of visual art, and that this emotion is provoked by every
kind of visual art, by pictures, sculptures, buildings, pots, carvings, textiles, &c., is not disputed, I think, by anyone capable of
feeling it. This emotion is called the aesthetic emotion; and if
we can discover some quality common and peculiar to all the
objects that provoke it, we shall have solved what I take to be
the central problem of aesthetics. We shall have discovered the
essential quality in a work of art, the quality that distinguishes
works of art from all other classes of objects.

For either all works of visual art have some common quality,
or when we speak of 'works of art' we gibber. Everyone speaks of
'art', making a mental classification by which he distinguishes
the class 'works of art' from all other classes. What is the
justification of this classification? What is the quality common
and peculiar to all members of this class? Whatever it be, no
doubt it is often found in company with other qualities; but
they are adventitious – it is essential. There must be some one
quality without which a work of art cannot exist; possessing
which, in the least degree, no work is altogether worthless.
What is this quality? What quality is shared by all objects that

provoke our aesthetic emotions? What quality is common to Sta Sophia and the windows at Chartres, Mexican sculpture, a Persian bowl, Chinese carpets, Giotto's frescoes at Padua, and the masterpieces of Poussin, Piero della Francesca, and Cézanne? Only one answer seems possible – significant form. In each, lines and colours combined in a particular way, certain forms and relations of forms, stir our aesthetic emotions. These relations and combinations of lines and colours, these aesthetically moving forms, I call 'Significant Form'; and 'Significant Form' is the one quality common to all works of visual art.

---

8 Fernand Léger (French): 'Beauty and the Hierarchies of Art' (1924)

It is my opinion that plastic beauty in general is totally independent of sentimental, descriptive and imitative qualities. Every object, picture, building and ornamental arrangement has a value in itself, absolute in the strictest sense and independent of what it may represent.

A number of people would *unintentionally* be sensitive to beauty in the commonplace object if they were not blinded by a preconceived idea of the art object. Poor visual education is at fault, and the modern mania to classify at any cost, whether categories of people or of tools. People are *afraid of free judgment* which is nonetheless the only state of mind open to the appreciation of beauty. Victims of a period marked by criticism, skepticism and intelligence, people are bent on understanding instead of letting their sensitivity function unhampered. They believe in *art makers* because they too have a trade. They are dazzled and stumped by titles and distinctions. My objective is to try and establish the following: no more cataloguing of beauty into hierarchies – that is the most clumsy mistake possible. Beauty is everywhere, in the arrangement of saucepans on the white wall of your kitchen, perhaps more there than in your eighteenth century salon or in official museums.

---

9 Eileen Gray (Irish, resident in France): 'Value' (1929)

Like music, a work acquires its value only through the love it manifests.

10   Jan Mukarovsky (Czech): 'The Artefact as an External Signifier' (1934)

It becomes increasingly evident that the basic constitution of the individual consciousness, even at its innermost levels, derives from content belonging to the collective consciousness. As a consequence, crucial importance accrues to problems of sign and meaning, seeing that any mental content that exceeds the bounds of the individual consciousness acquires the character of a sign by the very fact of its communicability. The science of signs (called semiology by Saussure, sematology by Buhler, semiotic by Peirce) needs to be elaborated to its fullest extent. As contemporary linguistics (see the investigations of the Prague School, that is, the Prague Linguistic Circle) expands the field of semantics by treating all the elements of the system of language, even including sounds, from the semiotic point of view, the results of linguistics need to be applied to other domains of sign usage and to be differentiated according to their special characteristics. There are a number of sciences particularly concerned with the problem of signs (as well as with the problems of structure and value, which problems, incidentally, are closely related to those of signs – a work of art, for instance, is at one and the same time sign, structure, and value). In fact, all sciences known as humanities (sciences morales, Geisteswissenschaft) deal with phenomena that have the more or less pronounced character of signs due to their double existence both in the world of sense perception and in the collective consciousness.

A work of art is not identifiable, as psychological aesthetics would like to think it is, with the state of mind and spirit of its creator or with any of the possible states of mind and spirit induced in its perception. Clearly, every state of the subjective consciousness involves something individual and momentary that makes it impossible to grasp and communicate in its entirety, whereas the work of art is meant expressly to serve as an intermediary between its creator and the community. Moreover, there is always some 'thing', some 'artifact,' that represents the work of art in the outside world and may be perceived by one and all. However, it is not possible to reduce the work of art to that 'artifact,' since it may happen that the artifact, shifted in time or space, will completely alter its appearance and inner structure. Such changes are readily detectable if, for instance, we compare several different, successive translations of the same poetic work. The artifact, thus, functions merely as an external signifier ('signifiant' in Saussure's terminology) for which in the collective consciousness there is a corresponding signification (often labelled 'aesthetic object') given by what is common to subjective states of mind aroused in individuals of any particular community by the artifact.

11   Anthony Bertram (British): 'What is Design?' (1938)

By design, then, we do not mean a drawing made in his studio by the designer – a design *for* something – but rather the thing itself, but with that drawing, the preceding idea of the thing and the succeeding process of manufacture all implicit.

But though the use of the word 'design' in this way may be comparatively new, the idea certainly isn't. In the fourth century B.C., Plato wrote in *The Republic*: 'Are not the excellence, beauty and correctness of every manufactured article, or living creature, or action, to be tried only by a reference to the purpose intended in their construction, or in their natural constitution?' This reference to purpose immediately suggests the idea of honesty, which is fundamental to good design. A well-designed object should not only serve its purpose well but should look as if it were made for that purpose and no other. For example, an electric grandfather clock which houses a cocktail cabinet in its case does not suggest cocktails, but weights and a pendulum. Similarly, stained deal laths tacked on to the front of a building suggest that it is a timber-frame building. It isn't. But this dishonesty is not about purpose but about method of construction. Or again, paper painted to imitate marble or the grain of oak and pasted on to white wood is dishonest about material. So that we may say that a well-designed object must be honest in three ways. It must confess the purpose for which it is constructed, the method by which it is constructed and the material of which it is constructed. But these three elements of honesty in design are not really independent. The purpose will usually suggest and sometimes dictate the method of construction and material. The material will often dictate the method of construction, and so on.

So it might seem that to judge the design of an object is a more or less mechanical process, for which we only need a little common sense to know if it is fit for its purpose, and a little technical knowledge to know if it is honestly made. But is this really how we judge? Do we not, in fact, in the case of all not strictly utilitarian objects, choose by looks? Ask any furniture dealer or house agent. He will tell you that it is looks that sell.

There is no space to discuss here why this is so. It has been true ever since man began to make things. And here we are up against the real difficulty. Very few of us agree as to what good looks are : or whether any given object has them or is a work of art. The most popular of all Latin tags is *De gustibus non est disputandum* – you can't argue about taste. But can't you? Is there any subject on earth people argue about more? And when they've finished up by being really rude to one another, they mutter *De gustibus* and go away convinced that they're right.

The faculty of distinguishing good from bad design in the familiar objects of domestic life is a faculty which most educated people – and women especially – conceive that they possess. How it has been acquired, few would be able to explain.' That remains as true to-day as when Eastlake wrote it, except that we can cut out the word 'educated'.

---

12   Raymond D. Havens (American): 'On Simplicity' (1953)

Simplicity, it would seem, is a simple matter. We all know what it means although, not thinking it important, we have given it little attention. But it has not always been so. In the eighteenth century, critics, essayists, and poets were constantly referring to it as the supreme excellence in almost every field, the 'open sesame' to every door, whether of conduct, thought, taste, or artistic production. 'The best and truest ornament of most things in life,' Swift called it, and Shaftesbury, 'this beauty above all beauties.' Lord Kames declared, 'The best artists . . . have in all ages been governed by a taste for simplicity,' and Horace Walpole said, 'Taste . . . cannot exist without Simplicity.' Joseph Warton went even further, maintaining 'SIMPLICITY is with justice esteemed a supreme excellence in all the performances of art.' William Mason held this to be the case at least in the two arts with which he dealt. For he began his poem on landscape architecture by invoking 'divine SIMPLICITY ! . . . Best arbitress of what is good and fair', and in his *Art of Painting* affirmed, 'Beauty's best handmaid is Simplicity.'

The extraordinary regard in which simplicity was held during the eighteenth century came in part from the support it received from science. Kepler, Galileo, Torricelli, Descartes, Pascal, Huygens, Robert Boyle, and Newton through their epoch-making discoveries had given unprecedented authority to science and the mathematical interpretation of nature. Science, in its turn, threw the full weight of this authority behind simplicity.

This principle likewise received from Newton its supreme illustration in the law of gravity. All generalisation is simplification, and the law of gravity, the greatest of scientific generalisations, simplified a confusing mass of phenomena by showing it to be the manifestation throughout space of a single simple law. In view of this and other triumphs of scientific generalisation it is not surprising that the Copernican theory was accepted, not because it furnished a more complete explanation of the known facts than its predecessors, but because it was simpler than they. Nor is it surprising that many eighteenth-century thinkers sought to apply the physico-mathematical method of science to all aspects of life. Simplicity was their goal and they accepted without question the notion that the simpler a thing is the better . . .

. . . But even apart from science simplicity had great allies, for it was inseparably linked with the two authorities held in the highest reverence: nature and the Ancients. Phrases like 'the simplicity of nature' or 'the true [or real] simplicity of nature' are to be met with at every hand and in the most diverse places; yet the conception they embody is often implied rather than expressed. This conception, usually vague enough, was constantly changing, but the principal element in it seems to have been that the simple is what is spontaneous, free from artifice and sophistication. The external world of tree, meadow, and stream is obviously simple in this sense and so, relatively, are the farmers and shepherds who live close to this world. Still simpler are savages who are in intimate contact with external nature and not far removed from 'the state of nature.' Furthermore, the ever-recurring antithesis between nature and art implies that the former, in contrast with the man-made work of art, has the simplicity of the spontaneous. But commonly when associated with nature simplicity carried with it something of the most usual of all its meanings, the uncomplicated. So deeply convinced was the eighteenth century of the freedom from intricacy of the natural that even external nature came to be regarded as uncomplicated and orderly.

The supreme illustration, it was felt, of rising above the complex and elaborate was furnished by the Ancients, whose noble or majestic or beautiful simplicity was repeatedly praised. Vicesimus Knox asserted: 'To renounce the models of the ancients, is to renounce the most captivating embellishment of art, an adherence to simplicity and nature. While a *Venus de Medicis* and an *Apollo Belvedere,* shall continue to be standards of excellence, no one can with reason apprehend, lest the chaste graces of real elegance should be sacrificed to the false glare of

Gothic affectation.' Collins, who personifies Simplicity, describes her as coming 'In *Attic* Robe array'd' – which is the garb his contemporaries would have expected her to wear – and as having lived chiefly in Greece. He does not, however, suggest a conception which was usually implied in references to the simplicity of the Ancients. This was largeness, grandeur, freedom from petty details, the simplicity befitting Gods and heroes. The many opponents of the Gothic, for example, never tired of contrasting its 'multiplicity of minute ornaments' with the noble simplicity of classic architecture. But it was held that among the Ancients, especially the Greeks, all the arts were marked by simplicity. This was notably the case with sculpture – which, as known, consisted mainly of single figures, nude or lightly clad, and in repose. The costume, or lack of it, of the ancients also was simple, as was their mode of life: Cincinnatus at the plough, Nausikaa washing soiled clothes. It was the same with literature: Homer was direct and naive, as were his heroes; Greek drama was singularly uncomplicated; Virgil wrote a book of husbandry and Horace told of his Sabine farm.

---

13 Isaiah Berlin (German): 'The Hedgehog and the Fox' (1953)

There is a line among the fragments of the Greek poet Archilochus which says: 'The fox knows many things, but the hedgehog knows one big thing'. Scholars have differed about the correct interpretation of these dark words, which may mean no more than that the fox, for all his cunning, is defeated by the hedgehog's one defence. But, taken figuratively, the words can be made to yield a sense in which they mark one of the deepest differences which divide writers and thinkers, and, it may be, human beings in general. For there exists a great chasm between those, on one side, who relate everything to a single central vision, one system less or more coherent or articulate, in terms of which they understand, think and feel – a single, universal, organising principle in terms of which alone all that they are and say has significance – and, on the other side, those who pursue many ends, often unrelated and even contradictory, connected, if at all, only in some *de facto* way, for some psychological or physiological cause, related by no moral or aesthetic principle; these last lead lives, perform acts, and entertain ideas that are centrifugal rather than centripetal, their thought is scattered or diffused, moving on many levels, seizing upon the essence of a vast variety of experiences and objects for what they are in themselves, without, consciously or unconsciously, seeking to fit them into, or exclude them from, any one unchanging, all-embracing, sometimes self-contradictory and incomplete, at times fanatical, unitary inner vision. The first kind of intellectual and artistic personality belongs to the hedgehogs, the second to the foxes; and without insisting on a rigid classification, we may, without too much fear of contradiction, say that, in this sense, Dante belongs to the first category, Shakespeare to the second; Plato, Lucretius, Pascal, Hegel, Dostoevsky, Nietzsche, Ibsen, Proust are, in varying degrees, hedgehogs; Herodotus, Aristotle, Montaigne, Erasmus, Molière, Goethe, Pushkin, Balzac, Joyce are foxes.

---

14 Roland Barthes (French): 'Myth' (c.1954)

What is a myth, today? I shall give at the outset a first, very simple answer, which is perfectly consistent with etymology: *myth is a type of speech* . . .

. . . Of course, it is not *any* type: language needs special conditions in order to become myth: we shall see them in a minute. But what must be firmly established at the start is that myth is a system of communication, that it is a message. This allows one to perceive that myth cannot possibly be an object, a concept, or an idea; it is a mode of signification, a form. Later, we shall have to assign to this form historical limits, conditions of use, and reintroduce society into it: we must nevertheless first describe it as a form.

It can be seen that to purport to discriminate among mythical objects according to their substance would be entirely illusory: since myth is a type of speech, everything can be a myth provided it is a conveyed by a discourse. Myth is not defined by the object of its message, but by the way in which it utters this message: there are formal limits to myth, there are no 'substantial' ones. Everything, then, can be a myth? Yes, I believe this, for the universe is infinitely fertile in suggestions. Every object in the world can pass from a closed, silent existence to an oral state, open to appropriation by society, for there is no law, whether natural or not, which forbids talking about things. A tree is a tree. Yes, of course. But a tree as expressed by Minou Drouet is no longer quite a tree, it is a tree which is decorated, adapted to a certain type of consumption, laden with literary self-indulgence, revolt, images, in short with a type of social *usage* which is added to pure matter.

Naturally, everything is not expressed at the same time: some objects become the prey of mythical speech for a while, then they disappear, others take their place and attain the status of myth. Are there objects which are *inevitably* a source of suggestiveness, as Baudelaire suggested about Woman? Certainly not: one can conceive of very ancient myths, but there are no eternal ones; for it is human history which converts reality into speech, and it alone rules the life and death of mythical language. Ancient or not, mythology can only have an historical foundation, for myth is a type of speech chosen by history: it cannot possibly evolve from the 'nature' of things.

15 Gerrit Rietveld (Dutch): 'Space' (1957)

If, for a particular purpose, we separate, limit, and bring into a human scale a part of unlimited space, it is (if all goes well) a piece of space brought into life as reality. In this way, a special segment of space has been absorbed into our human system.

16 Johannes Itten (German): 'Colour' (c.1961)

Developments in color chemistry, fashion, and color photography have aroused a broad general interest in colors, and the color sensitivity of the individual has been greatly refined. But this contemporary interest in color is almost wholly visual, material in character, and not grounded in intellectual and emotional experience. It is a superficial, external toying with metaphysical forces.

Colors are forces, radiant energies that affect us positively or negatively, whether we are aware of it or not. The artists in stained glass used color to create a supramundane, mystical atmosphere which would transport the meditations of the worshipper to a spiritual plane. The effects of colors should be experienced and understood, not only visually, but also psychologically and symbolically.

17 Clement Greenberg (American): 'Art is Strictly a Matter of Experience' (1961)

Art is strictly a matter of experience, not of principles, and what matters first and last in art is quality; all other things are secondary . . .

To hold that one kind of art must invariably be superior or inferior to another kind means to judge before experiencing; and the whole history of art is there to demonstrate the futility of rules of preference laid down beforehand: the impossibility, that is, of anticipating the outcome of aesthetic experience.

---

18   Umberto Eco (Italian): 'Two Types of Objects' (1970)

What would be a better way to initiate a column devoted to signs and myths – which we will try to carry forward without any obsession with regularity, responding instead to the suggestions that arrive from all sides – than by making a devout pilgrimage to one of the sanctuaries of mass communication, the Milan Trade Fair? And with the awareness that we are going there on a specific mission. Because it's one thing to enter as an economic operator: For him the Fair doesn't spout any false talk, it gives him a chance to find what he's looking for, touch it, buy it. This is a game with no double meanings, at least as honest as any commercial competition is honest in a market economy. But it's another thing to go there as spectator (as most visitors do): For him the Fair is a great kermesse of triumphant merchandise, and it takes on the characteristics, to a minor degree, of the big international expos, the world's fairs. If – as Marx said – 'the wealth of those societies in which the capitalist mode of production prevails presents itself as an "immense accumulation of commodities"', then world's fairs are the temple in which this merchandise loses all real contact with its value in use and most of its contact with its barter value, to become a series of pure connotative signs, at an emotional fever pitch. The goods almost lose their concrete individuality to become so many notes in an anthem of progress, a hymn to the abundance and happiness of consumption and production.

But a trade fair is an international expo only halfway, because the merchandise is there to be sold. The products are signs of an undifferentiated desire, but they are also objective terms of an individuated and precise desire. The immense population of objects collected here refers us to that 'sociology of objects' that is developing in France, of which we will speak on another occasion. But a sociology (or a semiology) of objects means that they must be seen within the concrete system of the society that creates them and receives them, so they must be seen as a language listened to as it is being spoken, and of which we try to discern the regulating system. Here, on the other hand, the objects appear lined up as if in a dictionary, or in a grammar, verbs with verbs, adverbs with adverbs, lamps with lamps, tractors with tractors. Wouldn't it be right to conclude that this collection of objects, which is a trade fair, actually leaves the visitor free, because it imposes on him no logic of the accumulation of objects and allows him to gaze coldly, to choose? On the contrary, however, the ideological message of a fair emerges only at a second glance, when we have almost been taken in by the persuasive game it establishes.

The objects are of two types. The first are the 'beautiful' objects, desirable, fairly accessible. They include easy chairs, lamps, sausages, liquors, motorboats, swimming pools. The visitor loves them and would like to own them. He cannot perhaps buy a motorboat but he can think of the remote possibility – one day, who knows? – of making such a purchase. But there is one thing he doesn't desire: to accumulate objects of a single type. He may want an ashtray, but not a hundred ashtrays; a rubber boat, but not a thousand rubber boats. So his desire is keen but but frantic; it can be postponed, but its difficulty never creates the drama of impossibility. When you think about it, these 'beautiful' objects are all consumer goods.

Then there are the others. They are 'ugly,' because they are cranes, cement mixers, lathes, hods, excavators, hydraulic presses (actually, they are very beautiful, more beautiful than the first, but the visitor doesn't know this). Since they are ugly and cumbersome, they are undesirable, also because they seem strangely defunctionalized, with their wheels spinning pointlessly, their blades striking the air without slicing anything . . . They are inaccessible, but the visitor doesn't care. He knows that even if he could buy a machine tool, it would be of no use to him. Because these objects, unlike the others, function only if they are accumulable. A thousand ashtrays are useless, but a thousand machine tools make big industry. At the end of his rounds, the ordinary visitor believes he has chosen. He desires beautiful objects, accessible, and not accumulable, and rejects those that are ugly and accumulable (but inaccessible). In reality, he has not chosen; he has only accepted his role as consumer of consumer goods since he cannot be a proprietor of means of production. But he is content. Tomorrow he will work harder in order to be able to buy, one day, an easy chair and a refrigerator. He will work at the lathe, which is not his because (the fair has told him) he doesn't want it.

19 Soetsu Yanagi (Japanese): 'Beauty and True Freedom' (1972)

Let us look at a beautiful piece of pottery. Its provenance does not concern us. If the article is beautiful, we may say that it has achieved Buddhahood, for it is not man alone that may become a Buddha. A beautiful artifact may be defined as one that reposes peacefully where it aspires to be. A man who achieves Buddhahood has entered the realm that lies beyond that of duality; by the same token, beauty is that which has been liberated – or freed – from duality.

Freedom is a word that is now being used rather too carelessly, and Buddhists prefer the word *muge* (literally, 'liberation,' 'being free from impediment'), which refers to the absence of that impediment or restriction arising from relativity. It means the state of liberation from all duality, a state where there is nothing to restrict or be restricted. Beauty, then, ought to be understood as the beauty of liberation or freedom from impediment. It should be noted that true freedom is not fettered even by the idea of freedom. In this sense, liberalism cannot be said to realize the true meaning of freedom, because it is enthralled by principle. Even less does freedom mean selfish or lawless behavior. True freedom must mean liberation from both one's self and others: it must not be in bondage to itself nor may it be restricted by others. Everything that is beautiful is, in one sense or another, a manifestation of this sort of freedom.

20 Victor Papenek (American): 'Design is the Conscious Effort to Impose Meaningful Order' (1974)

All men are designers. All that we do, almost all the time, is design, for design is basic to human activity. The planning and patterning of any act towards a desired, foreseeable end constitutes the design process. Any attempt to separate design, to make it a thing-by-itself, works counter to the inherent value of design as the primary underlying matrix of life. Design is composing an epic poem, executing a mural, painting a masterpiece, writing a concerto. But design is also cleaning and reorganising a desk-drawer, pulling an impacted tooth, baking an apple pie, choosing sides for a back lot baseball game, and educating a child.

Design is the conscious effort to impose meaningful order.

21   Herbert Marcuse (German): 'Art and Revolution' (1978)

The political potential of art lies only in its own aesthetic dimension. Its relation to praxis is inexorably indirect, mediated, and frustrating. The more immediately political the work of art, the more it reduces the power of estrangement and the radical, transcendent goals of change. In this sense, there may be more subversive potential in the poetry of Baudelaire and Rimbaud than in the didactic plays of Brecht.

22   Pierre Bourdieu (French): 'The Meaning of a Work of Art' (1979)

A work of art has meaning and interest only for someone who possesses the cultural competence, that is, the code, into which it is encoded. The conscious or unconscious implementation of explicit or implicit schemes of perception and appreciation which constitutes pictorial or musical culture is the hidden condition for recognising the styles characteristic of a period, a school or an author, and, more generally, for the familiarity with the internal logic of works that aesthetic enjoyment presupposes. A beholder who lacks the specific code feels lost in a chaos of sounds and rhythms, colours and lines, without rhyme or reason. Not having learnt to adopt the adequate disposition, he stops short at what Irwin Panovsky calls 'the sensible properties', perceiving a skin as downy or lacework as delicate, or at the emotional resonances aroused by these properties, referring to 'austere' colours or a 'joyful' melody. He cannot move from the 'primary stratum of the meaning we can grasp on the basis of our ordinary experience' to the 'stratum of secondary meanings', i.e. the 'level of meaning of what is signified', unless he possesses the concepts which go beyond the sensible properties and which identify the specifically stylistic properties of the work. Thus, the encounter with a work of art is not 'love at first sight' as is generally supposed, and the act of empathy, *Einfühlung*, which is the art lover's pleasure, presupposes an act of cognition, a decoding operation, which implies the implementation of a cognitive requirement, a cultural code.

This typically intellectualist theory of artistic perception directly contradicts the experience of art lovers closest to the legitimate definition; acquisition of legitimate culture by insensible familiarisation within the family circle tends to favour an enchanted experience of culture which implies forgetting the acquisition. The 'eye' is the product of history reproduced by education. This is true of the mode of artistic perception now accepted as legitimate, that is, the aesthetic disposition, the capacity to consider in and for themselves, as form rather than function, not only the works designated for such apprehension, i.e. legitimate works of art, but everything in the world, including cultural objects which are not yet consecrated – such as, at one time, primitive arts, or, nowadays, popular photography or kitsch – and natural objects. The 'pure' gaze is a historical invention linked to the emergence of an autonomous field of artistic production, that is, a field capable of imposing its own norms on both the production and the consumption of its products.

---

23   Ettore Sottsass (Italian): ' I Don't Understand why the President's Speeches are Better than Love Whispering in a Room at Night' (1983)

If a society plans obsolescence, the only possible enduring design is one that deals with that obsolescence, a design that comes to terms with it, maybe accelerating it, maybe confronting it, maybe ironizing it, maybe getting along with it. The only design that does not endure is the one that in such a society looks for metaphysics, looks for the absolute, for eternity. And then I don't understand why enduring design is better than disappearing design. I don't understand why stones are better than the feathers of a bird of paradise. I don't understand why pyramids are better than Burmese straw huts. I don't understand why the president's speeches are better than love whispering in a room at night. When I was young I gathered information only from fashion magazines or from very ancient, forgotten, destroyed, dusty civilizations. I gathered information from those areas where life is either just germinating or from the nostalgia of life – never from institutions, never from solidity, never from 'reality', never from crystallizations, never from hibernations. So I must admit that obsolescence for me is just the sugar of life.

---

24   Marco Zanuso (Italian): 'A Definition of the Design Process' (1983)

With the separation of design from the place and act of production and , consequently, with the increased ties with scientific and technological research, an ever-larger number of specialised working groups contributes to the total definition of a product. The result is that both the industrially produced object and the process leading to its definition and design acquire an ever-greater degree of complexity. This becomes true to the point that, unlike the case of the artisan's workshop, no single person can be said to have complete grasp of every aspect of the design process. This very important phenomenon means that in response to the complex nature of the structure of the object and the various contributions of specialised working groups, the role of the designer becomes increasingly concerned with the integration of these various components and the management and control of the interactions among them.

An example of this can be found in the early sewing machines I designed for Borletti. The starting point was the concept of manufacturing the machine casing in die-cast aluminium rather than in cast iron, as had hitherto been done, so that the resulting pieces could be given a more complex and precise form. This meant joining the entire internal mechanism with the supports that would become an integral part of the interior of the housing. It was thus necessary to redesign the entire machine inside and out; the design process required the coordination of the technicians who had knowledge of the various functional aspects.

A similar example can be found in the Brionvega 'Doney' television set. As this was to be the first completely transistorised television designed in Europe, precedents for the circuit layout design were lacking. Again the job had to be done from scratch, and the problem again involved coordination of the various experts involved in tandem with various phases of research and experimentation. The end result, as in the case of the Borletti sewing machine, is distinguished by a total integration of formal, structural, operative, and manufacturing solutions through a procedure comparable to systems engineering. I believe the absolutely innovative characteristics of the design of these products are largely due to the level of integration achieved in response to the complexity of the factors originally generated by scientific and technological research.

A significant result of these factors can be seen in the modified nature of the object of the design process. In this context, the design moment is aimed not uniquely toward the formal definition of a single object but rather toward the configuration of a systematic process in which the original object is 'open' to programmed modifications. These can thus grow naturally out of the original physical configuration, not in a casual and contradictory manner but as an extension of the evolutionary possibilities explicitly inherent in the overall governing concept and concretely embodied in the original realisation. It is evident that in this conception of the design process, the formulation of the systemic structure that governs these transformations assumes primary importance for the role of the designer.

---

25 Achille Castiglioni (Italian): 'A Definition of Industrial Design' (1983)

I define the enterprise of industrial design as the result of a creativity that is truly collective, in which the most important activities usually take place in realising the prototype, activities that require the collaboration of specialised workers that even in this day I would call artisans . . .

I think that the success of so-called Italian design is due to the fact that design, in my opinion, is not a discipline but an attitude growing out of one's humanistic, technological, economic, and political beliefs. In our society the function of productivity is entrusted to industry. To ensure that the bonds between teaching and production have positive results, future designers must become involved during their education in developing their own personalities as part of the continuous inquiry into products and methods of production. In this way practitioners will participate more knowledgeably in bringing about the products that enter society and contribute more and more to shaping them.

---

26 Stephen Bayley (British): 'Taste' (1983)

The architect Owen Jones, the author of *The Grammar of Ornament* (1856), made some observations about the Indian merchandise on display at the Great Exhibition of 1851. He had in mind the horrors of mid-Victorian mass-production when he wrote of the Indian stuffs: '. . . There are . . . no carpets worked with flowers wherein the feet would fear to tread, no furniture the hand would fear to grasp, no superfluous and useless ornament which a caprice has added and which an accident might remove . . . nothing could be removed and leave the design equally good or better.'

Is *that* the eternal rule of good taste?

27 Dieter Rams (German): 'Omit the Unimportant' (c.1984)

One of the most significant design principles is to omit the unimportant in order to emphasise the important. The time has come for us to discover our environment anew and return to the simple basic aspects, for example, to items that have unconstricted obvious-seeming functionalism in both the physical and the psychological sense. Therefore, products should be well designed and as neutral and open as possible, leaving room for self-expression of those using them.

Good design means as little design as possible. Not for reasons of economy or convenience. Arriving at a really convincing, harmonious form by employing simple means is surely a difficult task. The other way is easier and, paradoxical as it may seem, often cheaper, but also more thoughtless with respect to production. Complicated, unnecessary forms are nothing more than designer's escapades that function as self-expression instead of expressing the product's functions. The reason is often that design is used to gain a superficial redundance . . .

Design is the effort to make products in such a way that they are useful to people. It is more rational than irrational, optimistic and projected toward the future rather than resigned, cynical, and indifferent. Design means being steadfast and progressive rather than escaping and giving up. In a historical phase in which the outer world has become less natural and increasingly artificial and commercial, the value of design increases. The work of designers can contribute more concretely and effectively toward a more humane existence in the future.

28 Terrence Conran (British): 'Simplicity and Pleasure' (1985)

I have a taste for austerity and utility, but that's certainly not to say I have no appetite for pleasure. Quite the contrary. I firmly believe that plain, simple things are superior to flashy, complicated ones, precisely because ultimately they are more pleasurable.

29 Milner Gray (British): 'There Cannot be Absolute Canons of Taste' (c.1986)

It seems to me that, in the intensely design conscious period of the last twenty five years, all but a small fraction of what has been said and written on this whole subject has really been about abstractions; such concepts as 'good design', 'fitness for purpose', 'the aesthetics of expendability', 'the American idiom', 'the contemporary style'. These phrases are traps. They tempt us to confuse words with the things they refer to, and from there to argue merely about words – words which, moreover, do not necessarily mean the same thing to everyone.

On the other hand, sitting round a table to consider the design of this actual bottle or that particular label we understand each other because we are all concentrating on the same thing. Whisk the bottle away, and back comes that word 'design', what the semanticists call a 'high order abstraction'. And the term 'good design' – while it is unattached to definite examples – is simply a high order abstraction qualified by a value judgment. 'Good design', absolute and universal, does not exist. There cannot be absolute canons of taste: there can be standards, which should always be high, but should never become rigid. It follows that there is no universal formula by which good design can ever be produced or assessed. It *can* be recognised – but we recognise it subjectively. We can pronounce *our* judgments; we cannot predict the future's. The question, 'What is good design?' is a purely verbal dilemma.

30 Vico Magistretti (Italian): 'Collaboration' (1991)

I have always felt that design, at least as far as my experience in Italy is concerned, is the outcome of close collaboration between the manufacturer and the designer. The task of the designer is to come up with a design concept – the overall sense of the image and use of each project – and rely on the sophisticated technical ability of the manufacturer as far as the design's realisation is concerned. Design objects are not born on the drawing board, but come into being where they are actually produced, in a continual exchange of observations and suggestions.

SOURCES

Where no author is cited, assume that the author of the quotation is also the author of the book/article listed. Publishers are omitted for items before 1940.

Chapter 1

1 *The True Principles of Pointed or Christian Architecture* (1841, London)
2 *Journal of Design* (1849), in Heskett, John, *Industrial Design* (1980, London, Thames & Hudson)
3 The Exhibition as a Lesson in Taste, in the *Art Journal Illustrated catalogue of the Crystal Palace Exhibition, London 1851* (Reprint 1970, New York, Dover)
4 *The Grammar of Ornament*,1856, London, (Reprint 1986, London, Studio Editions)
5 Modern Manufacture and Design, from *Sesame and Lilies, The Two Paths & the King of the Golden River* (1859, London, Everyman)
6 *Hints on Household Taste* (1872, London)
7 *The Encyclopaedia of Ornament*, 1873, London (Reprint 1988, London, Studio Editions)
8 *Manual of Design* (1876, London)
9 *The Education of the Artist* (1886, Paris and London), translated from the French by Clara Bell
10 *The Writings of a Savage* (1978, New York, Viking)
11 Ornament in Architecture from *The Engineering Magazine* (1892), and later *Kindergarten Chats* (1918), (Reprint 1979, New York, Dover)
12 *The Claims of Decorative Art* (1892, London)
13 *Artistic America* (1895, Paris) reprinted as *Artistic America, Tiffany Glass, and Art Nouveau* (1970, Chicago, MIT)
14 *The Principles of Ornament* (1896, London)
15 Quoted by Cantacuzino, Sherban, in Pevsner and Richards (eds): *The Anti-Rationalists* (1973, London, Architectural Press)
16 Stylisation, (*Art et Decoration*, 1907)
17 *Nature and Ornament* (1908, London)
18 *Ornament and Crime*, 1908, Vienna, reprinted in Pevsner, Nikolas, *Adolf Loos* (London, Thames & Hudson)
19 *The Principles of Design* (1913, London)
20 *L'Art decoratif d'aujourd'hui*, 1925, Paris, Editions Cres (Reprint, *The Decorative Art of Today*, translated by J. I. Dunnett, 1987, London, Architectural Assocation)

21 *The Fundamental Spirit of Modern Architecture*,1930, Paris reprinted in Baljeu, Joost, *Theo Van Doesburg* (1974, New York, MacMillan)

22 *The International Style* (1932 and 1966, New York, Norton)

23 *Art and Industry* (1934, London, Faber & Faber)

24 Morano, E. and Vreeland, D., *Sonia Delaunay: Art into Fashion* (1986, New York, George Braziller)

25 *Post-modern Architecture* (1977, London, Academy Editions)

26 A Definition of Architecture as Shelter with Decoration on it and another Plea for a Symbolism of the Ordinary in Architecture (*A+U*, January 1978), reprinted in Arnell, P., Bickford, T. and Bergart, C., *A View from the Campidoglio – Selected Essays 1953-1984* (1984, New York, Harper & Row)

27 *From Bauhaus to Our House* (1981, New York, Farrar, Straus, Giroux)

28 'On Being a Designer', in *Eva Zeisel: Designer for Industry* (1984, Montreal, Musée des Arts Decoratifs)

29 *A Vision of Britain: A Personal View of Architecture* (1989, London, Doubleday)

Chapter 2

1 *An Inquiry into the Requisite Cultivation and the present State of the Arts of Design in England* (1806, London)

2 Yapp, G.W., *Art Education at Home and Abroad* (1852, London)

3 Extracts from the Economic Philosophical Manuscripts,1844, reprinted in Clayre, Alasdair (ed.) *Nature and Industrialization* (1977, Milton Keynes, Open University Press)

4 'Letter to the King of the Belgians', in *The Letters of Queen Victoria 1837-1861*, Volume 2 of 3 (1908, London)

5 *The Stones of Venice* (1851, London)

6 *Art Education at Home and Abroad* (1852, London)

7 *North and South*, 1854-5, London (1974, London, Penguin)

8 *Hard Times*,1854, London, reprinted in Clayre, Alasdair (ed.) *Nature and Industrialization* (1977, Milton Keynes, Open University Press.)

9 Memorandum of 1854 on the subject of the first French Exposition Universelle, from *The British Reports on the Paris Universal Exhibition of 1855* (1856, London)

10 *Capital* volume 1 chapter 10, 1867, London (1976, London, Penguin)

11 *Art Instruction in England* (1882, London)

12 'The Lesser Arts', reprinted in Thompson, Paul, *The Work of William Morris* (1977, London, Quartet)

13 'The Soul of Man Under Socialism', reprinted in *De Profundis and Other Writings*, (1986, London, Penguin)

14 Bancroft, H.H., *The Book of the Fair: An Historical and Descriptive Presentation of the Worlds . . . Exposition at Chicago 1893*, (1893, Chicago). I have attributed the quote to Palmer, as chair of the Lady Board of Managers at the Fair, though Bancroft credits it only to the Board as a whole.

15 *Anna of the Five Towns* (1902, London)

16 *Art et Decoration* (1904, Paris)

17 *The Ragged Trousered Philanthropists*, written c.1910, first published 1914 (1984, London, Granada)

18 The Factory System and Christianity, in *Essays by Eric Gill*, introduction by Mary Gill (1947, London, Jonathan Cape)

19 *International Convention Relating to International Exhibitions; Agreed Definition of the term International Exhibition* (1928, Paris)

20 'The Culture Industry: Enlightenment as Mass Deception', in *Dialectic of Enlightenment*, 1944, New York (Reprint 1979, London, Verso)

21. *The Human Condition* (1958, Chicago, Chicago University Press.)

22 Interview with Gretchen Berg, *Cahiers du Cinéma*, No. 10, 1967, reprinted in *Andy Warhol: Film Factory* (1989, London, BFI)

23 'Why have there been no Great Women Artists?' from Gornick, V. and Moran, B.K. *Woman and Sexist Society: Studies in Power and Powerlessness* (1971, New York, Basic Books)

24 *Art and Society* (1973, London, Merlin)

25 *The Dinner Party – A Symbol of our Heritage* (1979, New York, Doubleday)

26 *Distinction*, (1984, London, Routledge & Kegan Paul)

27 'The Obstacle'

28 *Albert Speer 1932-1942* (1985, Brussels)

29 'The Masses: The Implosion of the Social in the Media' , translated by Maclean, Marie, in *New Literary History*, Volume 16, No. 3, spring 1985 reprinted in full in Poster, David, *Jean Baudrillard Selected Writings*, (1988, Stanford, Polity)

30 *Potters and Paintresses: Women Designers in the Pottery Industry 1870-1955* (1990, London, The Women's Press)

Chapter 3

1 Letter of 9 October 1766, from *The Letters of Josiah Wedgwood*, Volume I (1903, Stoke, Wedgwood Museum)

2 *An Enquiry into the Nature and Causes of the Wealth of Nations*,1776, London, reprinted in Clayre, Alasdair (ed.) *Nature and Industrialization* (1977, Milton Keynes, Open University Press.)

3 Letter to Davies Giddy, printed in Dickinson, H.W. and Titley, A., *Richard Trevithick 1934*, reprinted in Jennings, Humphrey *Pandaemonium 1660-1886: The Coming of the Machine as Seen by Contemporary Observers* (1985, London, André Deutsch)

4 In *ibid*.

5 *Signs of the Times*, 1829, London, reprinted in Clayre, Alasdair (ed.) *Nature and Industrialization* (1977, Milton Keynes, Open University Press)

6 *The Industrial Revolution of the Eighteenth Century in England* (1886, London)

7 Volume IV of the *American Reports on the Exposition Universelle Paris 1889* (1890, Washington)

8 'The Soul of Man under Socialism' (1891), in *Plays, Prose Writings and Poems* (1975, London, Everyman)

9 *Cassells Book of the Household*, Volume II (c.1905, London)

10 *Vackrare Vardagsvara*, 1919, Stockholm, quoted from Naylor, Gillian, *Swedish Grace*, in Greenhalgh, Paul (ed.), *Modernism in Design* (1990, London, Reaktion)

11 *Style*, 1922, reprinted in Bayley, Stephen, *In Good Shape* (1979, London, Design Council)

12 Anonymous 'A Bungalow Fitted out at the Usual Cost', in *The Daily Mail Bungalow Book* (1922, London)
13 Theo van Doesburg and C. Van Easteren Paris 1923, from Baljeu, Joost, *Theo van Doesburg* (1974, New York, Macmillan)
14 *The Ideal Home*, Volume X, 1924, London.
15 *Bauhausbauten Dessau* Volume 12,1925, Dessau)
16 *Technics and Civilization* (1934, London, Routledge)
17 *The Architect and the World Today* (1935, London)
18 *Better Houses for Budgeteers* (1941, New York, Architectural Book Publishing Company)
19 *Cannery Row* (1945, New York)
20 *Plastics and Industrial Design* (1945, London, Allen & Unwin)
21 *The Industrial Revolution 1760-1830* (1948, London)
22 Aalto, Schildt, Wrede, *Sketches* (1978, Chicago, MIT)
23 *Theory and Design in the First Machine Age* (1960, London, Architectural Press)
24 *Working for Ford* (1973, London, Allen Lane)
25 *Plastics, Designs and Materials* (1978, London, Studio Vista)
26 *The Future of the Automobile: The Report of M.I.T.s International Automobile Program* (1984, London, Allen & Unwin)
27 *Objects of Desire* (1986, London, Thames & Hudson)
28 *Learning from Milan: Design and the Second Modernity* (1988 Cambridge, M.I.T.)

Chapter 4

1 'Minutes of Evidence of the Select Committee on Arts and Manufactures', Parliamentary Papers, 1836, Volume XI, quoted by Forty, Adrian, *Objects of Desire* (1986, London, Thames & Hudson)
2 *Useful Work Versus Useless Toil* (1884-5), reprinted in full in Clayre, Alasdair (ed.) *Nature and Industrialization* (1977, Milton Keynes, Open University Press)
3 *Katalog mit Arbeitsprogramm der Wiener Werkstatte*, 1905, Vienna, reprinted in full in Benton, C., Benton, T., and Sharp D.: *Form and Function: A Source Book for the History of Architecture and Design 1890-1939* (1975, Milton Keynes, Open University Press.)
4 *Designing for Machine-made Goods* (1911, Manchester, Manchester School of Art)
5 *Art et decoration*, Volume XXIX, 1911
6 *The New Architecture and the Bauhaus* (1935, London, Faber)
7 *Design this Day*, 1940, reprinted in Bayley, Stephen, *In Good Shape* (1979, London, Design Council)
8 'Pottery', in Farleigh, John, *Fifteen Craftsmen on their Crafts* (1945, London, Sylvan Press)
9 Chicago, Judy, with Susan Hill, 'Embroidering Our Heritage – The Dinner Party Needlework' in *The Dinner Party: A Symbol of Our Heritage* (1979, New York, Doubleday)
10 Crafts Council, *The Makers Eye* (1981, London, Crafts Council)
11 *The Makers Eye* (1981, London, Crafts Council)

12 'Quilts: The Great American Art' in Broude and Garrard, eds. *Feminism and Art History* (1982, New York)
13 *The English Rebels* (1984, London, Journeyman Press)
14 'Applied Art', from *Design in Sweden* (1985, London, The Swedish Institute)
15 *The New Ceramics: Trends and Traditions* (1986, London, Thames & Hudson)
16 *Women and Craft* (Elinor, Richardson, Scott, Thomas, Walker) (1987, London)

Chapter 5

1 Letter to Sir William Meredith (2 March 1765) from *The Letters of Josiah Wedgwood*, Volume I (1903, Stoke, Wedgwood Museum)
2 Scarf, Aaron, from *Art and Industry* (1971, Milton Keynes, Open University Press)
3 *Capital*, Volume 1, 1867, London (Reprint 1976, London, Penguin)
4 *The Principles of Decorative Design*, 1873, London (Reprint 1973, London, Academy Editions)
5 *Au bonheur des dames* (Lausanne: Editions Rencontre, n.d.), quoted in Williams, Rosalind, *Dream Worlds: Mass Consumption in Late Nineteenth Century France* (1982, Berkeley and Los Angeles: California University Press)
6 *Theories of the Leisure Class* (1899, New York, reprinted Unwin)
7 'Scenes from Shop and Store in London', from *Living London*, 1902, London reprinted as *Edwardian London*, (1990, London, Village Press)
8 Quoted from Burgess-Wise, David: *The Motor Car: An Illustrated International History* (1977, New York, Putnams)
9 The Machine Aesthetic, The Manufactured Object, The Artisan and the Artist, *Bulletin de l'effort moderne*, 1924, reprinted in J. Golding and C. Green *Leger and Purist Paris* (1971, London, Tate Gallery)
10 Letter written 19 August 1925, Charlottenburg, in O. Beyer, ed., *Eric Mendelsohn: Letters of an Architect*, translated by G. Strachan (1967, London, Abelard-Schuman)
11 *Horizons*,1935, New York, Horizons, reprint 1977, New York, Dover
12 Artistic Design and Commercial Imitation, 1935, reprinted in Frampton and Vellay, *Pierre Chareau* (1985, London, Thames & Hudson)
13 *Essays by Eric Gill* (1947, London, Jonathan Cape)
14 *The Hidden Persuaders* (1962, London, Pelican)
15 *Art and Confrontation: France and the Arts in an Age of Change* (1968, London, Studio Vista)
16 *Commodity Aesthetics*,1971, reprinted in Bayley, Stephen (ed.), *Commerce and Culture: From Pre-Industrial Art to Post-Industrial Value* (1989, London, Design Museum)
17 *Industrial Design* (1979, London, Faber & Faber)
18 *Cult Objects: The Complete Guide to Having It All* (1985, London, Paladin/Granada)
19 *An Introduction to Design and Culture in the Twentieth Century* (1986, London, Allen & Unwin)

20 *Love for Sale: the Works and Pictures of Barbara Kruger,* text by Kate Linker (1990, New York, Abrams)
21 'Teleshopping', in Bayley, Stephen, *Commerce and Culture: From Pre-Industrial Art to Post-industrial Value* (1989, London, Design Museum)
22 'The Designer Housewife in the 1950's', in *A View from the Interior,* edited by J. Attfield and P. Kirkham (1989, London, The Women's Press)
23 *The Independent on Sunday,* 4 October 1992

Chapter 6

1 Journal of a Tour and Residence in Great Britain by a French Traveller, 1815, in Fastnedge, Ralph, *English Furniture Styles 1500-1830* (1955, London, Penguin)
2 *Modern Domestic Cookery* (1851, London)
3 *Rustic Adornments for Homes of Taste,* 1856, London (Reprint 1987, London, National Trust)
4 *Hints on Household Taste* (1872, London)
5 *American Reports for the Vienna Exposition of 1873,* Volume IV (1876, Washington)
6 *A rebours* (1884 Paris) (translated as *Against Nature*)
7 Hughes *Domestic Economy* (1893, London)
8 *Warnes Everyday Cookbook* (c.1894, London)
9 *Ibid.*
10 *The House Beautiful and Useful* (1911, London)
11 *The Servantless House* (1920, London)
12 *The Ideal Home* (Feb. 1922, London)
13 Advertisement by Parker, Winder & Achurch Ltd, in *The Daily Mail Bungalow Book* (1922, London)
14 *Vers un architecture,* 1924, Paris, translated as *Towards a New Architecture,* 1927, London (Reprint 1946 and subsequently, London, Architectural Press)
15 Frampton, Kenneth, *Modern Architecture: A Critical History* (1980, London, Thames & Hudson)
16 'The Dwelling as a Problem', 1930, in Aalto, Schildt, Wrede, *Sketches* (1978, Chicago, MIT)
17 *Modern Architecture,* the Kahn Lectures, 1931, quoted from Benton, C., Benton, T., and Sharp, D., *Form and Function: A Source Book for the History of Architecture and Design 1890-1939* (1975, Milton Keynes, Open University Press)
18 *Ibid.*
19 *Estrid Ericson, Founder of Svenskt Tenn* (1939, Stockholm, Carlsson Bokforlag)
20 *Decorative Art* (1943-8, London)
21 *Art in Industry,* Volume, No. 3, 1947
22 *An Autobiography* (1977, London, Quartet). Wright died in 1959; it is unclear exactly when the various parts of the autobiography were written. The date given here is an estimate based on the retrospective tone of the passage.
23 *The Woodworker Annual,* Volume LVIII, 1954, London

Chapter 7

1 *Rapport sur lExposition Universelle de 1855, Presenté a l'Empereur* (1855, Paris)
2 *The Ethnological Exhibitions of London* (1855, London)
3 *The Grammar of Ornament*, 1856, London (Reprint 1986, London, Studio Editions)
4 Volume III of the *British Reports on the Exposition Universelle of Paris 1867, Fabrics, Clothing, Education and Dwellings.*
5 'Chinese and Japanese Art, and its Importance for Modern Art-Industry,' *The Workshop*, No. 21, 1870, pp. 321-4
6 *The Descent of Man*, (1871, London, 2 volumes)
7 'Les Arts arabes et le trait général de l'art arabe', 1873, in d'Avennes, Prisse, *The Decorative Art of Arabia* (Reprint 1989, London, Studio Editions)
8 *Principles of Decorative Design*, 1873, London (Reprint 1973, London, Academy Editions)
9 *Handbook to the British Indian Section, Paris Exhibition 1878* (1878, London)
10 *Official Catalogue of the Colonial and Indian Exhibition 1886* (1886, London)
11 *American Reports to the Exposition Universelle, Paris 1889*, Volume 2, (1890, Washington)
12 Attributed, not located.
13 *The Birth and Development of Ornament* (1894, London)
14 *Ibid.*
15 'La Culture artistique en Amerique',1895 in *Artistic America,Tiffany Glass, and Art Nouveau* (1970, Cambridge, MIT)
16 *Historic Ornament* (1899, London)
17 *Dangle's Guide to the Paris Universelle Exposition* (1900, London)
18 'Avant et Après',1903, reprinted in Guerin, Daniel (ed.) *The Writings of a Savage* (1978, New York, Viking)
19 'Das Englische Haus' 1904, Berlin, translated as 'The English House' in Benton, C., Benton, T., and Sharp, D., *Form and Function: A Source Book for the History of Architecture and Design 1890-1939*, (1975, Milton Keynes, Open University Press)
20 'On the Business Morals of Japan', *The Century Magazine* (American), 1908, pp. 395-400.
21 *The Basis of Passional Psychology*, 2 Volumes (1908, Paris and London)
22 *Penny Guide to the Japan-British Exhibition* (1910, London)
23 *Official French Report of the Latin-British Exhibition* (1912, Paris)
24 *Since Cézanne* (1914, London, Chatto & Windus)
25 'The Great Seal of Saorstat Eireann', *The Irish Sketch and Lady of the House*, Christmas 1924, pp. 13-14
26 *Journal of the Manchester College of Technology Textile Society*, Session 1928-9, Volume XIX.
27 *Your Guide to the Exposition*, International Colonial Exposition Paris 1931 (1931, Paris)
28 'Nuremberg Speech', Teut, Anna, *Architectur in Dritten Reich 1933-1945*, 1967, Berlin, quoted from Krier, L.,(ed), *Albert Speer, Architecture 1932-1942* (1985, Brussels)

29 'The Industrial Designer', *Art in Industry*, December 1946.
30 'American Architecture Today', in *Decorative Art 1951-52* (1952, New York)
31 *The Cultural Geography of the United States* (1973, New Jersey, Prentice-Hall)
32 *Orientalism* (1978, London, Routledge & Kegan Paul)
33 *English Culture and the Decline of the Industrial Spirit 1850-1980* (1985, London, Penguin)
34 *Black Athena: The AfroAsiatic Roots of Classical Civilization*, Volume 1, (1987 London, Free Association Books)
35 Coad, Emma Dent, *Javier Mariscal: Designing the New Spain*, (1991, London, Fourth Estate)

Chapter 8

1 'La Culture artistique en Amerique',1895, in *Artistic America,Tiffany Glass, and Art Nouveau* (1970, Cambridge, MIT)
2 In Holt, Elizabeth, ed., *The Expanding World of Art 1874-1902*, vol. 1 (1988, New Haven, Yale University Press)
3 On the Usefulness of the Applied Arts-Industry, *Umelecky Mesicnik* Vol I 1911-12, reprinted in Margolius, Ivan, *Cubism in Architecture and the Applied Arts* (1979, London, David & Charles)
4 *Exhibition of Works by the Italian Futurist Painters* (1912, London, Sackville Galleries)
5 'Glass Architecture' *Der Sturm*, 1914.
6 From Ness, June, L., *Lyonel Feininger* (1974, New York, Praeger)
7 De Stijl Manifesto: Towards a Newly Shaped World, from Baljeu, Joost, *Theo van Doesburg* (1974, New York, Macmillan)
8 'Towards Collective Construction',1923, reprinted in Baljeu, Joost, *Theo Van Doesburg* (1974, New York, Macmillan)
9 *Towards a New Architecture* (1923, Paris, 1927, London) (Reprinted 1978, London, Architectural Press)
10 *Regulations for the International Exhibition of Modern Decorative and Industrial Art Paris 1925* (1924, Paris)
11 Adam, Peter, *Eileen Gray: Architect/Designer* (1987, New York, Abrams)
12 'Le Nouveau', 1929, in *Deblaiment d'art* (1979, Brussels, Archives d'Architecture Moderne)
13 'Wood or Metal?' reprinted in Benton,C., Benton, T., and Sharp, D., *Form and Function: A Source Book for the History of Architecture and Design 1890-1939* (1975, Milton Keynes, Open University Press)
14 Speech delivered at a Werkbund meeting in Vienna, quoted in Conrads, U., *Programmes and Manifestos of Twentieth Century Architecture* (1964, London, Lund Humphries)
15 'Progress: The Swedish Contribution' (*Architectural Review*, 1930)
16 *Horizons*,1935 (Reprint 1977, New York, Dover)
17 *The New Architecture and the Bauhaus* (1935, London, Faber)
18 Thoughts on the Modern Period, radio broadcast WBAI New York, reprinted in Coplans, John (ed.) *Roy Lichenstein* (1972, London, Penguin)

19 'Contra una arquitectura adjetivada',1969, quoted in Julier, Guy, 'Radical Modernism in Spain', in Greenhalgh, Paul, *Modernism in Design* (1990, London, Reaktion)
20 Coe, Peter and Reading, Malcolm, *Lubetkin and Tecton: Architecture and Social Commitment* (1981, Bristol, Bristol University)
21 *The Sadeian Woman* (1978, New York, Pantheon)
22 'Syberbergs Hitler', in *Under the Sign of Saturn* (1983, London, Writers & Readers)
23 'Art and Industry', reprinted in *Images of God* (1986, London, Chatto & Windus)
24 *All That Is Solid Melts Into Air: The Experience of Modernity* (1983, London, Verso)
25 *The Bauhaus Reassessed: Sources and Design Theory* (1985, London, Herbert)
26 *Modernism: A Guide to European Literature 1890-1930* (1976, London, Pelican)

Chapter 9

1 *The Critique of Judgment* (1790)
2 *Two Lectures on Taste* (1834, London)
3 'L'Architecture et le style' in the *Dictionnaire raisonné de l'architecture française du XIe au XVIe siècle* From Hubert Damisch (ed.) *L'Architecture Raisonneé* (1978, Paris, Hermann)
4 Kleine Schriften, 1883, in *Some Architectural Writers of the Nineteenth Century* Pevsner, Nikolas, (1972, Oxford, Oxford University Press.)
5 Seemliness, 1902, reprinted in Robertson, P. (ed.), *Charles Rennie MacIntosh, the Architectural Papers* (1990, Glasgow, White Cockade Press)
6 'Empathy and Aesthetic Pleasure' , in *Aesthetic Theories: Studies in the Philosophy of Art* (1965, New Jersey, Prentice Hall)
7 *Art*, (1914, London)
8 'The Machine Aesthetic, the Manufactured Object, the Artisan and the Artist' *Bulletin de l'effort moderne*,1924, reprinted in Golding, J., and Green, C., *Léger and Purist Paris* (1971, London, Tate Gallery)
9 Adam, Peter, *Eileen Gray: Architect/Designer* (1987, New York, Abrams)
10 'Art as Semiotic Fact' in *Semiotics of Art* edited by Matejka and Titunik (1976, Cambridge, MIT)
11 *Design* (1938, London, Penguin)
12 'Simplicity, a Changing Concept', *Journal of the History of Ideas*, Volume XIV, January 1953.
13 *An Essay on Tolstoy's View of History* (1953, London, Weidenfeld & Nicolson)
14 *Mythologies* (1973, London)
15 Friedman, M., Jaffe, H., and others, *De Stijl 1917-1931: Visions of Utopia* (1982, Oxford, Phaidon)
16 *Itten, The Elements of Colour* (1970, New York, Van Nostrand Reinhold)
17 *Art and Culture* (1961, Boston, Beacon)
18 'Reading Things' , in *Travels in Hyperreality* (1986, Florida, Harcourt, Brace, Joranovich)

19 'The Buddhist Idea of Beauty', from Clark, Garth, *Ceramic Art: Comment and Review 1882-1977* (1978, New York, Dutton)
20 *Design for the Real World* (1974, London, Paladin)
21 *The Aesthetic Dimension* (1978, London, MacMillan)
22 *Distinction: A Social Critique of the Judgment of Taste* (1979 Paris, 1984, London, Routledge & Kegan Paul)
23 *Design since 1945* (Thames & Hudson, Philadelphia Museum of Art, 1983)
24 'Society', in *Design since 1945* (1983, Thames & Hudson, Philadelphia Museum of Art)
25 *Design since 1945* (1983, Thames & Hudson and Philadelphia Museum of Art)
26 *Taste: An Exhibition about Values in Design* (1983, London, The Conran Foundation)
27 'Omit the Unimportant', in Margolin, Victor (ed.) *Design Discourse* (1989, Chicago, Chicago University Press)
28 *Terrence Conran's Book of the Home* (1985, London, Octopus)
29 'The Creative Urge', in McCarthy, Z., ed., *Royal Designers on Design* (1986, London, Design Council)
30 *Vico Magistretti: Elegance and Innovation in Postwar Design* (1991, London, Thames & Hudson)